ASIAN ECONOMIC INTEGRATION REPORT 2015

HOW CAN SPECIAL ECONOMIC ZONES CATALYZE ECONOMIC DEVELOPMENT?

ADB

ASIAN DEVELOPMENT BANK

© 2015 Asian Development Bank
6 ADB Avenue, Mandaluyong City, 1550 Metro Manila, Philippines
Tel +63 2 632 4444; Fax +63 2 636 2444
www.adb.org; openaccess.adb.org

Some rights reserved. Published in 2015.
Printed in the Philippines.

ISBN 978-92-9257-246-4 (Print), 978-92-9257-247-1 (e-ISBN)
Publication Stock No. RPT157770-2

Cataloging-In-Publication Data

Asian Development Bank.
        Asian economic integration report 2015: How can special economic zones catalyze economic development?
Mandaluyong City, Philippines: Asian Development Bank, 2015.

1. Regionalism.   2. Subregional cooperation.   3. Economic development.   4. Asia.   I. Asian Development Bank.

Contents

Abbreviations

ADB	Asian Development Bank
ADO	Asian Development Outlook
AFC	Asian financial crisis
APEC	Asia-Pacific Economic Cooperation
ARIC	Asia Regional Integration Center
ASEAN	Association of Southeast Asian Nations (Brunei Darussalam, Cambodia, Indonesia, the Lao People's Democratic Republic, Malaysia, Myanmar, the Philippines, Singapore, Thailand, and Viet Nam)
ASEAN+3	ASEAN plus the People's Republic of China, Japan, and the Republic of Korea
ASEAN-4	Indonesia, Malaysia, the Philippines, and Thailand
ASEAN-5	Indonesia, Malaysia, the Philippines, Thailand, and Viet Nam
ASEAN+6	ASEAN+3 plus Australia, India, and New Zealand
BEC	Broad Economic Categories
BEPZA	Bangladesh Export Processing Zone Authority
CAREC	Central Asia Regional Economic Cooperation
CLMV	Cambodia, Lao People's Democratic Republic, Myanmar, and Viet Nam
CPIS	Coordinated Portfolio Investment Survey
DMC	developing member country
DVA	domestic value-added absorbed abroad
EFTA	European Free Trade Association
EOE	electrical and optical equipment
EPZ	export processing zone
EPZA	Export Processing Zone Authority
ETDZ	Economic and Technological Development Zone
EU	European Union
euro area	Austria, Belgium, Cyprus, Estonia, Finland, France, Germany, Greece, Ireland, Italy, Latvia, Luxembourg, Malta, the Netherlands, Portugal, Slovakia, Slovenia, and Spain
FDI	foreign direct investment
FTAAP	Free Trade Area of Asia-Pacific
FTA	free trade agreement
FTZ	free trade zone
FVA	foreign-value added
FY	fiscal year
G20	Group of Twenty (Argentina, Australia, Brazil, Canada, the People's Republic of China, France, Germany, India, Indonesia, Italy, Japan, the Republic of Korea, Mexico, Russian Federation, Saudi Arabia, South Africa, Turkey, the United Kingdom, the United States, and European Union)
G3	Group of Three (euro area, Japan, and the United States)
GDP	gross domestic product
GFC	global financial crisis
GME	growth miracle economies (the People's Republic of China; Hong Kong, China; the Republic of Korea; and Singapore)

GMM	generalized method of moments
GMS	Greater Mekong Subregion
GVC	global value chain
HTDZ	High-Tech Development Zone
IMF	International Monetary Fund
ICT	information and communication technology
IP	intellectual property
ISDS	investor-state dispute settlement
LHS	left-hand scale
M&A	mergers and acquisitions
MNC	multinational corporations
MTR	multilateral trade resistance
NIES	newly industrialized economies
OECD	Organisation for Economic Co-operation and Development
OLS	ordinary least squares
PDC	purely double-counted terms
PPP	public-private partnership
PRC	People's Republic of China
RCEP	Regional Comprehensive Economic Partnership
RCI	regional cooperation and integration
REC	regional economic corridor
RHS	right-hand scale
RKC	Revised Kyoto Convention
ROW	rest of the world
SASEC	South Asia Subregional Economic Cooperation
SEZ	special economic zone
SGZ	special governance zone
SME	small and medium enterprise
SOE	state-owned enterprise
SVAR	structural vector autoregression
TFA	Trade Facilitation Agreement
TFP	Trade Finance Program
TTIP	Transatlantic Trade and Investment Partnership
TPA	trade promotion authority
TPM	technological protection measure
TPP	Trans-Pacific Partnership
UNCTAD	United Nations Conference on Trade and Development
UNESCAP	United Nations Economic and Social Commission for Asia and the Pacific
US	United States
VSI	vertically specialized industrialization
WB	World Bank
WBES	World Bank Enterprise Survey
WCO	World Customs Organization
WEO	World Economic Outlook
WIOD	World Input-Output Database
WTO	World Trade Organization
y-o-y	year-on-year

Acknowledgments

The Asian Economic Integration Report (AEIR) 2015 was prepared by the Regional Cooperation and Integration Division (ERCI) of ADB's Economic Research and Regional Cooperation Department (ERCD), under the overall supervision of former Division Director Arjun Goswami and current Director Cyn-Young Park.

ERCI Principal Economist Jong Woo Kang coordinated production assisted by ERCI Economics Officer Mitzirose Legal. Consultants from the Asia Regional Integration Center (ARIC), led by ARIC Principal Economic Analyst Mara Claire Tayag, contributed data, research, and analysis.

Contributing authors to "Progress of Regional Cooperation and Integration" include James Villafuerte and Marthe Hinojales (Asian Economies under Changing Global Environment); Jong Woo Kang, Renz Calub, Marthe Hinojales, and Jessel Crispino (Updates on Trade and Investment Integration); Jong Woo Kang, Thiam Hee Ng, and Marthe Hinojales (Updates on Financial Integration); Guntur Sugiyarto and Suzette Dagli (Updates on Movement of People); and Jong Woo Kang, Haruya Koide, Shintaro Hamanaka, Mara Claire Tayag, Dorothea Ramizo, and Ana Kristel Molina (Updates on Trade Policy). The regional value chain analysis in "Updates on Trade and Investment Integration" benefitted from construction of input-output tables for five countries—Bangladesh, Malaysia, the Philippines, Thailand, and Viet Nam—by a team headed by Mahinthan J. Mariasingham from ERCD's Development Economics and Indicators Division.

Jong Woo Kang and Shahid Yusuf wrote the "Special Chapter: How Can Special Economic Zones Catalyze Economic Development?" Background papers were provided by Aradhna Aggarwal, Mohiuddin Alamgir, Zhenshan Yang, Peter Warr, Jayant Menon, Benjamin Endriga, and Grendell Vie Magoncia. Econometric analysis was provided by Ana Kristel Molina, Marthe Hinojales, Renz Calub, and Suzette Dagli. Pilar Dayag provided data and research support.

The AEIR also benefitted from comments provided by ADB regional departments during the 12-13 August 2015 workshop and subsequent interdepartmental reviews.

Guy Sacerdoti edited the manuscripts. Ariel Paelmo typeset and produced the layout, and Erickson Mercado created the cover design. Support for AEIR printing and publishing was provided by the Printing Services Unit of ADB's Office of Administrative Services and by the Publishing Team of the Department of External Relations. ERCI Senior Operations Assistant Pia Asuncion Tenchavez and ARIC Project Specialist Susan Monteagudo provided administrative and secretarial support, and helped organize the AEIR workshop. Erik Churchill, communications specialist of the Department of External Relations, coordinated the dissemination of AEIR 2015.

AEIR 2015—Highlights

Asia's trade has slowed faster than world trade; trade growth has been below economic growth since 2012. Structural factors such as slower expansion of global value chains and growth moderation in the People's Republic of China may be at play, but the region must embrace further efforts to make trade and investment regimes more open. Regional trade blocs such as the Trans-Pacific Partnership and the proposed Regional Comprehensive Economic Partnership could facilitate freer trade if supported through open, flexible accession.

Asia has emerged as an important source of outward foreign direct investment (FDI). Asia's outward FDI increased faster than inward FDI—growing 45.3% in 2014 compared with 2010, led by both the region's high income and emerging market economies. FDI is the most stable source of capital for the region compared with more volatile equity, debt, and bank-related flows.

Special economic zones (SEZs) can play a catalytic role in economic development, provided the right business environment and policies are put in place. In Asia, SEZs can facilitate trade, investment, and policy reform at a time the region is experiencing a slowdown in trade and economic growth. For SEZs to be successful, they must establish strong backward and forward linkages with the overall economy. Effective SEZs must be an integral part of dynamic national development strategies and evolve as economies develop by transforming from manufacturing bases to technological platforms for innovation and modern services.

Shang-Jin Wei

SHANG-JIN WEI
Chief Economist
Asian Development Bank

Trade Integration

- **Asia's trade growth has slowed due to slower global value chain (GVC) expansion and growth moderation in the People's Republic of China (PRC).** By volume, Asia's trade growth has fallen faster than world trade and has been below gross domestic product (GDP) growth since 2012. Asia's income elasticity of trade declined from 2.69 before the global financial crisis (GFC) to 1.30 afterwards—meaning trade is growing less for the same one-percentage increase in GDP than before. There are several interrelated structural reasons: (i) in general, Asia's economies are rebalancing away from exports and investment toward consumption and services; (ii) global and regional value chains appear to be maturing after decades of rapid expansion; in Asia, intermediate goods trade—almost 60% of the region's total—declined 2.6% in 2014 in value; and (iii) given the PRC's high weight in intraregional trade, its growth moderation reduces export growth across the region.

- **The Trans-Pacific Partnership (TPP) could be a stepping stone toward further global trade liberalization.** Intraregional trade has hovered at 55% of total Asian trade since 2011—below the European Union's (EU) 65%, yet above North America's 42%. When in force, the 12-member TPP (Australia, Brunei Darussalam, Chile, Canada, Japan, Malaysia, Mexico, New Zealand, Peru, Singapore, the United States [US], and Viet Nam) will likely affect Asia's production networks and trade links significantly. The TPP could also stimulate structural reforms beyond trade liberalization. Regional trade blocs such as the TPP—and the proposed Regional Comprehensive Economic Partnership (RCEP), which includes the 10 ASEAN members plus Australia, the PRC, India, Japan, the Republic of Korea, and New Zealand—could facilitate freer global trade, particularly with open accession.

- **The PRC's transformation toward more consumption- and services-led growth presents both challenges and opportunities for other economies.** With PRC growth moderating and its moving from an investment and export driven growth strategy to one led more by consumption and services, many economies in East Asia, Southeast Asia, and Oceania that supply raw materials or export parts and components to the PRC could face growing challenges in adjusting to these. However, expanding consumption in the PRC could expand market opportunities for consumption goods exports and investments in the related industries from the region.

Financial integration

- **The composition of capital flows matters for financial stability.** Inward foreign direct investment (FDI)—from outside and within the region—grew 26.3% (to $495 billion) from 2010 to 2014. Equity and debt inflows, however, decreased 20.1% and 59.4%, respectively, while bank credit has fluctuated across years. FDI is the most stable source of capital compared with more volatile equity, debt, and bank-related flows. Using the standard deviation of inflows into Asia as a percentage of GDP, inflow volatility was 0.6 for FDI during 2005Q1–2014Q1, 1.4 for equity and 1.5 for debt. Uncertainty over US interest rate policy contributed to capital flow volatility.

- **Asia has become an important source of outward FDI.** External and intraregional Asian FDI outflows increased faster than FDI inflows—growing 45.3% in 2014 compared with 2010, led by investments from traditional investors—including Japan; Hong Kong, China; and Singapore. While outward equity investment increased 91.6%, outward debt investment fell 178%. In 2014, outward equity investment mostly went to the euro area and other advanced economies, while outward debt investment to the US rose.

- **Investments from emerging Asian investors are also rising, particularly in developed economies.** Emerging Asian investors—such as the PRC, India, Malaysia, and Thailand—are increasing investments into Europe, the US, and Latin America. India has become the third largest source of inward FDI for the United Kingdom (UK) after the US and France in number of projects, while Thailand has increased investment in Italy and other European countries. The PRC increased its investments in utilities and logistics in particular in countries like Italy, Portugal, and Spain.

People Movement

- **Asia is the world's largest source of international migrants.** In 2013, 79.5 million people from Asia migrated to other countries—accounting for 34% of the global total (231.5 million). South Asia was the largest source, contributing 44% of the Asian total. Second was Southeast Asia, as ASEAN integration boosted both migration and tourism. Income disparities and demographics drive Asian migration. In general, economies with low income and large numbers of young (20-34), working age populations (Afghanistan, Bangladesh, and India, for example) are net sources of migrants. Those with high income and ageing populations (Australia, Japan, and New Zealand, for example) are net recipients.

- **Remittances and tourism remain important sources of income for many Asian economies.** Asia accounted for nearly 50% of global remittances ($583.4 billion) in 2014. India, the PRC, and the Philippines received the most—$163 billion, or 61% of the Asian total. As % of GDP, however, Tajikistan, Nepal, and the Kyrgyz Republic were largest with 41.9%, 29.9%, and 29.4% of GDP, respectively. Economies that rely heavily on remittances for income also tend to experience high volatility in remittance inflows. These economies should continue to pursue industrialization and economic diversification to make their economies more resilient and provide more domestic job opportunities.

Special Chapter: How Can Special Economic Zones Catalyze Economic Development?

Evolution of Special Economic Zones (SEZs)

- **Economic zones are proliferating, yet performance is mixed.** From an estimated 500 SEZs in 1995, there are now some 4,300 in over 130 countries (by the most recent count), employing more than 68 million workers. While many are successful, others are poorly run or never take off. Nonetheless, they are attracting renewed attention with more developing Asian economies using SEZs as a policy tool to promote industrialization and economic growth.

- **Economic zones have played a key role in economic development in many Asian economies.** The earliest SEZs in Asia grew within a context of relatively closed economies. They were designed to circumvent trade restrictions and earn foreign exchange revenues. The rationale was that large, nationwide economic benefits from these experiments far outweighed fiscal and other economic costs incurred by the temporary price and incentive distortions within SEZ enclaves. They also aimed to widen the manufacturing base and begin establishing a foothold in the global marketplace. Over time, in many countries, SEZs have paid high dividends in job creation, increased exports, and larger FDI—even if over-ambition or lack of strategic focus at times led to failure. SEZs were also used as testing grounds for incentives and structural reforms that could later spread across the economy to overcome development constraints.

- **Different SEZ stages coexist in developing Asia.** First stage enclave-type SEZs help generate employment and foreign exchange revenues. For example, SEZs in Cambodia remain relatively small and new, employing low-skilled workers in industries such as garments, electronics, and household furnishings. Second stage zones help diversify an economy's production base by strengthening linkages with the domestic economy—for example, Malaysia and Thailand moved from assembling imported inputs to increasing sales of their own branded merchandise in domestic and global markets. Third stage zones can bring nationwide developmental impact facilitated through certain reforms in areas such as the labor market and service sector. This improves productivity, promotes innovation, and strengthens skill development—as seen in the PRC; the Republic of Korea; and Taipei,China.

Economic impact of SEZs

- **Successful SEZs help expand exports and investments.** According to estimations conducted on Asian economies, the number and presence of SEZs in an economy are positively related to overall export performance and volume of inward FDI. On average, a 10% increase in the number of SEZs increases manufacturing exports by 1.1%—based on estimations for the region's economies with available data. This suggests SEZs do more than just reallocate exports and inward FDI into SEZs.

- **Still, SEZ performance varies widely across economies.** Measured by firm-level output (proxied by sales), exports, and productivity, SEZs in some countries have a clear, positive impact, while those in others have a less positive or even negative impact. Raw survey data show political instability; poor business environment; limited access to infrastructure, finance, and utilities; and undue regulations are key obstacles in doing business inside SEZs.

Success factors and possible future directions

- **SEZs are not cost-free; with governance issues often behind failures.** Foregone tax revenues and the costs for providing infrastructure, land, and subsidized utilities should not be overlooked. Poor governance and oversight sometimes lead to rent-seeking and poor SEZ performance. However, these costs and failures do not overshadow the large economic potential SEZs offer, as seen by the many successful examples.

- **Successful SEZs have several common features.** These include (i) the fiscal incentives which are important for initial firm investments along with institutional factors—such as an independent SEZ governing authority and enabling legal framework—that prove to be a much greater draw over time; (ii) cheap factory sites, abundant labor supply, strategic location, and multimodal connectivity with resources and major trading destinations; (iii) institutional efficiency, dependable judicial systems, adequate security, and transparent standards; and (iv) strong state and local government commitment along with consistent policies.

- **SEZs should be an integral part of national development strategies to enhance their nationwide effect.** A clear link to an economy's development strategy increases the likelihood SEZs will have broad nationwide impact. They can become a major engine for national development through backward and forward linkages with the rest of the domestic economy. Thus, they offer significant opportunities for domestic participation, knowledge sharing, innovation, and skills development—supported by priorities defined by the economy's development strategy. This happened with SEZs in the PRC; the Republic of Korea; Malaysia; and Taipei,China. For many other SEZs in the region, while some are connected to global value chains, others remain largely enclave-type SEZs without the backward and forward domestic linkages and operate below capacity. These economies need to improve the business enabling environment and work toward moving up the industrial value chain.

- **SEZs can support services, a knowledge-based economy, and innovation.** For Asia's low- and lower middle-income economies, manufacturing may remain the staple for SEZs. However, even these economies—and those at higher income levels—must examine the potential of services, such as logistics, finance, information technology, and other business services. High technology and knowledge-based SEZs can combine with research and development centers, e-governance systems, and training and recreational centers to evolve into innovation clusters.

PROGRESS IN REGIONAL COOPERATION AND INTEGRATION

1

Asian Economies under Changing Global Environment

Updates on Trade and Investment Integration

Updates on Financial Integration

Updates on Movement of People

Updates on Trade Policy

Progress in Regional Cooperation and Integration

Asian Economies under Changing Global Environment

I n the past decade, Asia emerged as a growth leader of the global economy. This strength was largely supported by deepening regional economic integration, anchored on expanding global production networks as well as positive external conditions during this period. For instance, in the decade after the Asian financial crisis (AFC), global trade grew 5.7% on average, benefitting Asia's relatively more open economies than the rest of the world. From 2000 to 2007, the share of intraregional cross-border trade grew two percentage points and financial flows five percentage points. As a result, economic growth in developing Asia continued to increase steadily—peaking at 10.1% in 2007.

The strength of Asia's growth was also supported by the set of structural reforms. Generally, these (i) fostered greater macroeconomic stability, (ii) liberalized trade and investment regimes, (iii) strengthened economic policy making, and (iv) made markets more efficient. Infrastructure investment—particularly in transport and logistics—helped reduce trade costs, providing an impetus to growth. Resilience strengthened by stockpiling reserves, declines in public deficits and debt, lower inflation, and in some economies more flexible exchange rate regimes helped the region withstand several episodes of global financial volatility.

Amid slowing demand from advanced economies during the global financial crisis (GFC) of 2008/09, domestic and regional demand cushioned the fall in output. This occurred as most economies in the region cut interest rates and used fiscal stimulus to support domestic consumption and investment growth. Meanwhile, regional supply chains continued to benefit from unilateral and regional liberalization arrangements—boosting regional demand and regional resilience. In 2014, intra-Asian trade remained 55.6% of its total trade, slightly higher compared with intraregional foreign direct investment (FDI) (52.6%).

The GFC's impact on growth was much more modest than that of the AFC **(Figure 1)**. And since the GFC, Asia's economic growth remains strong relative to other regions. But growth has slowed in recent years—after recovering to 9.3% in 2010, aggregate growth declined to 6.2% in 2014—still well above the 3.4% global average, but lower than the region's precrisis growth rates.

Figure 1: Real GDP Growth (%, y-o-y)

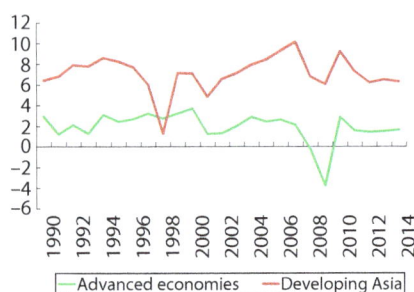

Note: Advanced economies refer to the major advanced economies (G7) by IMF definition: Canada, France, Germany, Italy, Japan, the United Kingdom, and the United States. Developing Asia refers to the 45 developing regional members of ADB, for which data is available. Based on local currency units and weighted using gross national income, Atlas method.
Source: ADB calculations using data from various issues of the *Asian Development Outlook*, ADB; *World Economic Outlook October 2015 Database*, International Monetary Fund (IMF); and *World Development Indicators*, World Bank.

Structural reasons for Asia's recent growth slowdown

Empirical analysis suggests that income convergence could be one reason for the slowing growth trend across developing Asia.[1] Generally, given a certain fixed level of technology, growth decelerates as an economy reaches higher income levels. This pattern emerges as the marginal contribution to growth of capital accumulation tends to be much higher for low-income than high-income economies. Ito (2015) examined the growth of four "growth miracle economies" (GME)—the People's Republic of China (PRC); Hong Kong, China; the Republic of Korea; and Singapore—the growth of four ASEAN economies (ASEAN-4) and the growth of Cambodia, Lao PDR, Myanmar, and Viet Nam (CLMV) during the pre-AFC (1985–1996), post-AFC/pre-GFC (1999–2007), and post-GFC (2010–2015).[2] He finds that PRC growth followed the GME growth path, with others following several decades later. The same correlation was observed for the ASEAN-4, although the correlation appears less tight. It is notable that CLMV economies are approaching the ASEAN-4 convergence growth path; while Malaysia and Thailand have thus far failed to reach the higher GME convergence growth path **(Figure 2)**. Some other results include (i) the Philippines showing a continuously increasing growth trajectory, and (ii) Singapore remaining above the GME growth path from the start.

To test these results further, an income convergence model is estimated following Barro and Sala-i-Martin (1990)—using 111 economies with growth rates calculated for 1999–2007 and 2010–2014.[3] The results confirm Ito's finding of two income convergence paths in the region, with GME economies tracking a higher income convergence path **(Figure 3)**.

The PRC remains the region's center of gravity in economic expansion. Its shift to a slower but more sustainable growth path is another primary reason behind the mild deceleration in both regional and global economic growth. Moreover, the growth slowdown in the region can be explained

Figure 2: Income Convergence— Selected Asian Economies

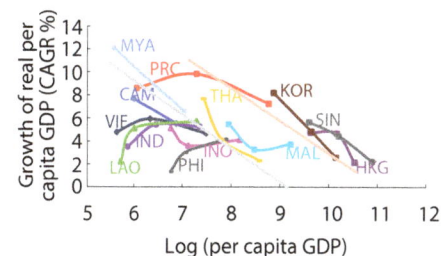

CAM = Cambodia; PRC = People's Republic of China; HKG = Hong Kong, China; IND = India; INO = Indonesia; KOR = Republic of Korea; LAO = Lao People's Democratic Republic; MAL = Malaysia; MYA = Myanmar; PHI = Philippines; SIN = Singapore; THA = Thailand; VIE = Viet Nam.
Note: Per capita levels and growth rates computed over three subperiods: 1985–1996, 1999–2007, and 2010–2015, where 2015 is the IMF forecast.
Source: T. Ito. 2015. Lessons for Global Financial Crisis for Asia. Presentation at the 7th International Policy Advisory Group Meeting. Manila. 3–4 August. Using data from *World Economic Outlook April 2015 Database*, International Monetary Fund.

Figure 3: Income Convergence—GMEs vs ROW

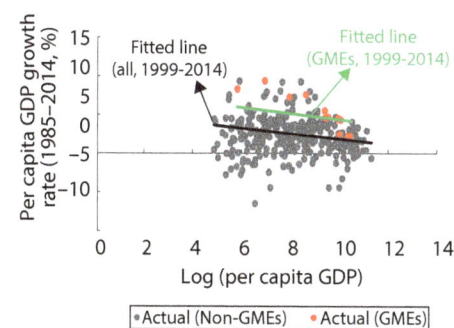

GME = "growth miracle economies" (PRC; Hong Kong, China; Republic of Korea; Singapore), ROW = rest of the world.
Note: Dataset comprises of 111 economies from the World Bank's WDI database with GDP per capita data beginning 1985 (96); 1999 (110) and 2010 (111). Log per capita GDP in the x-axis corresponds to values per these 3 years. The model follows work done by Barro and Sala-i-Martin (NBER, 1990). The dependent variable is log(GDPcap$_{2014}$/GDPcap$_{1999}$)*1/T, where T is the years within each interval (1999-2007 and 2010-2015). The independent variables are per capita GDP (1999) and a GME dummy.
Source: ADB calculations using data from *World Development Indicators*, World Bank.

---

[1] As in Barro and Sala-i-Martin (2003), ".... conditional convergence applies when the growth rate of an economy is positively related to the distance between this economy's level of income and its own steady state. Conditional convergence should not be confused with absolute convergence, a concept that applies when poor economies tend to grow faster than rich ones (and, therefore, the poor tend to "catch up." .....The two concepts are identical if a group of economies tend to converge to the same steady state."

[2] T. Ito. 2015. Lessons of Global Financial Crisis for Asia. Presentation for the 7th International Policy Advisory Group Meeting. Manila. 3–4 August.

[3] R. Barro and X. Sala-i-Martin. 1990. Economic Growth and Convergence Across the United States. *NBER Working Papers*. No. 3419. Cambridge, MA: NBER.

Figure 4: Number of Economies by Type of Working Age Population—Asia

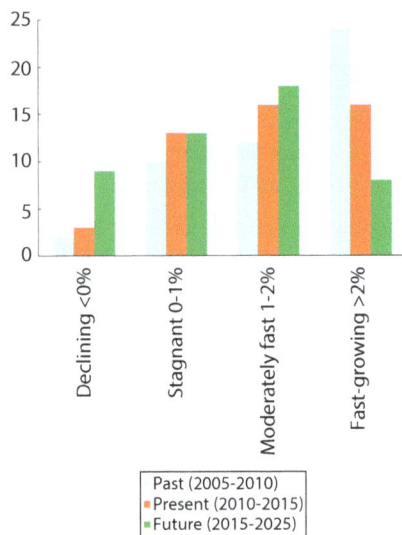

Past (2005-2010)
Present (2010-2015)
Future (2015-2025)

Note: Economies were classified by type of growth of their working age population (those aged 15–64). They are considered as fast growing if their working age population expands by at least 2% per year; moderately fast if their working age population growth is between 1% and 2%; stagnant if their working age population growth is between 0 and 1%; and declining if their growth is negative.
Source: ADB calculations using data from *World Population Prospects: The 2015 Revision*, United Nations.

Figure 5: Labor Productivity Growth—Asia (%, y-o-y)

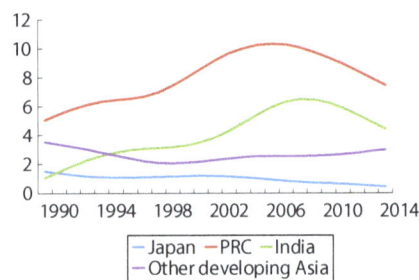

Japan — PRC — India
Other developing Asia

PRC = People's Republic of China.
Note: Growth rates were de-trended using Hodrick-Prescott filter.
Source: ADB calculations using data from Conference Board Total Economy Database, May 2015 edition.

in part by the demographic dividend—which has turned from positive to negative. An analysis of labor force growth in Asia shows the number of economies with rapidly growing labor force (greater than 2%) is decreasing **(Figure 4)**. More so, the number of economies with stagnant labor force growth (between zero to 1%) has stabilized and includes some of the biggest economies in the region—the PRC; Hong Kong, China; the Republic of Korea, and Thailand, for example. The number of economies with negative labor force growth rates has also grown.

The region's growth slowdown also coincides with slowing labor productivity growth. From 1990 to 2014, labor productivity has slowed for most of developing Asia **(Figure 5)**. The PRC's labor productivity growth began to fall in 2007, while India's labor productivity slowed subsequently. The slowdown in labor productivity in agriculture is mainly due to falling investment, diversion of productive agricultural land to nonfarm purposes, and climate change—which reduced most farm yields. Similarly, labor productivity growth in manufacturing eased as benefits from trade reform were exhausted and skilled labor shortages sparked wage increases across the region. In services, labor productivity also stalled from the rising share of low-productivity informal sector and household-orientated services. Efforts to boost fertility to shore up the future working age population in some economies—the PRC's shift from a one-child to a two-child policy is an example—must be accompanied by efforts to shore up productivity by investing in human capital as well as promoting creativity and innovation.

External impact on economic growth

To analyze how external conditions have affected growth in Asia over time, a structural vector autoregression (SVAR) model of the growth of Asian economies is estimated. Several external and domestic factors—grouped as external and internal blocks—are used as explanatory variables of Asian GDP growth.[4] External factors represent economic conditions outside the domestic economy that affect the growth of Asian economies. These include (i) US GDP growth, a proxy of growth in advanced economies; (ii) US Federal Funds Futures, a measure of US monetary policy; and (iii) VIX index, a measure of global risk.[5] Together, they comprise the external block in the baseline model, and are assumed to be unaffected contemporaneously by shocks from the internal block. Further, shocks to the external factors are assumed to be transmitted in the same order as above. In an alternate specification, the external block is expanded by including PRC GDP growth—to analyze the impact of PRC growth on emerging Asian economies.

The domestic block includes four variables: (i) the economy's GDP growth, (ii) the domestic short-term policy or money market rate, (iii) the

---

[4] The approach follows the International Monetary Fund analytical framework used in Chapter 4 of its *World Economic Outlook April 2014*. See IMF. 2014. On the Receiving End? External Conditions and Emerging Market Growth Before, During, and After the Global Financial Crisis. *World Economic Outlook April 2014*. Washington.

[5] We take the US Federal Funds Futures as the key explanatory variable representing QE tapering (and expected changes thereof). While we have modeled the SVAR assuming that it is not contemporaneously affected by the variables in the domestic block, this feedback loop is indeed possible, but not explored in the current specification of the model.

Figure 6: Impulse Response of Domestic Real GDP Growth to External Shocks
(percentage points; x-axis = number of quarters)

a: **Response to Real GDP Growth Shock in the US** (normalized to a 1 percentage point rise in US growth)

b: **Response to US Monetary Policy Changes** (normalized to a 100 basis point rise in US Federal Funds Futures)

c: **Response to Higher Global Volatility** (normalized to a 1 unit rise in the VIX index)

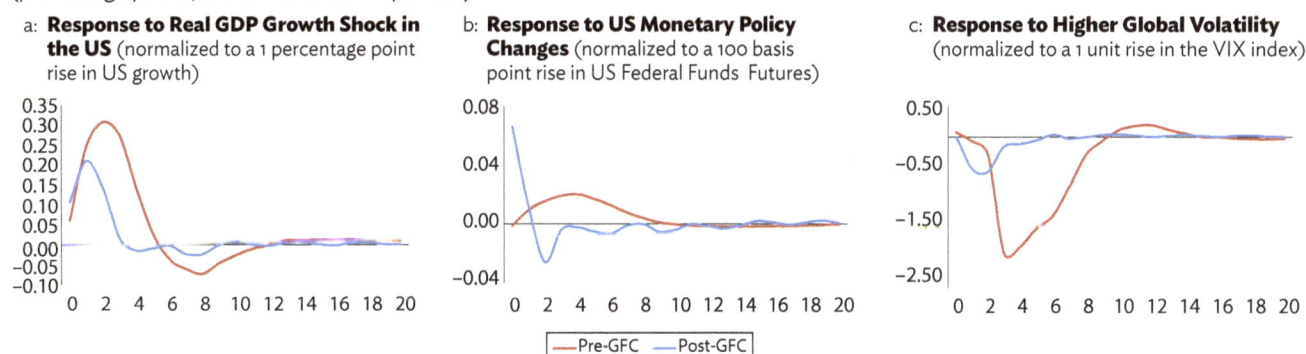

— Pre-GFC   — Post-GFC

GFC = global financial crisis.
Note: Pre-GFC = 2001Q1 to 2008Q1; Post-GFC = 2009Q1 to 2015Q2. Average for sample economies.
Source: ADB calculations using data from CEIC and national sources.

domestic inflation rate, and (iv) the growth of domestic credit. While the internal block does not affect the external factors contemporaneously, it affects the external block with a lag.[6] The SVAR model was estimated from 2000Q1 to 2015Q2, using economic data of 11 Asian economies— the PRC, India, ASEAN-4 and Viet Nam (collectively "ASEAN-5"), and the newly industrialized economies (NIEs).[7] To analyze the changing pattern of spillover effects on the region, the estimation period was split into "pre-GFC" (2001–2008Q1) and "post-GFC" (2009–2015Q2) periods.[8]

Consistent with results from similar studies, stronger growth in the US exerts a positive and persistent boost to economic growth in Asia. However, the US growth impact appears to have weakened and become less persistent after the GFC. Prior to the crisis, a one-percentage point increase in US growth typically boosted Asian economies' growth by about 0.3 percentage points. The effect lasted for about a year and gradually died down after 5 to 6 quarters. After the GFC, however, the impact was less—at about 0.2 percentage points. It also died down more quickly, by the end of first year **(Figure 6)**.

The expectation of tighter US monetary policy, represented by the US Federal Funds Futures (FF), appears to have a mixed effect on Asian growth. Prior to the GFC, a positive shock to the FF had a positive effect on Asian growth. However, after the GFC, a shock to the FF had a positive effect on growth initially, but turns negative after the second quarter.[9]

---

[6] All variables enter the model with two lags. Due to the short time period employed in the model, the use of higher than two lags results into nonconvergence and/or near-zero estimates.

[7] NIEs include Hong Kong, China; the Republic of Korea; Singapore; and Taipei,China.

[8] Pre-GFC period refers to quarters through 2008Q1; post-GFC refers to 2009Q1 through 2015Q2.

[9] Due to little variance in the FF in the post-GFC period, its impact on Asian growth warrants further analysis. It may be possible that before the GFC, the expectation for tighter monetary policy in the US could be associated with strengthening US economic growth—which had a positive spillover on Asian economies. In the post-GFC, while the expectation for tighter monetary policy still carries a positive US growth spillover effect, episodes of capital flow reversals—such as those during the "taper tantrum" between May and September 2013— could also introduce a negative spillover effect.

Figure 7: Share of Asian Output Variance Due to External and Local Factors—Baseline Model (%, x-axis = number of quarters)

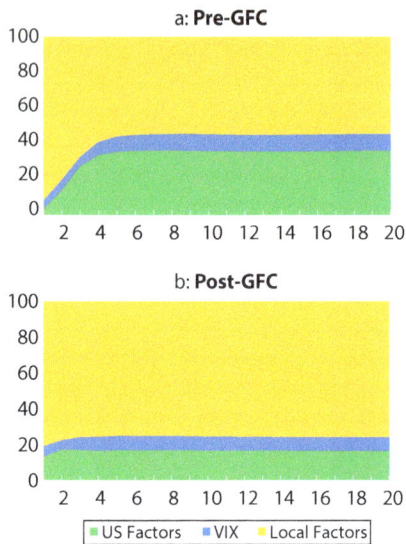

a: Pre-GFC

b: Post-GFC

■ US Factors ■ VIX □ Local Factors

GFC = global financial crisis, US = United States.
Note: Pre-GFC = 2001Q1 to 2008Q1; Post-GFC = 2009Q1 to 2015Q2. Average for sample economies.
Source: ADB calculations using data from CEIC and national sources.

Figure 8: Response to Real GDP Growth Shock in the PRC (percentage point response to a 1 SD rise in PRC growth)

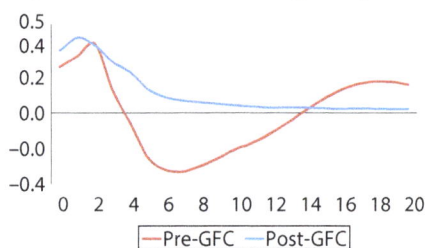

—— Pre-GFC —— Post-GFC

GFC = global financial crisis, SD = standard deviation, US = United States.
Note: Pre-GFC = 2001Q1 to 2008Q1; Post-GFC = 2009Q1 to 2015Q2. Average for sample economies.
Source: ADB calculations.

Finally, higher global risks—as measured by higher levels of VIX—exert negative effect on Asian economic growth, with the effect lasting for about 2 years. The negative effect appears much larger during the pre-GFC period compared with the post-GFC period.

Taking all three global factors into account, the variance decomposition analysis reveals that shocks to internal factors still tend to explain most of the growth variance **(Figure 7)**. Further, the importance of these internal factors also increased in the postcrisis period—not surprising given the change in the region's policy landscape. In the aftermath of the GFC, policy makers worked to rebalance growth away from exports to domestic demand. And this rebalancing effort could explain the increasing importance of internal factors. Another possibility, however, is the presence of other exogenous factors—such as the rising importance of the PRC—exerting a stronger influence on the growth dynamics of Asian economies.[10]

Consequently, the proportion explained by shocks to external factors declined between the two periods. In particular, while shocks to external factors used to account for about 41% of the growth variance in the precrisis period, it fell to about 24% in the postcrisis period. Results for the NIEs and ASEAN-5 shows the relatively more open NIEs saw a larger drop in the share of external factors' contribution to their growth variance—from about 41% pre crisis to about 17% postcrisis. The ASEAN-5, on the other hand, still derives 25% of its growth variance from external factors, down from about 44% in the precrisis period.

The baseline model is expanded to add PRC growth as another external (or "regional") factor. The model assumes PRC growth is unaffected by the growth of other Asian economies, but affected by US growth and monetary policy. In contrast, US growth is assumed not to be affected by PRC growth contemporaneously. This expanded model could help show how exposed Asian economies are to PRC growth slowdown.

As expected, a positive shock to PRC growth—controlling for the impact of other global factors—can boost Asian economic growth. The positive impact also tends to be more persistent after the GFC. More specifically, in the precrisis period, the positive effect only lasted for about four quarters. However, in the postcrisis period, the growth effect is much higher and long-lasting **(Figure 8)**.[11] This result confirms the PRC's increasing role as a major growth driver in the region.

---

[10]   The variance decomposition shows the proportion of the growth variance that can be explained by shocks to external as against internal factors.

[11]   A positive GDP shock from the PRC can affect Asian economies immediately through increased trade, but after a while, this increase in demand from the PRC can significantly raise commodity prices, which also in turn affects import prices. This increase in commodity prices appears to negatively impact Asian economies over time, which was quite pronounced pre-GFC due to a huge price increase in the run-up to the crisis, yet largely disappeared post-GFC.

Figure 9: Share of Asian Output Variance due to External and Local Factors—Expanded Model (%, x-axis = number of quarters)

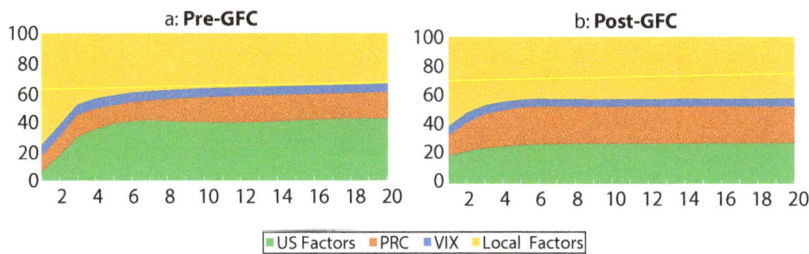

PRC = People's Republic of China, GFC = global financial crisis, US = United States.
Note: Pre-GFC = 2001Q1 to 2008Q1; Post-2009Q1 to 2015Q2. Average for sample economies.
Source: ADB calculations using data from CEIC and national sources.

Consistent with the baseline model, the variance decomposition for the "SVAR model with the PRC" confirms the declining importance of the US factor and increasing importance of the PRC to the region's growth **(Figure 9)**. While the share of US factors—as proportion of the growth variance—fell across the sample group of economies, the share of PRC factor increased from 16% to 24% over the same period. Among individual economies, the largest increases from the precrisis period are for Singapore; Indonesia; the Republic of Korea; and Taipei,China; while decreasing PRC contribution is observed for the Philippines, Malaysia, and Viet Nam.

Nonetheless, domestic factors still explain most of the variation in output growth as a whole across the two models. On average, domestic factors account for at least 40% of the variability in individual growth rates in the precrisis period, and slightly increasing to 43% in the postcrisis period.

Updates on Trade and Investment Integration

Asia's overall trade

While Asia's trade expansion has traditionally outpaced GDP growth—except during the 2008/09 GFC—it fell below GDP growth beginning in 2012. World trade growth has also been below 3% since 2012—lower than global GDP growth **(Figure 10)**. Even after excluding oil and other commodities, trade growth has fallen by volume as well. And the negative divergence is more pronounced in Asia.

Asia's income elasticity of trade has also dropped—from 2.69 pre-GFC (2000Q1–2007Q4) to 1.30 post-GFC (2009Q1–2015Q2)—implying that trade grows less now per one percentage rise in GDP **(Box 1)**.

Aside from protracted global economic recovery, there are several structural factors behind this phenomenon. The shift from exports and

Figure 10: Trade and GDP Growth—Asia and World (%, y-o-y)

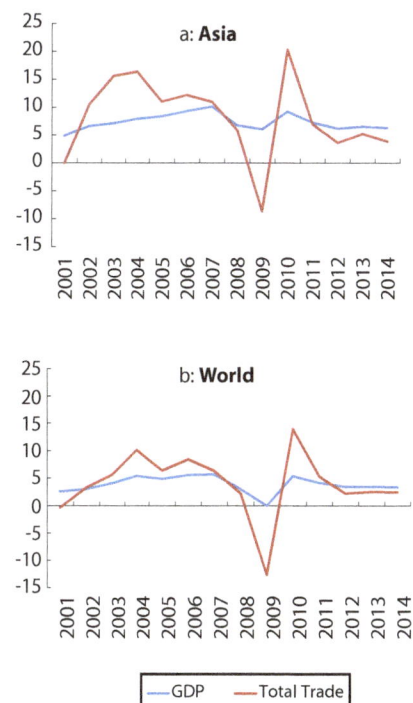

Note: GDP growth for Asia is weighted using gross national income, Atlas Method. For both Asia and world, trade refers to the total trade volume index of the World Trade Organization (WTO).
Source: ADB calculations using data from from various issues of the Asian Development Outlook, ADB; International Trade Statistics, WTO; World Economic Outlook April 2015 Database, International Monetary Fund; and national sources.

Box 1: Asia's Income Elasticity of Trade

We assess Asia's declining trade sensitivity using a vector error-correction model (VECM) of Asia's total imports and GDP. Using seasonally adjusted quarterly imports and GDP at 2005 constant prices, we estimate two models covering the pre-GFC (2000Q1-2007Q4) and post-GFC period (2009Q1-2015Q2). Long-run income elasticity of trade is measured by the coefficient of Asia's GDP in the cointegrating equation. Unit root and cointegration tests validate the use of VECM for this exercise. Due to limited data availability for quarterly GDP, the economies included in this analysis are Australia; the PRC; Hong Kong, China; India; Indonesia; Japan; Malaysia; the Philippines; Singapore; the Republic of Korea; Taipei,China; and Thailand.

Long-run coefficient estimates show that there has been a decline in income elasticity of trade. During the pre-GFC, elasticity was 2.69; after the GFC, elasticity fell to 1.30 **(Box table)**. The error-correction term is also consistent

and statistically significant, indicating a short term deviation of the two series converges to the long-term stable relationship relatively quickly.

Lower income elasticity of trade for Asia could have ramifications through trade-growth nexus: (i) overall economic growth is slowing; and (ii) for the same GDP growth level, import grows less than before. Lower exports to Asia implies less income generation for trading partners—particularly intraregional, which in turn induces even lower growth for the region **(Box figure)**. This highlights the need to make Asia's trade and investment environment more open by lowering trade barriers—particularly nontariff barriers and by supporting trade facilitation.

VECM Results: Income Elasticity of Trade—Asia

Dependent variable: Log (Asia Imports)
Independent variable: Log (Asia GDP)

Period	Cointegrating equation	Error-correction term
Pre-GFC (2000Q1–2007Q4)	2.69**	-0.28**
Post-GFC (2009Q1–2015Q2)	1.30**	-0.29**

** = significant at 5%, GFC = global financial crisis, VECM = Vector Error Correction Model.
Note: Coefficients in the cointegrating equation are multiplied by –1 for presentation purposes. Actual estimates are supposed to be negative since the cointegrating (error-correction) term is constructed by subtracting the right-hand side variable (GDP) from imports. GDP and imports are in constant 2005 US dollars, seasonally adjusted using Census X12.
Source: ADB calculations using data from Oxford Economics Databank.

Asia's Imports By Source
(% of total Asia imports)

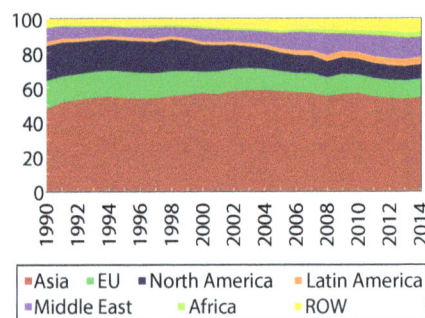

EU = European Union, ROW = rest of the world.
Source: ADB calculations using data from *Direction of Trade Statistics*, International Monetary Fund.

investment toward consumption and services as growth driver underlies this trend (See "Impact of the PRC's structural transformation", p. 12).

Global and regional value chains are not expanding as rapidly as before. Maturing global value chain linkages can be seen by slowing growth in intermediate goods trade—which accounts for about 60% of Asia's total trade **(Figure 11)**. While the region recovered quickly in 2010 following the GFC, trade across commodity groups began to fall afterward. Intermediate goods trade grew just 3.3% year-on-year (y-o-y) in 2013 and contracted 2.6% in 2014, pulling down Asia's overall trade growth **(Figure 12)**. Excluding highly volatile fuel, oil, and other primary goods, growth in intermediate goods trade fell from almost 5% in 2013 to just 0.5% in 2014. Trade in consumption and capital goods, however, continued to expand in 2014. But this was not enough to offset the sharp fall in intermediate goods as their share in Asia's total trade—though increasing—is still low. "Other goods" trade growth has fallen faster than intermediate goods, though its impact on Asia's overall trade is minimal given its small 5% share.

Given the PRC's large influence in Asia's intraregional trade, its moderating growth induces sluggish export growth across Asia. Asia's trade with the PRC since 1994 has followed a similar growth pattern as its trade with the rest of Asia. It has also been a buffer for the region, particularly during crises **(Figure 13)**. However, in 2014 Asia's trade growth with the PRC fell, coinciding with the sharp fall in Asia's total trade growth (see Figure 10).

Asia's intraregional trade

Despite declining trade growth, Asia's intraregional trade share has stabilized since the early 2000s at around 55% **(Figure 14)**. This implies roughly half of Asia's trade flows within the region. Indeed, gravity model estimates suggest Asia's intraregional exports are significantly higher than its exports to the rest of the world—after controlling for the impact of economic size, geographic, cultural, and economic proximity **(Box 2, Table 1)**. This is likely driven mostly by consumption goods—intraregional exports are significantly higher than Asia's exports to the rest of the world. Results also show that the region imports relatively more capital goods and intermediate goods from the rest of the world than its exports of these goods.

Subregional trade links

Assessing integration only at the regional level may mask certain patterns that are observed at the subregional level.[12] Subregional bias could show clearer patterns of trade linkages—as intraregional trade is dominated by "large" subregions (in terms of trade share) such as East Asia and Southeast Asia **(Figure 15)**. An estimation model is constructed with subregional dummies—subregional exports to outside Asia as the benchmark. After controlling for bilateral trade frictions and multilateral trade resistance, Central Asia, East Asia, and Southeast Asia trade significantly higher within their subregion across all commodities **(Table 2)**. This shows significant trade linkages occur subregionally. It is worth noting that these subregions have the most developed cooperation and integration initiatives—such as ASEAN, Central Asia Regional Economic Cooperation (CAREC), and Greater Mekong Subregion (GMS), among others.

Intersubregional trade—or trade flows with the rest of Asia—is also statistically significant across all Asian subregions, but it is strongest in South Asia and the Pacific and Oceania where intrasubregional trade links are the weakest. For the Pacific and Oceania, consumption goods are the main driver of intersubregional trade; while in South Asia, intermediate and consumption goods are the main drivers. It should be

Figure 11: Total Trade By Commodity Groups—Asia ($ billion)

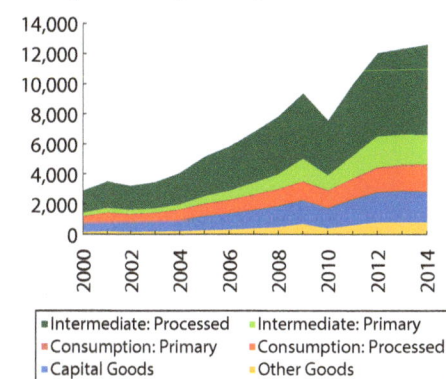

Note: Based on Broad Economic Categories.
Source: ADB calculations using data from United Nations Commodity Trade Database.

Figure 12: Total Trade Growth, By Commodity Groups—Asia (%, y-o-y)

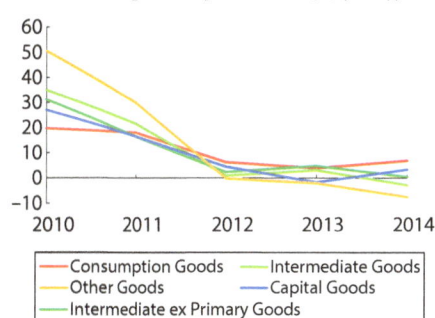

Note: Based on Broad Economic Categories.
Source: ADB calculations using data from United Nations Commodity Trade Database.

Figure 13: Asia ex PRC Trade Growth, by Partner (%, y-o-y)

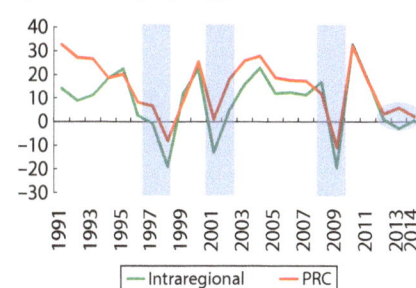

PRC = People's Republic of China.
Source: ADB calculations using data from *Direction of Trade Statistics,* International Monetary Fund.

---

[12]   See ADB. 2014. Updates on Trade Integration. *Asian Economic Integration Monitor April 2014.* Manila.

Box 2: A Dynamic Gravity Model in Measuring Regional Trade Integration

Using simple intraregional trade shares retain a problem in assessing regional trade integration. In particular, trade shares tend to increase as the number of members increase. Inclusion of members with large world trade weights also tends to increase intraregional trade shares (Plummer, Cheong, and Hamanaka 2010).[1] While trade bias represented by intraregional trade intensity can account for the size of the members relative to world trade, it also has problems in range variability, range asymmetry, and dynamic ambiguity which can make interpretation difficult (Iapadre and Tajoli 2014).[2] Furthermore, these two measures of trade integration may not control for the size of the economy, trade costs, and unobserved trade friction which can have a direct impact on trade flows.

In international trade literature, gravity models have been staple in measuring trade flows. Trade flows (either exports or imports) are determined by the size of the respective source and destination economies and distance, which appears to be an overall proxy for trade costs. However, this simple specification fails to capture the unobserved multilateral trade resistance (MTR). MTR measures the cost of country i to export to country j relative to the cost of exporting to other economies (outward multilateral resistance) or the cost of country i to import from country j relative to the cost of importing from all possible import sources (inward multilateral resistance).

Because of the structural weakness of the intuitive gravity model in assessing trade flows, international trade literature uses Anderson and van Wincoop's (2003) gravity model specifications that account for MTR.[3] To account for time-varying characteristics of each trading partner, the gravity model is augmented with country fixed effects interacted with year dummies—as in Olivero and Yotov (2012):[4]

$$\ln X_{ijt} = \beta_0 + \sum_{i=1}^{N} \delta_i F_{it} + \sum_{j=1}^{M} \delta_j F_{jt} + \sum_{i=1}^{N}\sum_{j=1}^{M} \beta_{ij}\,\tau_{ijt} + \rho_{ij} R_{ij} + v$$

In this specification, a set of exporter country dummies F_{it} accounts for all unobserved time-varying country effects that can enhance (GDP) or deter trade (outward multilateral trade resistance). A set of importer country dummies F_{jt} is included for the same purpose. This effectively captures trade resistance factors otherwise left out in traditional gravity models. The term τ_{ijt} captures the observed trade costs such as distance, shared border, and language, among others. R_{ij} is a vector of regional dummies. Depending on the sign of ρ_{ij}, we can test whether countries tend to trade more within the region or outside the region after controlling for trade costs and unobserved country effects. A positive ρ suggests high intra-Asia trade relative to Asia's exports to the rest of the world, while a negative ρ suggests otherwise. A statistically insignificant ρ indicates no difference between intra- and extra-Asia exports.

To account for missing bilateral trade, Heckman's (1979) sample selection estimator (called Heckit estimator) is used.[5] It is assumed that the missing bilateral trade data has a latent data-generating process that using ordinary least squares will result in sample selection bias. Indeed, it can be observed that certain country pairs have nonmissing data in one period, which vanish in subsequent periods. We use the common colonizer dummy from CEPII as the instrumental variable for the selection equation.

For trade data, the United Nations Commodity Trade Database (UN Comtrade) is used with Broad Economic Categories (BEC) commodity classification and regrouped into capital goods, consumption goods, and intermediate goods. Capital goods include capital goods (BEC 41) and industrial transport equipment (BEC 521). Intermediate goods include industrial food and beverage (BEC 111 and BEC 121), industrial supplies (BEC 21 and 22), fuels and lubricants (BEC 31 and 322), and parts and accessories of capital goods and transport equipment (BEC 42 and 53). Consumption goods include food and beverage for household consumption (BEC 112 and 122); transport equipment, nonindustrial (BEC 522); and consumer goods not elsewhere specified (BEC 61, 62, and 63). The model uses 2010-2014 data of 173 countries, of which 43 are from Asia.

---

[1]   M. Plummer, D. Cheong, and S. Hamanaka. 2010. *Methodology for Impact Assessment of Free Trade Agreements.* Manila: Asian Development Bank.

[2]   P. Iapadre and L. Tajoli. 2014. Emerging Countries and Trade Regionalization: A Network Analysis. *Journal of Policy Modeling.* 36 (1). pp. 89–110.

[3]   J. Anderson, and E. van Wincoop. 2003. Gravity with Gravitas: A Solution to the Border Puzzle. *The American Economic Review.* 93 (1). pp. 170–192.

[4]   M.P. Olivero and Y. Yotov. 2012. Dynamic Gravity: Endogenous Country Size and Asset Accumulation. *Canadian Journal of Economics.* 45 (1). pp. 64–92.

[5]   J. Heckman. 1979. Sample Selection Bias as a Specification Error. *Econometrica.* 47 (1). pp. 153-161.

Table 1: Gravity Model Estimation Results
[Dependent variable: Log (Exports)]

Variables	All goods	Capital goods	Consumption goods	Intermediate goods
Log(Distance)	-1.83**	-1.76**	-1.86**	-1.78**
	(0.02)	(0.02)	(0.02)	(0.02)
Colonial relationship dummy	0.82**	0.75**	0.92**	0.82**
	(0.11)	(0.10)	(0.11)	(0.11)
Common language dummy	0.95**	0.91**	1.03**	0.81**
	(0.04)	(0.05)	(0.04)	(0.05)
Contiguity dummy	0.86**	0.93**	0.98**	0.91**
	(0.12)	(0.11)	(0.12)	(0.12)
Regional dummies (base : Asia to ROW)				
Both in Asia dummy	0.95**	0.53	1.05**	0.30
	(0.34)	(0.33)	(0.37)	(0.35)
Importer in Asia dummy	1.04	0.18	2.56**	1.50**
	(0.66)	(0.64)	(0.62)	(0.68)
Both in ROW dummy	-0.57	-1.02**	0.67	0.64
	(0.49)	(0.49)	(0.44)	(0.52)
Rho (sample selection term)	0.05**	0.24**	0.13**	0.04**
Sample size	148,780	148,780	148,780	148,780
Censored observations	40,875	69,288	54,566	51,261
Uncensored observations	107,905	79,492	94,214	97,519

** = significant at 5%, ROW = rest of the world. Robust standard errors in parentheses.
Note: Time-varying country dummies are included but not shown for brevity. Heckman sample selection estimation was used. Data cover 2010–2014 for 173 countries, of which 43 are from Asia. Trade data based on Broad Economic Categories.
Source: ADB calculations using data from United Nations Commodity Trade Database.

Figure 14: Intraregional Trade Shares—Asia, EU, North America (%)

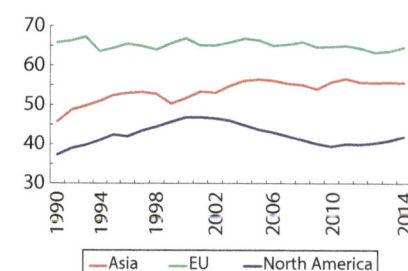

EU=European Union (27 members).
Note: North America covers the United States, Canada, and Mexico. Intraregional trade shares are calculated as $100 \cdot ((X_{ii}+M_{ii})/(X_{iw}+M_{iw}))$, where $X_{ii}+M_{ii}$ refers to region i's total intraregional trade and $X_{iw}+M_{iw}$ refers to region i's total trade with world.
Source: ADB calculations using data from *Direction of Trade Statistics*, International Monetary Fund.

Figure 15: Intrasubregional Trade Shares—Asia (%)

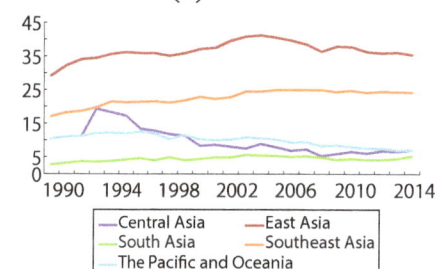

Note: Intra-subregional trade shares are calculated as $100 \cdot ((X_{ii}+M_{ii})/(X_{iw}+M_{iw}))$, where $X_{ii}+M_{ii}$ refers to region i's total intraregional trade and $X_{iw}+M_{iw}$ refers to region i's total trade with world.
Source: ADB calculations using data from *Direction of Trade Statistics*, International Monetary Fund.

noted, however, that there are differences in patterns when the model is estimated separately for the Pacific (excluding Oceania). For instance, consumption goods exports to the rest of Asia is slightly lower but still statistically significant; while intermediate goods trade now becomes insignificant. Meanwhile, the strongest subregions in intrasubregional trade (Central Asia, East Asia, and Southeast Asia) appear to have lesser trade links with Asian peers outside their respective subregions, although this linkage also appears significant for consumption goods. This implies that overall regional trade might be driven by trade in consumption goods, while capital and intermediate goods flows are sustained at the intrasubregional level.

Overall, trade integration has been progressing well subregionally— dominated by subregions such as East Asia and Southeast Asia. This leaves further room to improve intersubregional trade in strengthening Asian intraregional trade. Regional trade agreements spanning subregions and intersubregional infrastructure connectivity could help boost trade across subregions. In the meantime, South Asia and the Pacific could enhance trade more within their respective subregions.

Table 2: Gravity Model Estimation Results—Intra- and Intersubregional Trade

	Central Asia	East Asia	South Asia	Southeast Asia	The Pacific and Oceania
Intrasubregional trade dummy					
All goods	4.25**	3.34**	0.89**	4.29**	0.75
Capital goods	3.70**	1.22**	1.66**	2.47**	0.23
Consumption goods	4.52**	2.48**	1.08**	3.58**	−0.54
Intermediate goods	3.38**	3.74**	0.61	4.96**	−0.24
Intersubregional trade dummy					
All goods	0.67*	0.59*	3.84**	0.80**	1.70**
Capital goods	0.02	0.13	0.70	0.41	0.96**
Consumption goods	0.81*	0.75**	3.51**	0.70*	2.20**
Intermediate goods	−0.06	−0.08	3.79**	0.42	0.71*

** = significant at 5%, * = significant at 10%.
Note: Base category (benchmark) is subregion's trade with countries outside Asia. Heckman sample selection estimation was used. Data cover 2010–2014 for 173 countries, of which, 43 are from Asia. Trade data based on Broad Economic Categories.
Source: ADB calculations using data from United Nations Commodity Trade Database.

Figure 16: Sources of GDP Growth— PRC (% of GDP growth)

a: By Expenditure

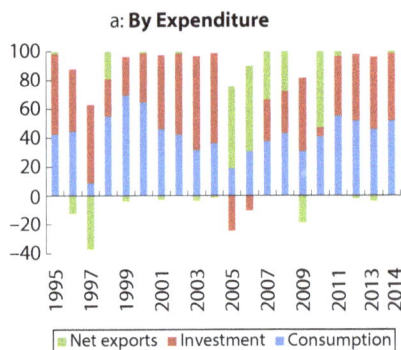

■ Net exports ■ Investment ■ Consumption

b: By Sector

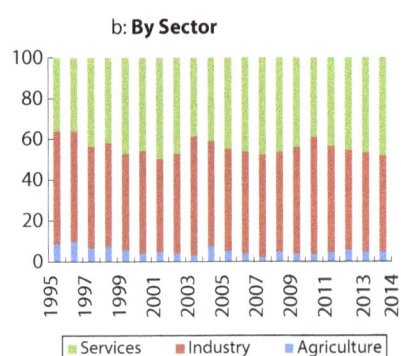

■ Services ■ Industry ■ Agriculture

Source: ADB calculations using data from *Asian Development Outlook April 2015*, ADB; and *World Development Indicators*, World Bank.

Figure 17: Asia's Trade Shares, By Partner (% of Asia's total trade)

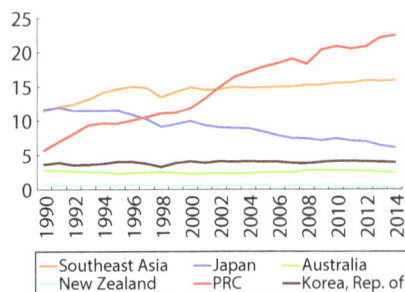

—Southeast Asia —Japan —Australia —New Zealand —PRC —Korea, Rep. of

PRC = People's Republic of China.
Source: ADB calculations using data from *Direction of Trade Statistics*, International Monetary Fund.

Impact of the PRC's structural transformation

The PRC is moving to a "new normal"—slower yet more sustainable and balanced growth. From 2010 to 2014, GDP growth moderated from 10.6% to 7.3%—as authorities shift away from growth led by exports and investment to one led more by consumption and services. Considerable progress has been made in terms of this rebalancing, with consumption expenditure's share of GDP growth in 2014 reaching 52%, compared with investment (47%) and net exports (1.4%) **(Figure 16a)**. By sector, the share of services in GDP growth (48%) now marginally exceeds industry (46%) **(Figure 16b)**. The slowdown and structural transformation are expected to continue for at least the medium term, given that the 13th Five-Year Plan (2016–2020) emphasizes economic rebalancing from heavy industry toward services, with a higher contribution of consumption in growth.

The PRC's economic slowdown and structural transformation will impact the rest of the region significantly, given the economy's weight in intra-Asia trade—which grew dramatically over the past 2 decades **(Figure 17)**. From just over 5% in 1990, Asia's trade with the PRC grew to more than 20% of total trade in 2014. In contrast, Japan's share in Asia's trade declined markedly over the same period in tandem with its outward production expansion through FDI. Others maintain steady shares in total intraregional trade. For both intrasubregional trade in East Asia and intersubregional trade across subregions, the trade linkage with the PRC has become significant.

PRC imports from Asia grew to over $800 billion in 2011, but have stabilized since—amid the slump in global and Asian trade **(Figure 18)**. Overall, PRC imports from Asia are heavily geared toward intermediate goods, followed by capital goods and finally consumption products. But while intermediate goods imports from Asia have grown minimally

Figure 18: The PRC's Imports from Asia—By Commodity Groups and Asian Subregions

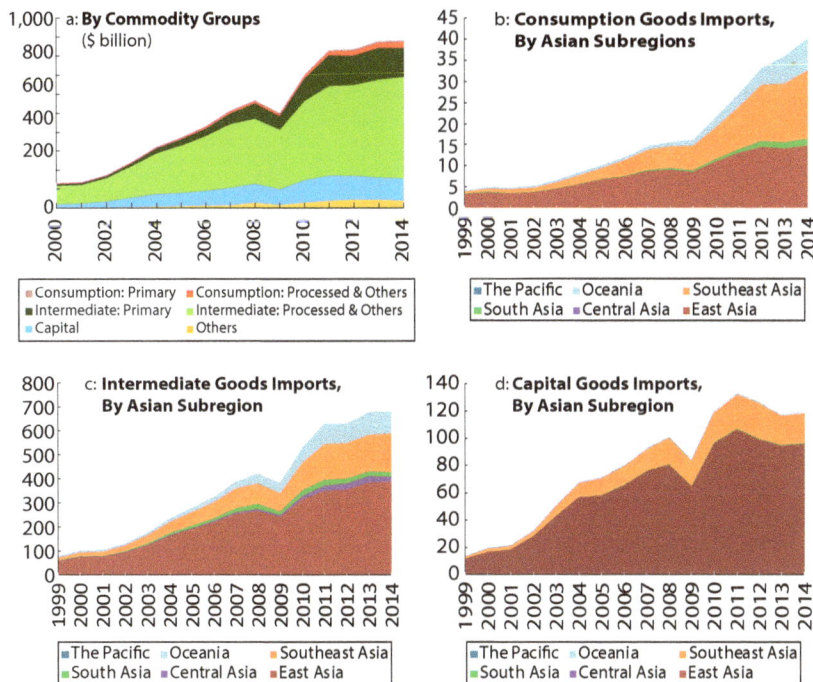

a: **By Commodity Groups**
($ billion)

Legend:
- Consumption: Primary
- Consumption: Processed & Others
- Intermediate: Primary
- Intermediate: Processed & Others
- Capital
- Others

b: **Consumption Goods Imports, By Asian Subregions**

Legend:
- The Pacific
- Oceania
- Southeast Asia
- South Asia
- Central Asia
- East Asia

c: **Intermediate Goods Imports, By Asian Subregion**

Legend:
- The Pacific
- Oceania
- Southeast Asia
- South Asia
- Central Asia
- East Asia

d: **Capital Goods Imports, By Asian Subregion**

Legend:
- The Pacific
- Oceania
- Southeast Asia
- South Asia
- Central Asia
- East Asia

PRC = People's Republic of China.
Note: Based on Broad Economic Categories.
Source: ADB calculations using data from United Nations Commodity Trade Database.

by less than 10% since 2010—PRC imports of consumption goods from the region has almost doubled. Subregionally, East Asia's share remains largest for all three categories—though declining over time. Recently, imports of consumption goods from Southeast Asia have surpassed those from East Asia, likely due to declining final goods trade with Japan. Although PRC intermediate goods imports are declining, the relative shares for Central Asia and the Pacific and Oceania have increased—mostly raw materials for PRC manufacturing. Increasing imports from Central Asia since 2008 derive from increased fuel imports from the subregion. In capital goods, however, the PRC imports its heavy machinery largely from the rest of East Asia and Southeast Asia.

The PRC's structural transformation could pose challenges for many Asian economies. Top Asian exporters to the PRC primarily sell raw materials and parts and components **(Figure 19)**. These economies could face severe challenges should the PRC demand for these commodities weaken drastically. Most of them come from East Asia and Oceania, with the rest from Southeast and Central Asia. Exports from East Asia and Southeast Asia are mostly processed intermediate goods, while those from Oceania and Central Asia are raw materials, which are subject to volatile global commodity and oil prices as well. While the PRC's economic transition poses challenges to these economies, its growing consumer market offers opportunities for consumption goods exports and investments in related industries from the region. Among Asian economies, New Zealand had the highest share of consumption

Figure 19: Top Asian Exporters to the PRC

(% of economy's total exports, 2014)

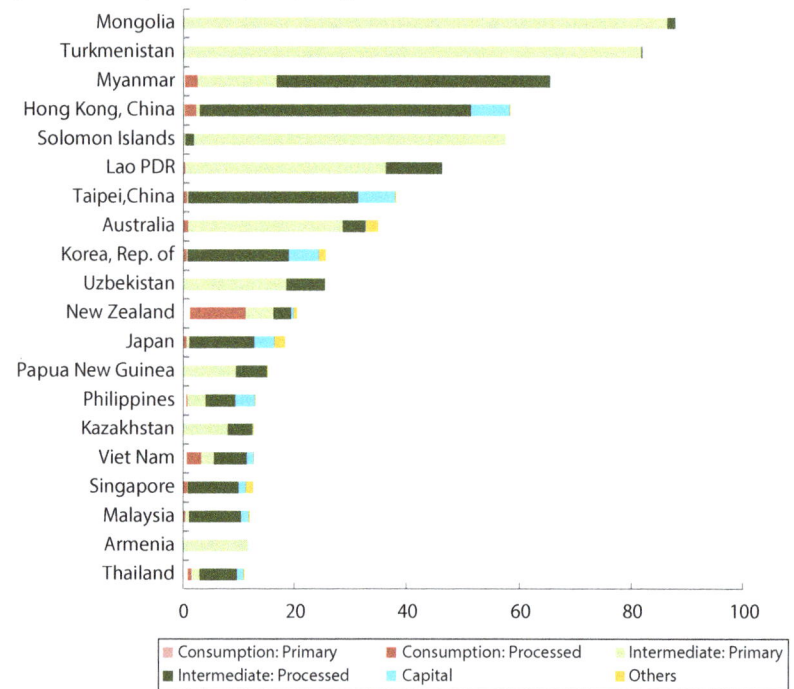

Note: Based on Broad Economic Categories.
Source: ADB calculations using data from United Nations Commodity Trade Database.

goods exports to the PRC out of its total exports in 2014, followed by some Pacific developing economies (Fiji, Kiribati, and Vanuatu) and Southeast Asian economies (Viet Nam, Cambodia, and Myanmar). These economies also had the highest increase in consumption goods exports to the PRC over the past 5 years.

Analyzing regional value chains

Measuring the depth of regional value chains is critical when analyzing trade integration. The build-up and changing patterns of regional value chains in Asia can be traced through the movement of economy market shares and the production weight between low- to high-technology manufactures—the higher-value exports. In 1996, for low-technology products, the PRC, the Republic of Korea, and Thailand ranked highest in terms of market share among the "+3" economies, India, and middle income ASEAN (Indonesia, Malaysia, the Philippines, and Thailand) **(Table 3)**. But by 2014, shares of the Republic of Korea and Thailand fell back with the PRC, India, and Indonesia taking higher shares. For high-technology products, Japan's share in 1996 was highest at 30%, followed by the Republic of Korea and Malaysia. But by 2014, the PRC was largest with a 43.7% share. For medium-high and medium-low technology products, the +3 economies held the largest market shares throughout the two periods. The Republic of Korea and the PRC, in particular, have been increasing their shares over time.

By export composition, Japan's highest weight was on medium-high technology products throughout the two periods **(Table 4)**. In 1990, the

Table 3: Share in Asia's Manufactured Goods Exports per Technology Level (%)

	High Technology			Medium-High Technology			Medium-Low Technology			Low Technology		
	1996	2000	2014	1996	2000	2014	1996	2000	2014	1996	2000	2014
+ 3 Economies												
PRC	5.9	9.4	43.7	6.3	10.1	36.5	10.8	14.9	34.6	21.2	26.3	55.4
Japan	30.0	25.5	7.7	52.8	49.8	23.6	27.6	24.7	11.1	5.4	5.1	2.0
Korea, Rep. of	7.3	10.7	9.4	9.9	9.7	14.4	15.4	16.2	15.1	7.6	6.7	2.4
India	0.4	0.3	1.7	1.1	1.2	3.6	1.9	2.5	9.6	6.0	6.7	9.4
ASEAN-4												
Indonesia	0.9	1.4	0.5	0.9	1.4	1.7	2.6	3.0	1.8	6.1	5.9	5.2
Malaysia	9.4	9.7	4.7	2.2	2.1	2.4	3.5	3.6	4.2	4.5	3.4	3.2
Philippines	2.6	4.5	1.6	0.4	0.6	0.7	0.8	0.8	0.5	1.7	1.5	0.9
Thailand	3.8	3.6	2.7	2.1	3.0	5.2	2.5	3.2	3.6	6.5	5.5	4.3
Rest of Asia	39.8	35.0	28.0	24.3	22.2	11.8	35.1	31.1	19.5	41.0	39.1	17.1
Total Asia	100.0	100.0	100.0	100.0	100.0	100.0	100.0	100.0	100.0	100.0	100.0	100.0

PRC = People's Republic of China.
Note: Based on direct R&D intensity measured relative to value-added and gross production statistics. Includes only manufactured goods, classified according to ISIC Rev. 3. High-technology industries include aircraft and spacecraft; pharmaceuticals; office machinery; telecommuncations equipment; and medical and precision instruments. Medium-high technology industries include electrical machinery; motor vehicles; chemicals sans pharmaceuticals; railroad equipment; and other machinery and equipment. Medium-low technology industries include ships and boats; rubber and plastic products; petroleum products; other nonmetallic mineral products; and basic metals. Low-technology industries include recycling; wood, pulp, and paper products; food and beverage; and textile products.
Source: ADB calculations using data from *STAN Bilateral Trade Database,* Organisation for Economic Co-operation and Development (OECD).

Table 4: Manufacturing Export Share by Technology Level (% of country's total exports)

	High Technology			Medium-High Technology			Medium-Low Technology			Low Technology		
	1990	2000	2014	1990	2000	2014	1990	2000	2014	1990	2000	2014
+ 3 Economies												
PRC	10.9	22.4	30.6	12.4	19.0	24.4	11.2	13.4	15.8	54.3	41.0	28.0
Japan	29.8	31.7	18.5	50.4	48.8	54.1	12.5	11.5	17.4	5.5	4.2	3.5
Korea, Rep. of	27.1	36.8	27.0	26.1	26.4	39.5	19.1	20.9	28.1	26.4	15.1	4.9
India	4.1	4.7	8.6	11.5	13.5	18.0	8.9	13.2	32.4	58.8	61.0	35.0
ASEAN-4												
Indonesia	1.0	13.2	5.1	3.3	10.3	15.0	11.9	10.8	11.2	35.6	36.6	35.0
Malaysia	31.3	58.5	33.0	6.9	10.1	16.4	8.9	8.2	19.0	24.3	13.4	16.0
Philippines	52.3	70.7	43.6	8.2	7.3	18.9	7.2	4.5	8.5	27.9	14.9	18.1
Thailand	17.2	31.1	19.2	8.5	20.2	35.9	6.2	10.5	16.9	55.8	30.8	22.5

PRC = People's Republic of China.
Note: Starting year for the Republic of Korea is 1994; the PRC, 1992; and the Philippines, 1996. See Table 3 for list of industries belonging to each technological level.
Source: ADB calculations using data from *STAN Bilateral Trade Database,* OECD.

PRC's highest weight was on low-technology products, at 54.3%. By 2014, however, it had moved up the value chain with high-technology products accounting for the highest portion of its exports at 30.6%—followed by medium-high technology products at 24.4%. For India, compared with 1990—when it focused mainly on low-technology exports—the economy gradually switched focus to higher technology products. This is also true for Thailand. The large decline in the PRC and the Republic of Korea's low-technology exports' weight over time was partly replaced by India and Indonesia's sustained production weight.

International production sharing has important implications for global value chains as well as Asian economic integration. Cross-border production networks—trade in parts and components and final assembly—have strengthened regional interdependence, as seen from increasing intraregional trade shares. With each stage of production now occurring in different economies, intermediate inputs cross borders multiple times, making it difficult to trace any particular economy's value-added to the regional supply chain—if relying on gross trade statistics. The discrepancy between value-added and gross trade (which "double-counts" this back-and-forth intermediate trade) has long been identified.[13] Accounting for this crisscrossing is particularly important for "Factory Asia", and could shed light on the structure of Asia's vertical specialization and integration.

Using the gross exports accounting framework by Wang, Wei, and Zhu (2014), integration in value-added trade was examined by decomposing the gross intraregional exports of 12 Asian economies into its various components.[14] Generally, an economy's exports (to any partner) can be decomposed into four major categories: domestic value-added absorbed abroad (DVA); value-added first exported but eventually returned home (RDV); foreign value-added (FVA); and purely double-counted terms (PDC).[15] While the relatively small number of economies—which comprise the "region" for this exercise—may allow for limited analysis, the economies included are arguably the major drivers of regional trade (in 2014, they accounted for 77% of Asia's intraregional exports).

The different components and their combinations allow us to gauge (i) whether there is significant difference from intraregional measures of gross exports and exports ultimately absorbed abroad, (ii) whether linkages among the 12 has also increased in terms of domestic value-added, (iii) the structure of the region's value-added trade, and (iv) economies and economy-pairs driving this trend. Three years were examined—2000, 2005, and 2011—for which data from Intercountry Input-Output (IO) tables are available. The available data covers 45 economies and the rest of the world (ROW) as an additional group—40 economies and the ROW were sourced from the World Input-Output Database, while an additional five Asian economies were constructed by ADB.[16]

Between 2000 and 2011, Asia's intraregional gross exports have increased about 3.6 times. And while the DVA accounts for the largest share in Asia's trade (some 70%), the increase between the two periods is mostly accounted for by an increase in PDC (4.4 times), followed by FVA (3.9 times), RDV (3.8 times) and finally DVA (3.4 times). Given the increasing

---

[13] R. Koopman, Z. Wang and S-J. Wei. 2014. Tracing Value-added and Double Counting in Gross Exports. *American Economic Review.* 104 (2). pp.459–494. Also available as NBER Working Paper No. 18579; Z. Wang, S-J Wei, and K. Zhu. 2014. Quantifying International Production Sharing at the Bilateral and Sectoral Levels. *NBER Working Paper.* No. 19677. Cambridge, MA: National Bureau of Economic Research.

[14] The 12 economies are Australia; Bangladesh; the PRC; India; Indonesia; Japan; the Republic of Korea; Malaysia; the Philippines; Thailand; Taipei,China; and Viet Nam.

[15] See footnote 14.

[16] Except for Bangladesh, Malaysia, the Philippines, Thailand and Viet Nam, which were constructed by ADB, the IOs of the rest were sourced from the World Input-Output Database (WIOD). While the WIOD and ADB IO tables have been constructed in a clear conceptual framework on the basis of officially published input-output tables in conjunction with national accounts and international trade statistics, level numbers are likely to remain different from those officially released by the respective economies.

role in Asian trade growth of the PDC component—which occurs from increasing production sharing across borders—this shows Asia's growing linkages in the regional production network.

Consistent with other findings of increasing intraregional shares using gross trade statistics, exports of DVA ultimately absorbed within the region—as a percent of all exported DVA—has likewise increased **(Figure 20)**. This increasing trend is not only in DVA, but in FVA and PDC as well. However, Asian economies' exports of domestic value that returns back via imports have been declining, consistent with the fact that most of DVA is now absorbed abroad.

Drivers of regional value chains

To examine the region's forward and backward cross-border production linkages, the portion embedded in intermediate goods (DVAint) is extracted from DVA to calculate the ratio of FVA+DVAint out of total intraregional exports.[17] In 2011, FVA+DVAint accounted for 53.5% of the intraregional trade—relatively stable with 52.2% in 2000. This illustrates the region's strong forward and backward intraregional linkages. Of the 12, the top three are the PRC, Japan, and Australia, followed by the Republic of Korea, Indonesia, and Taipei,China **(Figure 21)**.

Within Asia, the major drivers of the trend for each value-added trade component are gauged by examining share contributions **(Figure 22)**. For example, decomposing intraregional DVA trade shows the PRC accounted for the largest share in 2011. For FVA, the PRC and the Republic of Korea top the list, each accounting for almost a quarter of total intraregional FVA. In other words, almost half of Asian FVA comes from these two economies' exports. In terms of RDV, 85% of intraregional RDV is accounted for by the PRC and Japan. In terms of PDC, the top three slots in 2011 were the PRC, followed by the Republic of Korea and Taipei,China—an order reversed from 2005. Generally, one can see the relative dominance of East Asian economies in various components of regional value-added trade, partly due to the PRC's rise as a major player in intraregional trade over the span of a decade.

This relative dominance of East Asian economies is even more evident if trade links are broken down further into economy pairs. Ranking bilateral trade among the 12 economies by contribution to intraregional trade per component—a total of 132 economy-pairs—intra-East Asian links dominate the top 10 **(Table 5)**. More notably, the cumulative share of the top 10 economy-pairs account for over half of intraregional DVA and FVA trade. The concentration ratio is even higher for PDC and RDV trade, with the top 10 pairs accounting for about 60% and 75% of total intraregional PDC and RDV trade, respectively. Thus, trade by component appears to be dominated by a small number of economy-pair trades, in particular across East Asia, rather than with the rest of Asia.

Figure 20: Intraregional Trade by Components (% of component's exports to the world)

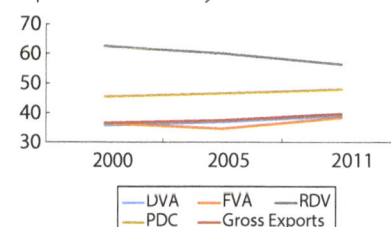

DVA = domestic value-added; FVA = foreign value-added; RDV = returned domestic value-added; PDC = pure double counting component.
Source: ADB calculations using data from World Input-Output Tables and ADB Input-Output Tables, and methodology from Wang Z., S-J. Wei, and K. Zhu. 2014. Quantifying International Production Sharing at the Bilateral and Sectoral Levels. *NBER Working Paper*. No. 19777. Cambridge, MA: NBER.

Figure 21: Intraregional FVA & DVA in Intermediates by Source (as % of intraregional exports)

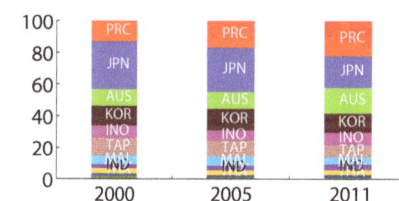

AUS = Australia; BAN = Bangladesh; PRC = People's Republic of China; IND = India; INO = Indonesia; JPN = Japan; KOR = Republic of Korea; MAL = Malaysia; PHI = Philippines; TAP = Taipei,China; THA = Thailand; VIE = Viet Nam.
Note: Viet Nam, the Philippines, and Bangladesh are not labeled in the figure; they comprise the smallest shares, with Viet Nam and the Philippines owning the last two horizontal bars, while the bar of Bangladesh is too small to be seen in the chart.
Source: ADB calculations using data from World Input-Output Tables and ADB Input-Output Tables, and methodology from Z.Wang, S-J. Wei, and K. Zhu. 2014. Quantifying International Production Sharing at the Bilateral and Sectoral Levels. *NBER Working Paper*. No. 19777. Cambridge, MA: NBER.

---

[17] DVAint refers to DVA in intermediate goods exported by an Asian economy to its Asian neighbors, while FVA in this case refers only to foreign value added from Asian economies that is embedded in one's exports after factoring out the FVA portion from the ROW.

Figure 22: Intraregional Value-Added Exports—Asia

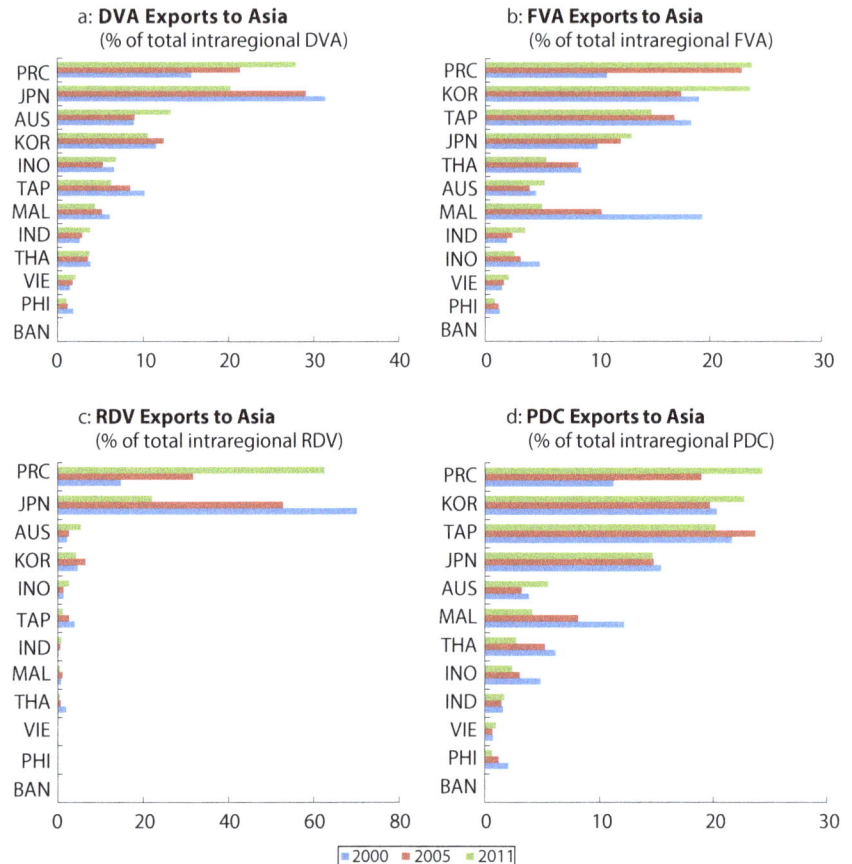

a: DVA Exports to Asia
(% of total intraregional DVA)

b: FVA Exports to Asia
(% of total intraregional FVA)

c: RDV Exports to Asia
(% of total intraregional RDV)

d: PDC Exports to Asia
(% of total intraregional PDC)

■ 2000   ■ 2005   ■ 2011

AUS = Australia; BAN = Bangladesh; PRC = People's Republic of China; IND = India; INO = Indonesia; JPN = Japan; KOR = Republic of Korea; MAL = Malaysia; PHI = Philippines; TAP = Taipei,China; THA = Thailand; VIE = Viet Nam.

DVA = domestic value-added; FVA = foreign value-added; RDV = returned domestic value-added; PDC = pure double counting component.

Source: ADB calculations using data from World Input-Output Tables and ADB Input-Output Tables, and methodology from Z. Wang, S-J. Wei, and K. Zhu. 2014. Quantifying International Production Sharing at the Bilateral and Sectoral Levels. NBER Working Paper. No. 19677. Cambridge, MA: NBER.

This pattern, indicating a possible intrasubregional bias, is also worth further examination.

Progress in sector-level value chains

Intraregional production activities within sectors appear to be changing as well, with shares within industrial exports showing interesting shifts between 2000 and 2011 **(Figure 23)**. For example, intraregional trade within the labor-intensive Asian textile industry, while still increasingly dominated by the PRC—which covers about two-thirds of intraregional exports—shows Bangladesh and Viet Nam emerging as important players; In the meantime, DVA shares of three East Asian economies—Japan; the Republic of Korea; and Taipei,China—have declined 6 to 8 percentage points during this period. With rising production costs in other economies in general, setting up operations—such

Table 5: Value-Added Trade—Asian Economy Pair Drivers

DVA Economy-Pairs (as % of Intraregional DVA Trade)						FVA Economy-Pairs (as % of Intraregional FVA Trade)					
2000		**2005**		**2011**	**Rank**	**2000**		**2005**		**2011**	**Rank**
JPN-TAP	7.62	JPN-PRC	10.17	JPN-PRC	9.31	1	TAP-PRC	7.81	PRC-JPN	11.13	KOR-PRC	12.48	1
JPN-PRC	7.55	PRC-JPN	8.76	PRC-JPN	8.97	2	MAL-THA	7.79	TAP-PRC	10.07	TAP-PRC	10.01	2
PRC-JPN	7.23	KOR-PRC	5.79	AUS-PRC	6.10	3	KOR-JPN	7.45	KOR-PRC	8.20	PRC-JPN	8.76	3
JPN-KOR	5.87	JPN-TAP	5.10	KOR-PRC	5.81	4	KOR-PRC	6.52	KOR-JPN	4.63	JPN-PRC	6.45	4
TAP-PRC	3.91	TAP-PRC	5.03	PRC-KOR	5.10	5	MAL-JPN	6.48	JPN-PRC	4.62	KOR-JPN	5.29	5
KOR-JPN	3.82	JPN-KOR	4.69	TAP-PRC	4.20	6	TAP-JPN	6.18	MAL-JPN	4.24	PRC-KOR	3.37	6
KOR-PRC	3.68	PRC-KOR	4.05	PRC-IND	3.93	7	PRC-JPN	5.97	THA-JPN	3.67	PRC-AUS	3.33	7
AUS-JPN	3.58	AUS-JPN	2.74	PRC-AUS	3.41	8	THA-JPN	4.62	PRC-KOR	3.58	PRC-IND	3.28	8
JPN-MAL	3.17	JPN-MAL	2.63	AUS-JPN	3.08	9	JPN-PRC	2.94	TAP-JPN	3.12	AUS-PRC	2.33	9
TAP-JPN	3.03	KOR-JPN	2.60	JPN-KOR	2.86	10	INO-JPN	2.30	PRC-AUS	2.42	TAP-JPN	1.86	10
Rest of Asia	50.53	Rest of Asia	48.44	Rest of Asia	47.22		Rest of Asia	41.92	Rest of Asia	44.31	Rest of Asia	42.86	
Top 10	49.47	Top 10	51.56	Top 10	52.78		Top 10	58.08	Top 10	55.69	Top 10	57.14	

RDV Economy-Pairs (as % of Intraregional RDV Trade)						PDC Economy-Pairs (as % of Intraregional PDC Trade)					
2000		**2005**		**2011**	**Rank**	**2000**		**2005**		**2011**	**Rank**
JPN-TAP	16.10	JPN-PRC	15.73	PRC-KOR	21.48	1	TAP-PRC	7.53	TAP-PRC	15.88	TAP-PRC	14.55	1
JPN-MAL	14.16	PRC-KOR	10.36	PRC-TAP	14.89	2	KOR-PRC	5.89	KOR-PRC	9.23	KOR-PRC	11.94	2
JPN-KOR	11.32	JPN-MAL	10.21	PRC-JPN	11.97	3	KOR-TAP	4.16	PRC-KOR	4.97	PRC-KOR	7.72	3
JPN-PRC	10.86	JPN-TAP	8.86	JPN-PRC	8.40	4	TAP-MAL	3.89	JPN-PRC	4.35	JPN-PRC	5.20	4
JPN-THA	10.49	PRC-TAP	8.57	JPN-TAP	4.22	5	TAP-JPN	3.78	PRC-TAP	3.63	PRC-TAP	4.86	5
PRC-KOR	4.78	JPN-KOR	7.94	PRC-AUS	3.98	6	JPN-TAP	3.75	KOR-TAP	3.27	PRC-JPN	4.45	6
PRC-TAP	4.13	JPN-THA	6.71	JPN-KOR	3.79	7	KOR-JPN	3.72	PRC-JPN	3.24	KOR-JPN	4.08	7
JPN-INO	3.43	PRC-JPN	5.89	PRC-IND	2.92	8	JPN-MAL	3.17	JPN-KOR	2.96	JPN-KOR	3.36	8
PRC-JPN	2.69	KOR-PRC	3.22	PRC-THA	2.52	9	JPN-KOR	3.03	KOR-JPN	2.78	KOR-TAP	3.04	9
THA-MAL	1.64	PRC-MAL	2.50	AUS-PRC	2.45	10	MAL-THA	3.01	JPN-TAP	2.77	JPN-TAP	2.94	10
Rest of Asia	20.42	Rest of Asia	20.01	Rest of Asia	23.36		Rest of Asia	58.05	Rest of Asia	46.90	Rest of Asia	37.84	
Top 10	79.58	Top 10	79.99	Top 10	76.64		Top 10	41.95	Top 10	53.10	Top 10	62.16	

AUS = Australia; PRC = People's Republic of China; IND = India; INO = Indonesia; JPN = Japan; KOR = Republic of Korea; MAL = Malaysia; TAP = Taipei,China; THA = Thailand.
DVA = domestic value added; FVA = foreign value added; RDV = returned domestic value added; PDC = pure double counting component.
Source: ADB calculations using data from World Input-Output Tables and ADB Input-Output Tables, and methodology from Z. Wang, S-J. Wei, and K. Zhu. 2014. Quantifying International Production Sharing at the Bilateral and Sectoral Levels. *NBER Working Paper.* No. 19777. Cambridge, MA: NBER.

as in Bangladesh and Viet Nam—has been on the rise.[18] The FVA in Bangladesh and Viet Nam exports are also increasing much faster than the rest of their peers (excluding the PRC).

More capital-intensive than textiles, the region's electrical and optical equipment (EOE) industry—including electronics—shows a similar trend in terms of intraregional DVA exports. Leading exporters in 2000 saw their shares decline after a decade, with their later industrializing

---

[18] McKinsey & Company. 2013. The Global Sourcing Map–Balancing Cost, Compliance, and Capacity: McKinsey's Apparel CPO Survey 2013. http://www.mckinsey.com/~/media/mckinsey/dotcom/client_service/retail/articles/the_global_sourcing_map_balancing_cost_compliance_and_capacity.ashx

Figure 23: Shares to Intraregional DVA Exports (y-axis = difference in shares, 2011 vs 2000; box numbers = shares as of 2011)

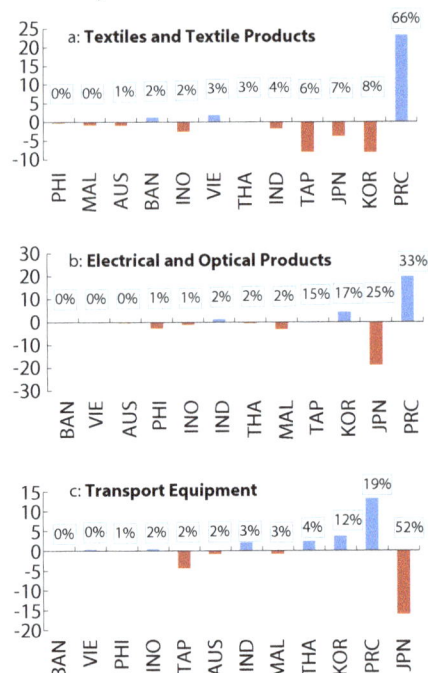

a: Textiles and Textile Products

0% 0% 1% 2% 2% 3% 3% 4% 6% 7% 8% 66%

PHI MAL AUS BAN INO VIE THA IND TAP JPN KOR PRC

b: Electrical and Optical Products

0% 0% 0% 1% 1% 2% 2% 2% 15% 17% 25% 33%

BAN VIE AUS PHI INO IND THA MAL TAP KOR JPN PRC

c: Transport Equipment

0% 0% 1% 2% 2% 2% 3% 3% 4% 12% 19% 52%

BAN VIE PHI INO TAP AUS IND MAL THA KOR PRC JPN

AUS = Australia; BAN = Bangladesh; PRC = People's Republic of China; IND = India; INO = Indonesia; JPN = Japan; KOR = Republic of Korea; MAL = Malaysia; PHI = Philippines; TAP = Taipei,China; THA = Thailand; VIE = Viet Nam; DVA = domestic value added.
Source: ADB calculations using data from World Input-Output Tables and ADB Input-Output Tables, and methodology from Z. Wang, S-J. Wei, and K. Zhu. 2014. Quantifying International Production Sharing at the Bilateral and Sectoral Levels. *NBER Working Paper*. No. 19677. Cambridge, MA: NBER.

neighbors gaining ground. This is typical of the Flying Geese paradigm.[19] For example, Japan controlled 44% of intraregional DVA exports in EOE in 2000. A decade later, its share had dropped 18.7 percentage points, while the rest of East Asia gained—the PRC share increased 19.8 percentage points, followed by the Republic of Korea (4.4 percentage points). Interestingly, India has entered the EOE picture (1.4 percentage points). As of 2011, the PRC holds the largest share of the region's intraregional DVA exports of EOE (33%), with Japan remaining second (25%).

The transport equipment manufacturing export sector—another capital-intensive industry—also shows increasing participation of smaller Asian economies. While Japan remains the biggest intraregional exporter of DVA in transport equipment, it has seen its share decrease from 68% in 2000 to 52% in 2011. This could be due to the (re)location of Japanese manufacturing bases in locations such as the PRC, Thailand, and Viet Nam, where the exports can originate. Transport equipment is among the top manufactures receiving Japanese FDI in the region. Before the GFC, it accounted for about 26% of Japan's outward FDI. In the years afterward, transport equipment manufacturing FDI again recovered, accounting for 21%.[20] As of 2011, more Asian economies are increasing their export shares in this sector—led by the PRC, the Republic of Korea, Thailand, and India.

Together with shifts in DVA shares are changing patterns of returned domestic value added (RDV). In EOE intraregional exports, for example, there was a notable drop in Japan's share of the region's RDV over the years. In 2000, it accounted for 78% of the region's total RDV; in 2011, it was barely 20%. It appears that Japan's EOE exports are no longer characterized by parts and components that need to be reimported back to Japan for further processing. This suggests that Japan is likely focusing on the higher-end of the value chain. On the other hand, the PRC now accounts for 73% of the region's RDV. Still, while comprising a big chunk of the region's intraregional exports, PRC electronic exports seem to be dominated by processed manufacturing, characterized by low-technology assembly.[21] Further, most high-technology producers tend to be foreign investors that use the PRC as an export platform.[22]

The RDV shares in intraregional exports of transport equipment has also changed significantly from 2000 to 2011. PRC's RDV climbed from a 3% share to 48% over the span of a decade, suggesting the PRC's increasing role in more capital-intensive production networks. This is also in line with the fact that the PRC now accounts for 28% of the pure double-counting in intraregional exports for transport equipment, up from only 7% in 2000.

[19] K. Akamatsu. 1962. A Historical Pattern of Economic Growth in Developing Countries. *Journal of Developing Economies*. 1 (1). pp. 3–15.

[20] Before GFC refers to 2005–2008, after GFC refers to 2012–2014.

[21] F. Lin and H.C. Tang. 2013. The People's Republic of China cracks electronic export sophistication: Fact or fallacy? *AIEN Blog*. 17 Sept. https://aric.adb.org/blog/the-peoples-republic-of-china-cracks-electronic-export-sophistication-fact-or-fallacy

[22] C. Qingqing, C.C. Goh, B. Sun, and L.C. Xu. 2011. Market Integration in the People's Republic of China. *Asian Development Review*. 28 (1). p. 87.

While patterns of DVA and RDV appear to be a toss-up between economies, Malaysia figures prominently when it comes to changes in shares of FVA and PDC components. Malaysia—well-known in the global electronics industry—used to hold the largest share in intraregional FVA in EOE exports in 2000, and second in PDC. However, a decade later it showed the biggest drop in FVA content and in PDC among the 12 economies. This may suggest its Asian neighbors might be using Malaysia less as a hub in the regional electronics production network. By 2011, the PRC had the largest share of FVA (increasing its share 23.4 percentage points) in intraregional EOE exports, while Taipei,China still has the largest PDC share—primarily driven by export links with the PRC. In transport equipment, Malaysia also experienced the biggest drop in FVA share between 2000 and 2011, moving from second in 2000 to fourth in 2011, behind Japan, the PRC, and the Republic of Korea.

Nonetheless, even within these three sectors, intra-East Asian pairs dominate. Within the EOE industry, the top bilateral link in gross exports is between Taipei,China and the PRC; however, a large portion of that is due to back-and-forth trading of intermediate products. However, interesting linkages outside East Asia are also emerging. For textiles, Indonesia has become a strong market for the PRC—the top PRC market among ASEAN and second to Japan as PRC's DVA export market in Asia by 2011. There is also growing intermediate goods trade between the Republic of Korea and Viet Nam in textiles, with the PDC component increasing by a factor of 13 from 2000 to 2011.

FDI integration in Asia

Total FDI inflows to Asia

Global FDI inflows totaled $1.2 trillion in 2014, down 16% from $1.5 trillion in 2013. Despite the decline, inflows to Asia from outside and within the region were up 9% in 2014 from 2013 ($495 billion), reaching 40% of the global total **(Figure 24)**. Around 80% of Asia's inflows went to East Asia ($247 billion) and to Southeast Asia ($133 billion), with multinational corporations (MNCs) providing much of the investment. In recent years, MNCs have become a major force in enhancing regional connectivity in these two subregions—through cross-border investment in infrastructure and production. The PRC and Hong Kong, China took in 94% of East Asia's FDI, while Singapore, Indonesia, Thailand, Malaysia, and Viet Nam absorbed 92% of the FDI going into Southeast Asia.[23]

In 2014, the PRC became the world's largest FDI recipient, attracting $129 billion (up 4% from 2013), mainly from new FDI in services— particularly retail, transport, and finance. Among major investing economies, investment from the Republic of Korea into the PRC rose the highest by 30% in 2014. FDI flows from the European Union (EU)—

---

[23]   However, taking into consideration that majority of Hong Kong, China-sourced FDI to the PRC are investments by PRC residents round-tripped through Hong Kong, China, the combined FDI inflows of the PRC and Hong Kong, China drops from $231.5 billion to $112.2 billion (from 94% to 45% of East Asia's FDI).

Figure 24: Total FDI Inflows—Asia ($ billion)

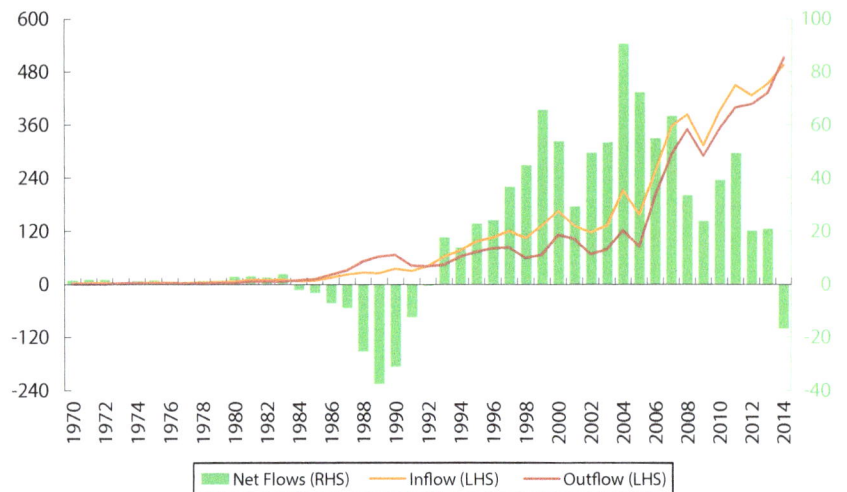

FDI = foreign direct investment, LHS = left-hand scale, RHS = right-hand scale.
Note: Asia does not include Bhutan, the Maldives, the Federated States of Micronesia, Myanmar, Nauru, Nepal, Palau, Tajikistan, Turkmenistan, and Tuvalu (FDI outflows) as data unavailable.
Source: ADB calculations using data from United Nations Conference on Trade and Development (UNCTAD).

the PRC's largest trading partner—increased slightly; but flows from Japan and the US declined by 39% and 21%, respectively. FDI inflows to Hong Kong, China saw a surge—associated with some large cross-border mergers and acquisitions (M&A)—such as the $5.7 billion purchase of a 25% stake in A.S. Watson Co. by Singapore's Temasek Holdings, and the $4.8 billion acquisition of Wing Hang Bank by OCBC Bank (also from Singapore). Investors from the PRC were major players in the M&A market in Hong Kong, China. For example, COFCO acquired a 51% stake in Noble Agri Limited, paying $4 billion to its parent Novel Group. In terms of greenfield projects, companies from the PRC accounted for about one fifth of all projects recorded by InvestHK in 2014.[24]

Singapore remained the dominant recipient of FDI in Southeast Asia, with its inflows rising by 4% to $68 billion. Inflows to Indonesia rose 20% to $23 billion, mostly coming from Singapore, Japan, Malaysia, the Netherlands, and the United Kingdom. Viet Nam saw inflows increase slightly—by 3% in 2014. Viet Nam still enjoys a labor cost advantage over the PRC, but rapidly rising wages have reduced the difference, which may affect relatively small investors in labor-intensive industries. In November this year, the Vietnamese government decided to raise the minimum wage by about 15%.[25]

---

[24] Greenfield FDI relates to investment projects that establish new entities and involve building offices, buildings, plants and factories from scratch. It is considered a kind of working capital. InvestHK is a government department responsible for FDI, supporting overseas businesses to set up and expand in Hong Kong, China.

[25] UNCTAD. 2015. *World Investment Report 2015*. Geneva.

Total FDI outflows from Asia

Historically, FDI outflows from Asia have been below inflows except for the periods 1984–1992 and recently in 2014 (see Figure 24). In fact, outflows from Asia were up 19% in 2014 ($512 billion) from 2013 ($432 billion). Asia is investing abroad more than any other region. According to the UNCTAD *World Investment Report 2015*, MNCs from Asia became the world's largest investors, accounting for almost one-third of the global total ($1.4 trillion). FDI outflows from Asia were primarily from East Asia ($416 billion) and Southeast Asia ($80 billion) as MNCs expanded foreign operations through greenfield investments and cross-border M&As. Traditional Asian investors come from these two subregions— Japan is the largest, accounting for an average of 31% of Asia's total FDI outflows since 2000, followed by Hong Kong, China (24%) and Singapore (8%). Investment from nontraditional Asian investors also increased in 2014, mostly to advanced economies **(Box 3)**. Investments by MNCs based in Asia increased 29% to $432 billion in 2014. Around 72% ($310 billion) were investments coming from Hong Kong, China ($143 billion), the PRC ($116 billion), Singapore ($41 billion), and India ($10 billion).

Box 3: Foreign Direct Investment from Emerging, Nontraditional Asian Investors

In 2014, Asia's total FDI outflows reached $512 billion, a 19% increase from 2013. Investments primarily came from East Asia, particularly Hong Kong, China, as well as from Southeast Asia, particularly Singapore. According to the UNCTAD *World Investment Report 2015*, investments by Asian multinational corporations (MNCs) were the main drivers of growth. In 2014, several emerging Asian investors such as the PRC, Malaysia, Thailand, and India have increased investment particularly to developed economies.

People's Republic of China (PRC)

Based on a report by Baker & McKenzie/Rhodium Group, the last 3 years have seen significant interest by PRC investors in the privatization of state-related industries (such as utilities or logistics) in countries including Portugal, Italy, and Spain.[1] In Italy, the PRC has made acquisitions in the energy and industrial equipment totaling $3.3 billion (targeted companies were CDP Reti acquired by the PRC's State Grid Corporation, and Ansaldo Energua Spa acquired by Shanghai Electric). The Economic Commission for Latin America and

Major Destination of FDI Flows from Emerging Asian Investors (2014)

Source	Major non-Asia Destinations	$ million	% of total investor's outbound FDI
PRC	Italy	23,394	28.2
	Peru	1,238	1.5
	US	788	1.0
Malaysia	Italy	441	7.5
	Turkey	423	7.2
	France	110	1.9
Thailand	Italy	1,487	61.7
	Netherlands	57	2.4
	Germany	32	1.3
	US	29	1.2
India	United Kingdom	489	23.9
	US	203	9.9
	Finland	187	9.2

PRC = People's Republic of China, US = United States.
Source: ADB calculations using data from ASEAN Secretariat, OECD, and UNCTAD database.

---

[1] Baker & McKenzie. 2015. [The People's Republic of China] investment into Europe hits record high in 2014. Firm News. 11 February. http://www.bakermckenzie.com/news/Chinese-investment-into-Europe-hits-record-high-in-2014-02-11-2015

Continued on next page

Box 3 continued

the Caribbean (ECLAC) reported that PRC MNCs participated in some of the biggest acquisitions in Peru, mainly the purchase of the Las Bambas mine for $7.0 billion.[2]

According to a report of Rhodium Group, PRC firms spent $3.7 billion on 30 FDI transactions in the US in the fourth quarter of 2014, which includes 18 acquisitions ($3.4 billion) and 12 greenfield projects $272 million. Most of the increase in investments went to finance and commercial real estate. The PRC's total annual spending on greenfield investments in the US also reached a new record high of $1.3 billion in 2014.[3]

Thailand

Overseas investments by Thai corporations have grown significantly, overtaking inward FDI. Thai firms are encouraged by the government to expand regionally and in developed markets, through cross-border M&As and greenfield investments. The government recognizes that to overcome domestic resource limitations and expand business, Thai entrepreneurs need to branch out overseas and assists them to do so. Target industries are predominantly labor intensive, such as textiles

and garments, shoes and leather, agriculture, food preparation, metal processing, auto parts and accessories, construction materials, and real estate development.[4]

Thailand's outbound investments primarily go to Europe—particularly Italy, the Netherlands, and Germany—as well as the US. For instance, ASEAN's largest fully-integrated flat steel-maker Sahaviriya Steel Industries seized on the strong baht and distressed assets in Europe to acquire Europe's second largest steel smelter (UK-based Teesside Cast Products) for $469 million in 2011. The world's largest canned tuna producer (TUF) acquired the European MW Brands for $489 million in October 2010. The Central Group—already active in Indonesia and the PRC—purchased Italian department store operator La Rinascente for $143 million in May 2011 and acquired the 120-year old Illum department store in Denmark in March 2013, with plans to invest $65.4 million for renovation.[5]

India

According to the Inward Investment Report 2014-2015 of UKTI (UK Trade and Industry), India is now the third largest FDI source for the UK after the US and France in number of projects. Key sectors include healthcare, agricultural technology, and food and beverages. Indian Venture Capital Fund Vistaar Group is a key foreign investor in establishing a postproduction studio at MediaCity, Manchester. The fund plans to invest $12 million this year and $18 million over the next 5 years.[6]

India is one of the fastest growing FDI sources for the US with investments in aerospace, textile, IT sectors and life sciences. Indian firms employ around 44,000 US workers and export more than $2 billion worth of goods from the US. Between January 2003 and October 2014, 362 US investment projects were announced by Indian firms.[7]

There are 30 Indian companies, mainly in software and consultancy, operating in Finland. Currently, there are about 400 Indian professionals working for Finnish high-tech companies and Indian software companies like TCS.[8]

[2] Economic Commission for Latin America and the Caribbean. 2015. *Foreign Direct Investment in the Region Fell 16% in 2014 after a Decade of Strong Expansion.* CEPAL Press Releases. 27 May. http://www.cepal.org/en/pressreleases/foreign-direct-investment-region-fell-16-2014-after-decade-strong-expansion

[3] T. Hanemann and C. Gao. 2015. [The People's Republic of China] FDI in the United States: Q4 and Full Year 2014 Update. *Rhodium Group Research Notes.* http://rhg.com/notes/chinese-fdi-in-the-united-states-q4-and-full-year-2014-update

[4] Thailand Board of Investment. 2015. *BOI Supports Government Policy to Promote Overseas Investment.* http://www.boi.go.th/tir/issue_content. php?issueid=119;page=352php?issueid=119;page=352. Accessed 6 November 2015.

[5] Oxford Business Group. *Outbound Investment: Local Corporates Move to Expand in Regional Markets and Further Afield.* http://www.oxfordbusinessgroup.com/analysis/outbound-investment-local-corporates-move-expand-regional-markets-and-further-afield

[6] UK Trade and Investment. 2015. *UKTI Inward Investment Report 2014 to 2015.*

[7] *The Economic Times.* 2015. India among fastest growing FDI sources for [US]. 29 June.

[8] *The Economic Times.* 2014. India eyes Finland for tech cooperation to give 'Make in India' a boost. 13 October.

Figure 25: Intraregional FDI Inflows—Asia

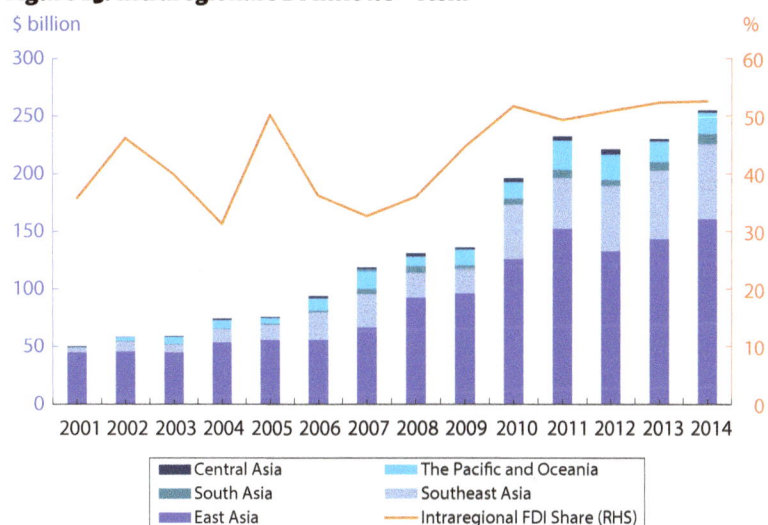

FDI = foreign direct investment, RHS = right-hand scale.
Note: Asia does not include Armenia, Azerbaijan, Bhutan, Brunei Darussalam, Georgia, the Lao People's Democratic Republic, the Maldives, Marshall Islands, Mongolia, Nepal, Sri Lanka, Timor-Leste, Tonga, and Solomon Islands as data unavailable. 2013 and 2014 data were estimated using actual values from previous period.
Source: ADB calculations using data from *ASEAN Investment Statistics Database,* ASEAN Secretariat; *Bilateral FDI Statistics,* United Nations Conference on Trade and Development (UNCTAD), and Organisation for Economic Co-operation and Development (OECD).

MNCs from Hong Kong, China made the economy the world's second largest investor after the US. Investment by MNCs in the PRC grew faster than FDI inflows. Overseas acquisitions have become an increasingly important means of international expansion by some financial institutions in the PRC. For instance, through six cross-border M&As during a short period between October 2014 and February 2015, the PRC's Anbang Insurance Group took over New York's Waldorf Astoria Hotel in the US at $1.95 billion, FIDEA Assurances (cost undisclosed) and Delta Lloyd Bank ($178 million) in Belgium, Vivant Verzekeringen in the Netherlands ($171 million), Tong Yang Life in the Republic of Korea ($1 billion), and a 26-story office tower in New York from Blackstone Group.[26] FDI outflows from India increased fivefold to $10 billion in 2014, as some large Indian MNCs resumed international expansion.

Asia's intraregional FDI inflows

Asia's intraregional FDI also increased in 2014—to an estimated $255 billion from $230 billion in 2013—and remains 52.6% of Asia's total FDI inflows **(Figure 25)**. FDI inflows in 2014 increased in all subregions except Central Asia. The proactive regional investment cooperation efforts in East and Southeast Asia have contributed to the rise in intraregional FDI inflows. The PRC, Japan, and the Republic of Korea, along with Singapore, Malaysia, and Thailand have been strong sources

---

[26] UNCTAD. 2015. *World Investment Report 2015.* Geneva.

of FDI in Southeast Asia. The establishment of the PRC-ASEAN free trade agreement in early 2010 strengthened regional economic cooperation and contributed to FDI flows, particularly from the PRC to Southeast Asia.

Main Destinations of Intraregional FDI

In East Asia, FDI flows are mostly between Hong Kong, China and the PRC. The majority of Hong Kong, China-sourced FDI to the PRC are investments by PRC residents "round-tripped" through Hong Kong, China—funds from the PRC intermediated as direct investment in Hong Kong, China to tap incentives available to foreign but not domestic investors. Investments from the rest of the world to the PRC are also intermediated through Hong Kong, China, the leading destination of PRC FDI outflows. As of December 2014, 876 PRC companies were listed on the Hong Kong[, China] Stock Exchange (HKSE), representing 60% of total HKSE market capitalization. The increase in FDI inflows to the PRC was driven mainly by an increase in FDI in services, particularly retail, transport and finance, while FDI fell in manufacturing, especially in industries sensitive to rising labor costs.

The bulk of Southeast Asian FDI inflows goes to Indonesia, the Philippines, Cambodia, and the Lao People's Democratic Republic (Lao PDR). An improvement in investment climate may have led to these increased FDI inflows. Based on the World Bank's *Doing Business Report 2014*, Indonesia has improved its credit information system through a new regulation that set a legal framework for establishing credit bureaus. These significantly improved access to credit. The increase in FDI inflows to Indonesia was driven by increases in key industries—mining; food; transportation and telecommunications; metal, machinery and electronics; and chemical and pharmaceuticals. For the Philippines, its Doing Business score increased to 62.08 in 2014 from 55.95 in 2013 as reforms on construction permits, obtaining credit, and paying taxes were implemented.[27] Better macroeconomic fundamentals and higher credit agency ratings may have also attracted more investments. Cambodia's score increased to 55.05 from 51.07 as access to credit and electricity improved. The Lao PDR has also seen its Doing Business score improve— to 49.10 from 48.40—partly due to a reduction in corporate income tax.

In South Asia, most FDI inflows go to India and Pakistan. By sector, India's manufacturing is gaining as policies to revitalize the sector are sustained. For instance, the launch of the "Make in India" initiative in mid-2014 may be bearing fruit. The increase in FDI inflows in Pakistan came from rising PRC flows in services, in particular a large investment made by the [People's Republic of] China Mobile in telecommunications. In addition, Pakistan will benefit significantly from the PRC-Pakistan

---

[27] The Doing Business Report provides objective measures of business regulations and their enforcement across 189 economies. The "Distance to Frontier" score aids in assessing the absolute level of regulatory performance and how it improves over time. This measure shows the distance of each economy to the "frontier," which represents the best performance observed on each of the indicators across all economies in the Doing Business sample since 2005. An economy's distance to the frontier is on a scale from 0 to 100, with 0 the lowest and 100 the frontier.

Industrial Corridor and associated PRC investment in infrastructure and manufacturing—in the overall context of "One Belt, One Road" initiative.

In the Pacific and Oceania, most FDI inflows go to Australia and New Zealand. Australia's FDI comes from Japan, the PRC, and Singapore, while the bulk of New Zealand's FDI inflows are from Australia, Singapore, and the PRC. Foreign MNCs in Australia remain in oil and gas projects, including 12 of 13 oil and gas projects at the "committed stage"—a combined value of $177 billion. In New Zealand, several acquisitions came from Asia; for example, Oji's acquisition of Carter Holt Harvey's pulp and paper operations for $1.036 billion (Japan), CKI's acquisition of Envirowaste for $490 million (Hong Kong, China), and Beijing Capital's acquisition of Waste Management from Transpacific Industries ($950 million).

In Central Asia, the moderate decline in FDI inflows may be attributed to regional conflicts coupled with falling oil prices and international sanctions, which dampened foreign investor confidence. In particular, FDI flows to Kazakhstan declined as a rise in equity investments was offset by a decline in intracompany loans. Geological exploration by foreign investors continued, accounting for more than half of FDI.

Main Sources of Intraregional FDI

Most intraregional FDI flows come from East Asia **(Figure 26)**. Japan was the top Asian investor in 2014, with 39.6% of Asia's intraregional FDI inflows, up from 38.9% in 2013. Singapore was second, contributing 27.6% (up from 25.3% in 2013) of intraregional FDI in 2014, followed by the PRC (and Hong Kong, China) at 11.2% (down from 13.8% in 2013), the Republic of Korea at 4.9% (down from 5.9%) and Malaysia at 4.0% (up from 2.6%).[28]

Japan's top investment destinations are Australia, Indonesia, and the PRC **(Table 6)**. They primarily go into manufacturing, particularly transportation equipment, chemicals and pharmaceuticals, and electric machinery. For non-manufacturing, investments are mainly in finance and insurance, wholesale and retail, and real estate.[29] Singapore's FDI flows to the region are twice those of ASEAN-4 outward investments combined—and Singapore is strengthening ties with the CLMV economies. Viet Nam is both a major recipient and source of FDI. From the PRC (and Hong Kong, China), FDI goes mostly to Singapore, Australia, and Japan.

Figure 26: Top 5 Sources of Intraregional FDI—Asia ($ billion)

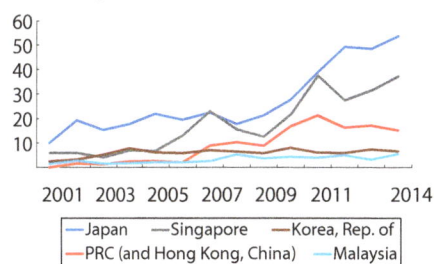

PRC = People's Republic of China, FDI = foreign direct investment.
Note: Asia does not include Bhutan, Georgia, Kiribati, the Maldives, the Federated States of Micronesia, Nauru, Palau, Papua New Guinea, Solomon Islands, Tajikistan, Timor-Leste, Tonga, Turkmenistan, Tuvalu, and Vanuatu as data unavailable.
Source: ADB calculations using data available from *ASEAN Investment Statistics Database,* ASEAN Secretariat; *Bilateral FDI Statistics,* United Nations Conference on Trade and Development (UNCTAD); and Organisation for Economic Co-operation and Development (OECD).

---

[28] The PRC and Hong Kong, China were combined as most of Hong Kong, China's investment (almost 98%) goes to the PRC.
[29] Bank of Japan. Outward/Inward Direct Investment 2013 CY. Balance of Payments. https://www.boj.or.jp/en/statistics/br/bop/index.htm/

Table 6: Major Destination of FDI from Asia's Top 5 Investors (2014)

Asian Investors	Top 3 Destinations in Asia	$ million	% Share to Economy's Outflows
Japan	Australia	9,460	17.7
	Indonesia	9,394	17.6
	PRC	8,457	15.8
Singapore	Indonesia	12,253	32.9
	PRC	7,252	19.5
	Hong Kong, China	3,244	8.7
PRC (and Hong Kong, China)	Singapore	3,848	25.3
	Australia	3,009	19.8
	Japan	1,134	7.5
Korea, Rep. of	PRC	3,494	53.0
	Indonesia	816	12.4
	Viet Nam	723	11.0
Malaysia	Singapore	2,491	45.8
	Indonesia	896	16.5
	Australia	748	13.7

PRC = People's Republic of China, FDI = foreign direct investment.
Source: ADB calculations using data from *ASEAN Investment Statistics Database*, ASEAN Secretariat; *Bilateral FDI Statistics*, United Nations Conference on Trade and Development (UNCTAD); and Organisation for Economic Co-operation and Development (OECD).

Updates on Financial Integration

Following the 2008/09 GFC, financial flows to and from Asia regained attention from the region's policy makers. The dual-track growth between Asia and advanced economies again drew large foreign capital inflows to the region, boosting financial markets and strengthening financial connectivity. They also underscored the challenges of greater capital flow volatility.

The increased exposure of regional economies—both to each other and outside Asia—increases the possibility of potential spillovers. The taper tantrum of May 2013 is a case in point, where a simple announcement by the US Federal Reserve about the possibility of tapering its quantitative easing program rattled several major Asian markets—even some with relatively strong domestic macrofundamentals. And today, while the forecast rise in US interest rates could raise capital flow volatility, it is not expected to rattle the region's markets as they did in 2013. Markets may have already factored in an eventual increase. Nevertheless, managing potentially volatile capital outflows remains an important issue for the region—especially given rising risk premiums and depreciating currencies.

The composition of capital flows matters for financial stability. Within the four types of capital flows, Asia's cumulative financial flows post-GFC have been largely dominated by FDI—with inflows to the region accounting for more than a third of global FDI flows in 2014 (see "FDI Integration in Asia", p. 21). The rest of the region's cumulative financial inflows—non-FDI flows—are split among equity (24%), debt (17%), and bank lending (17%) **(Figure 27)**. Over time, the FDI share of total inflows has increased as well—from 41% in 2010–2011 to 48% in 2013–2014, but

Figure 27: Sources of Financial Flows—Asia ($ billion, cumulative 2010–2014)

Total Inflows to Asia

Total Outflows from Asia

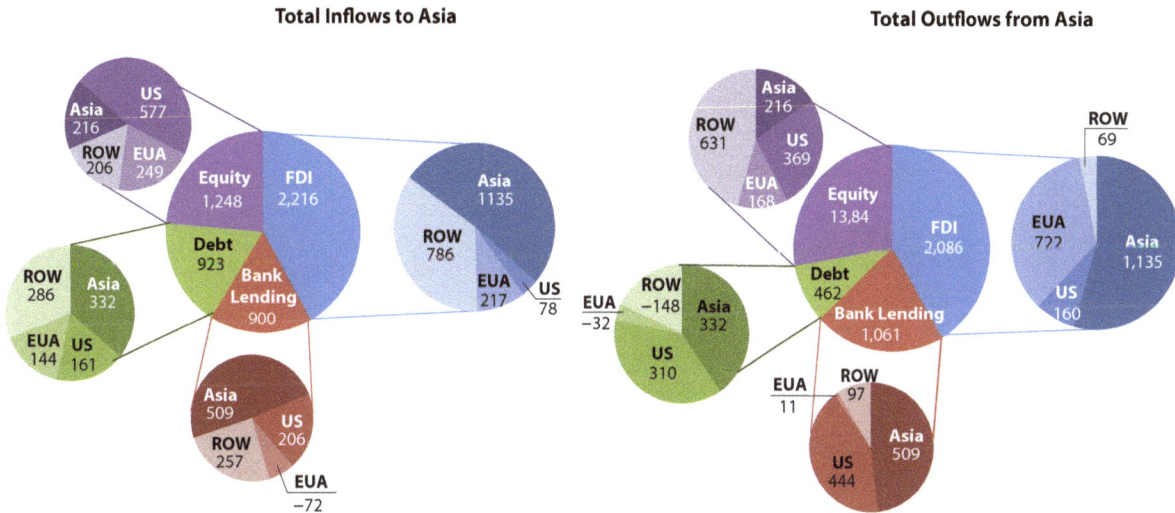

FDI = foreign direct investment, EUA = euro area, ROW = rest of the world, US = United States.
Source: ADB calculations using data from ASEAN Secretariat; Bank for International Settlements; *Coordinated Portfolio Investment Survey,* International Monetary Fund (IMF); Organisation for Economic Co-operation and Development (OECD); and United Nations Conference on Trade and Development (UNCTAD).

the increase in share of equities has been more notable—from less than 1% to 36% over the same period.[30] Shares of debt and bank credit, on the other hand, have been declining **(Figure 28a)**.

The picture is slightly different for Asia's capital outflows. While FDI still comprises the bulk of the region's outflows, followed by equity, bank credit outflows (intraregional included) exceed the region's debt outflows. Nonetheless, both bank credit and debt are seeing declining shares as a proportion of the region's total outflows over the last 5 years. FDI and equity shares to total outflows, in contrast, have been increasing over time; the share of FDI has more than doubled from 30% to 67% between 2010–2011 and 2013–2014, while the share of equity increased from 11.3% to 45% **(Figure 28b)**.

However, as a whole, non-FDI flows tend to be larger than the relatively stable FDI. Standard deviation measures show that FDI inflows in Asia—as % of GDP—appear to be the most stable flows among the four types, with bank-related flows the most volatile, followed by debt and equity **(Table 7)**.

The recent pattern of financial inflows also show Asian economies are generally more integrated with each other in FDI and bank borrowings, with intraregional inflows in each category accounting for about half the region's total. Geographic proximity, relocation of regional MNCs, and recent initiatives on regional cooperation likely contributed to this trend. In contrast, Asia's equity and debt markets are integrated more with global markets, as inflows are on the whole dominated by non-regional sources. While potential bank outflows appear large, most likely remain within the region, unlike portfolio investments. Sources of inflows

Figure 28: Capital Flows—Asia
(% share to total)

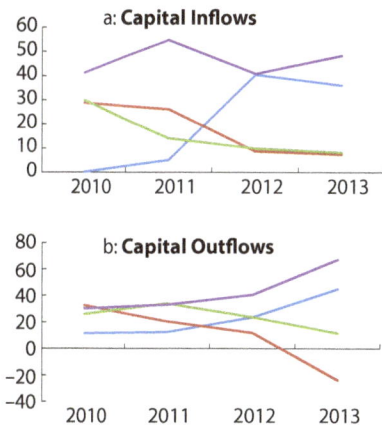

FDI = foreign direct investment. Uses two-year rolling values.
Source: ADB staff calculations using data from ASEAN Secretariat; Bank for International Settlements; *Coordinated Portfolio Investment Survey,* International Monetary Fund; Organisation for Economic Co-operation and Development; and United Nations Conference on Trade and Development.

---

[30] Using 2-year rolling values.

Table 7: Capital Flow Volatility—Asia (standard deviation of capital flow levels as % of GDP, 2005Q1–2014Q1)

	FDI	Equity	Debt	Bank
East Asia	0.54	1.59	1.68	2.89
Southeast Asia	0.99	0.88	1.35	4.99
Total Asia	0.60	1.36	1.57	2.38

FDI = foreign direct investment, Bank = bank-related flows.
Note: East Asia includes the People's Republic of China; Hong Kong, China; the Republic of Korea; and Japan. Southeast Asia includes Indonesia, Malaysia, the Philippines, Singapore, Thailand, and Viet Nam. Asia includes East Asia, Southeast Asia, Australia and New Zealand.
Source: ADB calculations using data from *International Financial Statistics,* International Monetary Fund (IMF); and national sources.

could add potential volatility, given that over half of non-FDI inflows—particularly equity and debt—are largely sourced outside the region.

The pace of Asia's financial integration on portfolio investment not simply lags trade integration, but its pace seems to be slowed down by several factors, including information asymmetries and differences in regulatory and institutional quality.[31]

Portfolio inflows to Asia[32]

Equity

Figure 29: Equity Inflows—Asia
($ billion, by source)

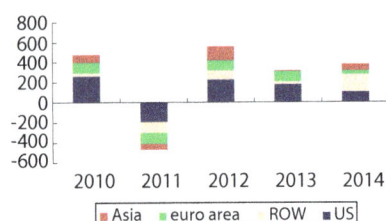

US = United States, ROW = rest of the world.
Source: ADB calculations using data from the *Coordinated Portfolio Investment Survey,* International Monetary Fund.

Equity inflows to Asia continue to recover since largely having disappeared in 2011, when global market confidence was hit by several external shocks—such as Japan's Tohoku earthquake and the deepening sovereign debt crisis in the euro area **(Figure 29)**.[33] Still equity flows remain 20.1% below the level in 2010. By 2014, equity inflows to the region was $377 billion, a large part accounted for by inflows from the rest of the world (ROW) with a 45.4% share, followed by the US (27.4%), intraregional inflows (16.1%), and finally the euro area (11.1%). Traditionally, inflows to Asia have been led by the US, followed by the euro area—in 2010, over half of Asia's equity inflows came from the US (55%), with the euro area accounting for 23.0%.

This trend changed notably in 2014, when flows from the ROW overtook combined US and euro area flows. Intraregional equity inflows by end-2014, in contrast, were just barely above its 15.3% share in 2010—even if recovering swiftly after nearly disappearing in 2013—likely due to the taper tantrum then rattling Asian financial markets.

---

[31]   N. Ananchotikul, S. Piao, and E. Zoli. 2015. Drivers of Financial Integration—Implications for Asia. IMF *Working Papers*. WP/15/160. Washington: IMF.

[32]   Only debt, equity and bank credit flows are discussed in this section. Trends in FDI integration can be found in the Updates on Trade and Investment Integration section, p. 21.

[33]   World Bank. 2013. *World Development Indicators 2013*. Washington.

Several economies outside the US and euro area returned to Asia after withdrawing investments in 2013 (for example, Norway, Mauritius, Bahrain, and the Russian Federation), while other economies further increased equity investments (such as Mexico, Chile, and Iceland). Among ROW, economies such as Norway, Mauritius, the UK, and Canada were the region's top investors in 2014. While investors in the US and euro area seem to have taken a more cautious approach to equity exposure, others have more actively expanded their equity portfolios into Asia. However, intraregional equity investments (a typical measure of financial integration) fell to 16.6% after peaking at 18.2% in 2012, indicating they have stalled compared with extra-regional inflows.

Among subregions, East Asia received the largest portion of Asia's total equity inflows globally—of cumulative flows from 2010 to 2014, 76% went to East Asian economies **(Figure 30)**. Even in 2013—during the taper tantrum—total inflows to East Asia from the US and the euro area increased, while all other subregions saw decline in inflows from 2012. East Asia is also the most integrated with the rest of Asia, receiving 76% of Asian equity inflows. Southeast Asia follows both globally and intraregionally, with a 14% and 17% share, respectively; third is South Asia (about 5% of total inflows from the world, and 5% from within the region). However, in 2013–2014, South Asia absorbed 24% of all Asia's inflows globally—against Southeast Asia's 11%—due to increased equity inflows to India, Pakistan, Sri Lanka, and Afghanistan. The relative attractiveness in 2014 of South Asian equity markets—compared with Southeast Asia—appears consistent across all types of investors, whether from within Asia, the US and euro area, or the ROW.

Each Asian subregion's source of equity investments remain largely extra-regional—a significant part come from the US and euro area **(Figure 31)**. From 2010–2014, about 60% of total equity inflows to Central Asia and East Asia came from these economies. In Southeast Asia it was 72%, and it topped 100% for South Asia (as US and euro area equity investments more than offset equity withdrawals from the ROW). East Asia, Southeast Asia, and South Asia likewise rely on Asia as an important source of equity investments. Of the total equity investments entering Southeast Asia over the past 5 years, some 21% originated within Asia, slightly higher than South Asia's 20% and above East Asia's 17%. Central Asia is not too far behind with 10%, while the Pacific and Oceania received only 2% of its total equity inflows from Asia.[34]

Among individual economies, the PRC and India had the largest increase in equity inflows, taking nearly 95% of the equity inflows that accrued to Asia from 2010 to 2014. Overall, top equity destinations in the region in 2014 are in East Asia—the PRC; Japan; and Taipei,China—and Singapore and India. Together, these five economies absorbed 92% of 2014 equity inflows to Asia. Equity inflows account for less than 10% of the nominal GDP of these five Asian economies, and no more than a third of their foreign reserve assets.

Figure 30: Equity Inflows to Asia—Asian Subregions ($ billion, by recipient)

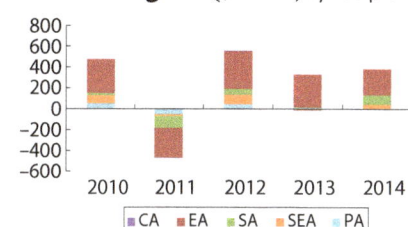

CA = Central Asia, EA = East Asia, SA = South Asia, SEA = Southeast Asia, PA = the Pacific and Oceania.
Source: ADB calculations using data from the *Coordinated Portfolio Investment Survey*, International Monetary Fund.

Figure 31: Equity Inflows—Asia
($ billion, by source, from 2010–2014)

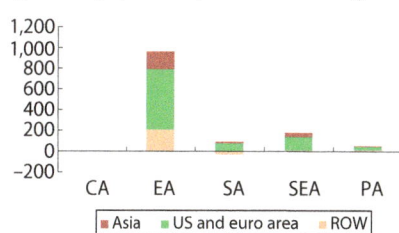

CA = Central Asia, EA = East Asia, SA = South Asia, SEA = Southeast Asia, PA = the Pacific and Oceania, US = United States, ROW = rest of the world.
Source: ADB calculations using data from the *Coordinated Portfolio Investment Survey*, International Monetary Fund.

---

34 Distinguishing the Pacific and Oceania, the former received 9% of its total equity inflows from the world during the review period. This number is pulled down when combined with Oceania, which receives less than 0.5% of its total equity inflows from Asia, as most of it is sourced from the US, euro area and the rest of the world.

Figure 32: Debt Inflows—Asia

($ billion, by source)

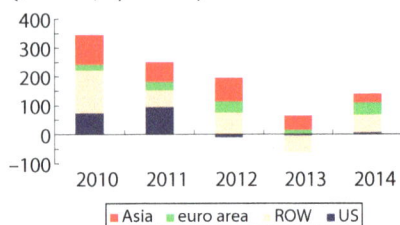

US = United States, ROW = rest of the world.
Source: ADB calculations using data from the
Coordinated Portfolio Investment Survey, International
Monetary Fund.

Figure 33: Yields Dispersion and Quantitative Easing (%)

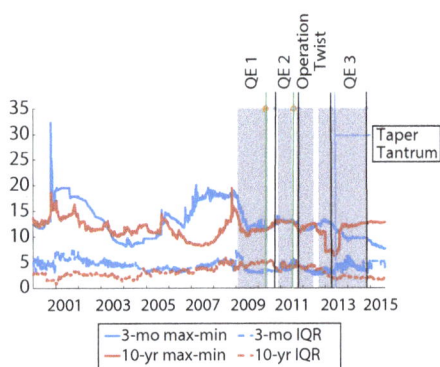

IQR = interquartile range.
Note: Green lines refer to Japan quantitative easing
(QE) episodes, while black lines refer to euro area QE
episodes.
Source: ADB calculations using data from Bloomberg,
US Federal Reserve, European Central Bank and Bank
of Japan.

Figure 34: Debt Inflows—Asia

($ billion, by recipient)

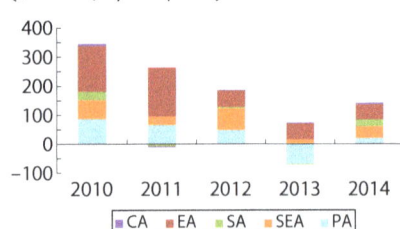

CA = Central Asia, EA = East Asia, SA = South Asia,
SEA = Southeast Asia, PA = the Pacific and Oceania.
Source: ADB calculations using data from the
Coordinated Portfolio Investment Survey, International
Monetary Fund.

Debt

Debt inflows to Asia has slowed over the past 5 years; in 2014, they totaled $140.2 billion, about 59.4% lower than 2010 **(Figure 32)**. Except for the euro area, debt inflows from the US, intraregionally, and from the ROW fell more than 50% compared with 2010. US debt investments to Asia fell the most—down 91% over the 5 years—gradually dwindling beginning 2012—in 2012–2013, the US withdrew more debt than it placed (a net outflow)—and while positive in 2014, accounts for only 4.6% of Asia's total debt inflows, well below the 21.4% in 2010. As the US share of Asia's debt inflows declines, more investments are coming from the euro area, with inflows expanding to 29.6% of the total in 2014 from 5.7% in 2010. In fact, among all debt inflows to the region in 2014, only those from the euro area increased—even doubling its inflows to Asia in 2010.

After a nearly 100% drop in 2013, debt inflows continued to recover in 2014, largely originated from the ROW (43.8%), followed by the euro area (29.6%), intraregional debt inflows (22.0%), and the US (4.6%). ROW debt inflows came primarily from European economies or territories such as Norway, Bermuda, and Switzerland. While there has been a renewed global appetite for Asian debt in 2014, debt inflows from within the region appear to have stalled—sliding slightly to 28.9% in 2014 from 29.3% in 2013.

Ample global liquidity from ultra-loose monetary policies seems to have attracted capital inflows to Asia—particularly as ROW and euro area investors search for higher yields. This likely helped narrow the dispersion of bond yields across the region. The dispersion of 3-month and 10-year government bond yields in Asian bonds—as measured by the min-max range and interquartile range—has declined significantly **(Figure 33)**. This suggests greater interest rate convergence and a narrowing risk perception in the region. However, this trend may not continue if monetary policies begin to tighten.

Like equity inflows, East Asia receives the bulk of the region's total debt inflows—from 2010 to 2014, 53% of the region's debt investment inflows went to East Asian markets, followed by Southeast Asia, with a 24% share **(Figure 34)**. The Pacific and Oceania, where Australia and New Zealand dominate, are more attractive as a debt flow destination than equity; the subregion received 16% of the world's debt inflows to Asia within the 5-year period—and some years beat out Southeast Asia.[35] South Asia, which accounted for less than 10% of Asia's total debt inflows before 2013, saw a surge in inflows in 2014 with a 17% share—almost double its 2010 share. This increase coincided with a decline in East Asia's share— from 46% in 2010 to 37% in 2014—and the Pacific (from 25% to 14%). Given different sources of financial inflows, Asian subregions' reliance on US and euro area investors is far more limited in debt markets than equity flows. From 2010 to 2014, debt flows into East Asia and South Asia were sourced mostly from Asia—44% of East Asia's debt and 51% of South Asia's. Debt inflows to other subregions are dominated by extraregional

---

[35] This 16% is driven primarily by Australia and New Zealand (Oceania), which receives 16% of Asia's debt inflows. The Pacific developing member countries (comprising the Pacific), on the other hand, receive only 1% of Asia's total inflows from the world.

markets—47% of Southeast Asia's debt flows are from the US and euro area, compared with 33% from Asia; for the Pacific and Oceania, 53% comes from the ROW (12% from Asia); while Central Asia gets nearly 100% of its debt inflows from the US and euro area **(Figure 35)**.

While East Asian economies are top equity destinations, several Southeast Asian economies have grown as prominent debt inflow destinations in recent years. Of total debt inflows to Asia between 2010 and 2014, Hong Kong, China took 59%, followed by Singapore (16%), the Philippines (15%), and Indonesia (5%). Collectively, the four account for 94% of Asia's total inflows from 2010 to 2014, partly due to their relatively stronger economic positions (such as in the case of the Philippines) and role as financial hubs (Hong Kong, China and Singapore). In 2014, the largest debt investments were made first in Hong Kong, China; followed by India, Japan, Indonesia, and the PRC. Nearly 65% of the region's total debt inflows in 2014 went to these five markets. Debt liabilities of these economies are not more than 2.5% of their respective GDPs and a fifth of their foreign reserve assests.

Together, this means Asia's intraregional inward portfolio shares remain stable, if declining slightly from 21.5% in 2013 to 21.2% in 2014. Investors from the ROW—particularly non-US and euro area economies—invested more capital into the region, even as total intraregional portfolio liabilities grew 7.7%, up from 4.7% a year ago.

Portfolio outflows from Asia

Equity

While equity inflows to Asia in the 5 years since 2010 declined, equity outflows have nearly doubled—up 91.6%—to $616 billion **(Figure 36)**. Equity investments have gone mostly into the euro area and ROW—rather than the US or the region itself. In 2010, the euro area's share of Asia's total equity outflows was 4.0%. It rose to 18.1% in 2014, with the ROW share up from 45.4% in 2010 to 59.4%. Intraregional and US shares have declined. During the 5-year period, Japan accounted for 96.6% of total outflows worldwide, while the Republic of Korea, middle-income ASEAN, and India also contributed.

In 2014, outflows bounced back sharply after a 33.6% decline in 2013 under global financial uncertainty. Asia's equity investments to all destinations, including the region itself increased—except to the US—given its renewed interest in Asian equities. As a share of total outflows, more equity investments flowed to the ROW and euro area during the year. Price may have been a factor, as the increase in euro area equity gains in 2014 was accompanied by an increase in its share in Asia's equity portfolio—almost double the US **(Figure 37)**. The large share of investment in ROW economies suggests some Asian economies are tapping nontraditional equity investment destinations.[36] Euro area

---

36 The sudden jump in the ROW share for 2014 was due to the jump in the share of Cayman Islands—from 23.7% to 51.3%—in Asia's total investments to the world. Australia, Japan, and Singapore are the primary Asian investors in the territory. The Cayman Islands stock exchange has more than $123 billion in market capitalization.

Figure 35: Debt Inflows—Asian Subregions ($ million, by source, from 2010–2014)

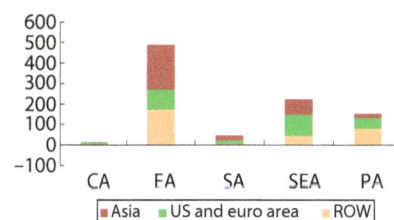

CA = Central Asia, EA = East Asia, SA = South Asia, SEA = Southeast Asia, PA = the Pacific and Oceania, US = United States, ROW = rest of the world.
Source: ADB calculations using data from the *Coordinated Portfolio Investment Survey*, International Monetary Fund.

Figure 36: Equity Outflows—Asia ($ billion, by destination)

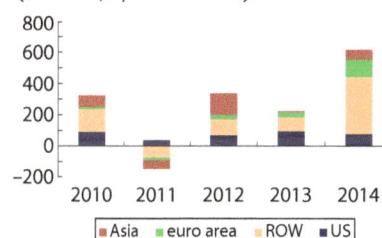

US = United States, ROW = rest of the world.
Source: ADB calculations using data from the *Coordinated Portfolio Investment Survey*, International Monetary Fund.

Figure 37: Equity Prices vs. Equity Flows from Asia

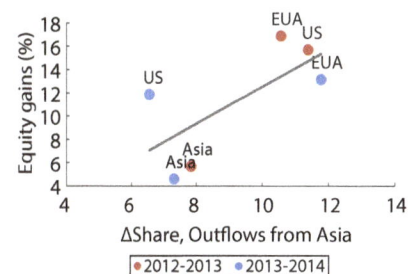

EUA = euro area, US = United States.
Note: ∆Share scaled up by 10 points for presentation purposes. Share refers to share to total Asian outstanding investments. Equity gains are y-o-y changes in the stock market indexes (Jan 2012 = 100). EUA uses the MSCI European Monetary Union Index for Europe, the Dow Jones Industrial Average for the US, and the MSCI Emerging Asia index for Asia.
Source: ADB calculations using data from Bloomberg.

Figure 38: Equity Outflows by Asia—Asian Subregions
($ billion, by source)

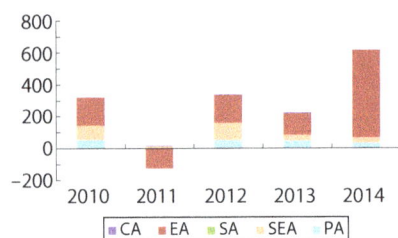

CA = Central Asia, EA = East Asia, SA = South Asia, SEA = Southeast Asia, PA = Pacific and Oceania.
Source: ADB calculations using data from the *Coordinated Portfolio Investment Survey,* International Monetary Fund.

Figure 39: Equity Outflows—Asia
($ billion, by destination, from 2010-2014)

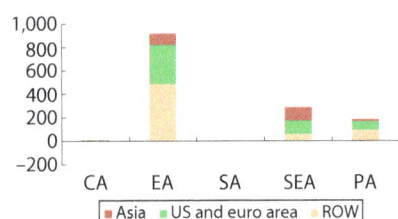

CA = Central Asia, EA = East Asia, SA = South Asia, SEA = Southeast Asia, PA = Pacific and Oceania, US = United States, ROW = rest of the world.
Source: ADB calculations using data from the *Coordinated Portfolio Investment Survey,* International Monetary Fund.

Figure 40: Debt Outflows—Asia
($ billion, by destination)

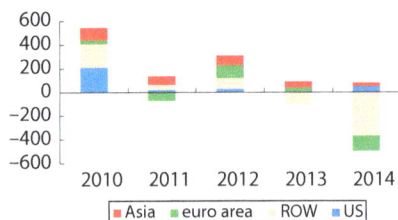

US = United States; ROW = rest of the world.
Source: ADB calculations using data from the *Coordinated Portfolio Investment Survey,* International Monetary Fund.

economies such as Luxembourg and Ireland have become preferred destinations for Asian investment, while the PRC and India in the region are also markets of choice. In 2014, the largest equity investor was Japan, accounting for 78% of Asia's total investments globally, followed by Hong Kong, China (8%); Australia (5%); and Singapore (4%).

Among subregions, East Asia is the most active equity investor. From 2010 to 2014, 66% of total Asian equity outflows came from East Asia, followed by Southeast Asia (20%) and the Pacific and Oceania (13%) **(Figure 38)**. At the other end is South Asia, with a lower share of Asia's equity outflows than Central Asia. Since 2010, intraregional equity outflows have equally moved to East Asia and Southeast Asia. Intraregional equity investments recovered in 2014, after the 2013 taper tantrum made Asian investors more cautious—intraregional equity investments fell 97.2% year-on-year in 2013. Still, in 2014 Southeast Asian equity investments within the region were subdued, against aggressive outflows from East Asia. During the year, 93% of intraregional equity flows came from East Asia.

By destination, most subregions generally place more equity investments in the ROW economies, except for Central Asia and Southeast Asia, where investors mostly look to the US and euro area **(Figure 39)**. In South Asia, for example, 84.5% of equity outflows go to ROW economies, as it appears to withdraw equity investments from Asia. East Asia and the Pacific and Oceania, on the other hand, have about 50% of equity outflows in ROW economies. By contrast, Central Asia invests nearly 70% of its equity portfolio in the US and euro area, with Southeast Asia investing 41%. Consistent across subregions, however, is the aversion to Asian markets. Southeast Asia has the highest intraregional share—38.7%. Low equity investment intraregionally could be due to fundamentals or rigidities across markets.

Debt

Debt outflows of Asia are less significant than equity outflows. Of all portfolio flows over the last 5 years, Asia's debt outflows contracted the most. In 2014, Asian economies withdrew $422 billion in debt investments globally after investing $540 billion in 2010—a 178% drop **(Figure 40)**. Over the 5-year period, the largest decline in outflows was in the euro area economies and the ROW. Asian and US debt markets fared relatively better. Intraregional debt investments have been sustained by a steady increase in issuance—with relatively higher bond yields. Active initiatives that promote local currency bond market development have helped.

The largest debt investors between 2010 and 2014 were the Republic of Korea, accounting for 56% of the region's increase in debt investments, followed by New Zealand (23%), Thailand (16%), and the Philippines (5%). Other Asian economies decreased in debt outflows over the period, with Japan and Hong Kong, China showing the largest drop between 2010 and 2014. By destination, debt outflows to some euro area economies increased markedly between 2010 and 2014, but this was likely due to low base effects—debt outflows in 2010 were largely negative. Meanwhile, debt outflows to Hong Kong, China; the Philippines; Singapore; and

Taipei,China increased significantly over the period. Intraregional debt outflows remained positive during the year, but were down 38.1% year-on-year. In 2014, the largest debt outflows came from Singapore, the Republic of Korea, Australia and New Zealand—a combined 85% of the region's debt outflows during the period.

Speculation over changes in US monetary policy—starting in 2013—likely influenced Asian investment decisions, and could shift further in the short-term. In 2014, Asian debt investors turned increasingly toward the US, which absorbed about 60% of Asian debt placements during the year, as investors shied away from the ROW and euro area. This trend could continue as bond investors who take advantage of expected higher yields of US securities and their safe haven status. Widening US-EU differentials for 10-year government bond yields have also accompanied the increasing US debt shares in Asia **(Figure 41)**.

East Asia generally dominates debt outflows among the five subregions, followed by Southeast Asia, and the Pacific and Oceania **(Figure 42)**. East Asia had 69% of cumulative intraregional debt outflows during the 5-year period. With the larger debt withdrawals (than placements) of East Asian economies in 2014 (mostly through Hong Kong, China), Southeast Asia took a larger share of intraregional debt outflows during the year (75%), followed by the Pacific and Oceania (22%), Central Asia (2%), and East Asia (1%).[37]

By destination, East Asia's intraregional debt outflows from 2010 to 2014 were above its debt investments outside the region—East Asia invested only in Asia, while withdrawing debt investments elsewhere **(Figure 43)**. Southeast Asia's flows during the 5-year period were 37% for the US and the euro area, 35.5% for Asia, and 27.4% for ROW. South Asia, on the other hand, invested 27.7% of its outflows within the region (though about half of its investments to the ROW[53.9%]). The Pacific and Oceania debt outflow composition is similar to South Asia's—investing more to the ROW (51.9%), followed by 30.8% for the US and euro area combined, and a 17.2% intraregional share. For Central Asia, the US and euro area accounted for 68.1% of the subregion's total outflows, while Asia and the ROW equally share the rest.

In sum, Asia's intraregional outward portfolio shares continue to increase—albeit marginally—from 18.7% in 2013 to 19.5% in 2014 **(Figure 44)**. However, as investors increase investments in equity outside the region more than within the region—the equity's share in Asia's total intraregional portfolio is plateauing **(Figure 45)**.

As a percentage of total debt, intraregional debt holdings rose from 15.9% to 18.7%, as Asian investors reduced exposure to European and non-US debt securities. However, they held more extra-regional equities in 2014, dropping intraregional equity holdings' share to total equity holdings to 20.5% from 23.1%. Yet, intraregional equities grew 10.8%, while debt grew a slower 4.9%.

Figure 41: US-euro Area Yield Differential and US Debt Share out of Asian Holdings

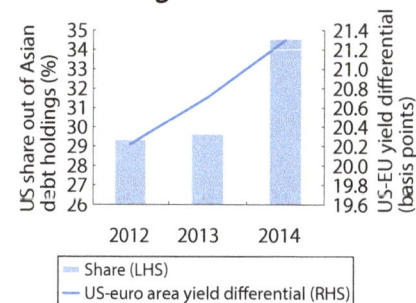

LHS = left-hand side, RHS = right-hand side, US = United States.
Note: Yield differential is equal to US yield less euro area yield. Uses 10-year government bond yields (Jan 2012 = 100). Differential scaled up by 20 points for presentation purposes only.
Source: ADB calculations using data from Bloomberg.

Figure 42: Debt Outflows—Asia
($ billion, by source)

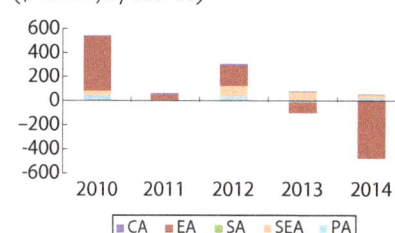

CA = Central Asia, EA = East Asia, SA = South Asia, SEA = Southeast Asia, PA = the Pacific and Oceania.
Source: ADB calculations using data from the *Coordinated Portfolio Investment Survey,* International Monetary Fund.

Figure 43: Debt Outflows—Asia
($ billion, by destination, from 2010-2014)

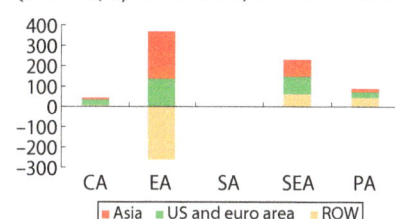

CA = Central Asia, EA = East Asia, SA = South Asia, SEA = Southeast Asia, PA = the Pacific and Oceania, US = United States, ROW = rest of the world.
Source: ADB calculations using data from the *Coordinated Portfolio Investment Survey,* International Monetary Fund.

---

[37]   In 2014, Hong Kong, China's "negative outflows" were largest for the PRC, Australia, Malaysia, and the Republic of Korea.

Figure 44: Outward Portfolio Investments (% share)

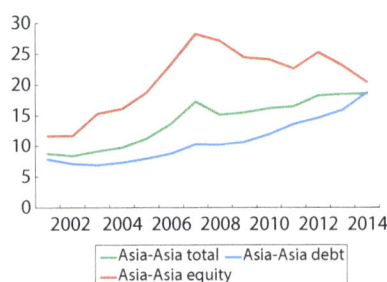

Note: The data refer to reporter economy's cross-border holdings of portfolio securities owned by the partner economy as a share of the reporter economy's total cross-border portfolio securities holdings. The data do not include reporting economy's holdings of securities issued by domestic issuers. Reporting economies classified under Asia include Australia; Bangladesh, Hong Kong, China; India; Indonesia; Japan; Kazakhstan; the Republic of Korea; Malaysia; Mongolia; New Zealand; Pakistan; the Philippines; Singapore; Thailand; and Vanuatu. Partner economies classified under Asia include all ADB regional member economies.
Source: ADB calculations using data from *Coordinated Portfolio Investment Survey*, International Monetary Fund.

Figure 45: Intraregional Portfolio Composition—Asia (% share to total portfolio)

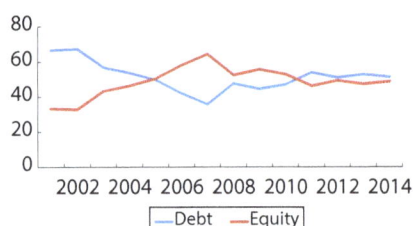

Source: ADB calculations using data from the *Coordinated Portfolio Investment Survey*, International Monetary Fund.

Figure 46: Bank Credit Inflows—Asia ($ billion, by source)

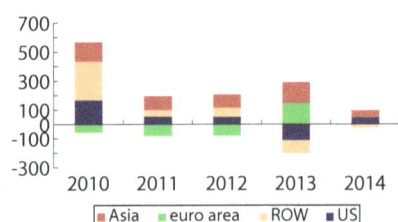

US = United States, ROW = rest of the world.
Source: ADB calculations using data from *Coordinated Portfolio Investment Survey*, International Monetary Fund.

Bank Credit Flows

Like portfolio inflows in general, bank credit inflows to Asia is below what it was 5 years ago; from $508 billion in 2010 to $69 billion in 2014, a decline of 86.4% **(Figure 46)**. The decrease is broad-based by source, except for the euro area, which increased its credit flows between 2010 and 2014 by 100%. However, this was largely due to the negative base in 2010, and euro area bank credit inflows only account for 3.2% of total 2014 credit inflows. The largest decline in credit inflows came from banks from the ROW, followed by the US, and then Asia.[38] Further, banks from the ROW are no longer a major source of credit inflows for the region. In 2010, these banks supplied about a 52% share. But beginning 2013, ROW banks began to retrench (negative inflows), with only minimal new lending—if any—to Asia. Instead, intraregional and US credit flows dominate, each accounting for 48% of the 2014 total (in 2010, Asia held a 24% share, with the US at 27% of the total inflows).

In 2014, cross-border bank credit inflows slowed year-on-year as well **(Figure 47)**. From about $88 billion in 2013, they fell to $69 billion, contracting 21.5% y-o-y. Intraregional bank credit dropped more than 60% y-o-y, and with euro area credit growth still negative, much of the 2013 bank credit inflows from the euro area nearly dried up in 2014. In contrast, US flows resumed in 2014.

Bank credit flows from Europe between 2010 and 2014 came primarily from France, the Netherlands, Ireland, Austria, and Belgium—76% of European credit inflows. Most went to Japan (81%), followed by—though rather far off—New Zealand (8%). In 2014, however, the largest recipients of euro area credit was the PRC (53.6% of the total); Japan (21.6%); Indonesia (10.1%); and Taipei,China (6.6%). An IMF review of the euro area in July pointed out that high nonperforming loans (NPLs) in some European banks were eroding profitability and discouraging new lending.[39] In the meantime, bank credit inflows from the euro area were just 1% when compared to these economies' GDP and 2.5% of foreign reserves.

East Asia drew the largest share of credit from the US, which returned as largest source of overseas credit for the region in 2014, accounting for 90% of US credit inflows in 2014.[40] India was also a prime destination for US bank credit. Still, the size of US bank credit relative to their nominal GDP remains relatively small at no more than 2%. While the direct impact of a US interest rate hike on the region's economies through the external bank credit channel could be minimal, widening interest rate differentials and depreciating local currencies could add to debt servicing costs, in particular for corporate borrowers.

Intraregionally, the role of Japanese and Australian banks has been increasing as a credit source for the rest of Asia. The two increased

---

[38] Reporting countries under ROW include Chile, Canada, and other European economies not included in the euro area (Sweden, Switzerland, Turkey, The United Kingdom).

[39] IMF. 2015. *Euro Area Policies: 2015 Article IV Consultation.* https://www.imf.org/external/pubs/ft/ser/2015/cr1204.pdf

[40] East Asia includes the PRC; Hong Kong, China; Japan; the Republic of Korea; and Taipei,China.

lending to Asia to $98.5 billion in 2014—a combined 24.2% share of the region's total foreign bank borrowings, and 32% of Asia's total borrowing for the year. Much of these credit flows went to East Asia (54%), followed by Southeast Asia (30%), then India (10%).

Asian credit outflows, on the other hand, declined between 2010 and 2014, down 93.3% over the period.[41] The decline, while broad-based—with Asian banks reducing new lending to all major destinations—was largest for the ROW, then the US **(Figure 48)**. After y-o-y increases in 2011 and 2012, credit outflows from Asian banks—though positive—slowed in terms of growth in the following years. Shrinking credit outflows to the ROW and the euro area continued, while credit outflows to the US rose in 2014.

Asian credit outflows used to focus on the region and the US. Prior to 2013, the US share of Asian credit outflows had always been higher than those received by Asian economies. By 2013 the trend had reversed; for example, in 2013, 69.5% of Asian credit outflows were absorbed intraregionally (from 25.4% in 2012), while the US only received 2.6% (from 28.6%). While credit outflows to the US rose again in 2014, the size remained just half the size of intraregional credit flows. Between 2010 and 2014, the economies with the largest increases in borrowings from the region were Malaysia, Japan, Indonesia and the Marshall Islands.

Updates on Movement of People

People in Asia keep moving and their numbers keep growing, with significant dynamic patterns across subregions. Their movement contributes to economic connectivity in addition to trade and capital flows. Movement growth, however, remains relatively slow—as economy level restrictions remain.

Movement occurs through tourism and labor migration—with most economies in Asia simultaneously both sources and destinations. Demographics and income disparities across economies and subregions continue to drive mobility. Tourism flows mainly come from higher income economies or subregions, while labor migration is the reverse. Remittance inflows—mostly from labor migrants—and tourism receipts remain important.

Remittance Inflows and Tourism Receipts

In 2014, Asia received the largest share of global remittances, accounting for 46.1% ($269 billion) of the total ($583 billion). India, the PRC, and the Philippines were the top three recipients in the region—together accounting for $163 billion (or 64%) of Asia's 2014 total **(Figure 49)**. As a percentage of GDP, Tajikistan, Nepal, and the Kyrgyz Republic topped

Figure 47: Foreign Bank Lending Flows to Asia ($ billion, 4-quarter moving average)

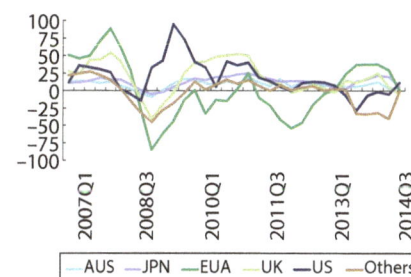

AUS = Australia, EUA = euro area, JPN = Japan, UK = United Kingdom, US = United States.
Source: ADB calculations using data from Bank for International Settlements (Table 9D). Data accessed in May 2015.

Figure 48: Bank Credit Outflows— Asia ($ billion, by destination)

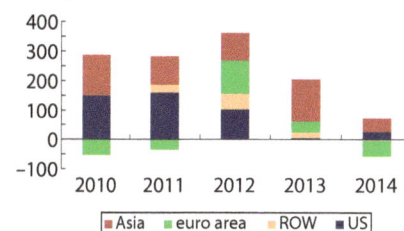

US = United States, ROW = rest of the world.
Source: ADB calculations using data from the *Coordinated Portfolio Investment Survey*, International Monetary Fund.

---

[41]   Asian credit outflows are from Australia, India, Japan, and the Republic of Korea (starting 2013). Data is sourced from the Bank for International Settlements Statistics (Table 9D).

Figure 49: Top 10 Remittance Recipient Economies—Asia

(based on net inflows, 2014)

a: $ billion

India
PRC
Philippines
Bangladesh
Viet Nam
Indonesia
Sri Lanka
Uzbekistan
Korea, Rep. of
Nepal

0   20   40   60   80

b: % of GDP

Tajikistan
Nepal
Kyrgyz Republic
Armenia
Samoa
Georgia
Tonga
Marshall Islands
Uzbekistan
Sri Lanka

0   10   20   30   40   50

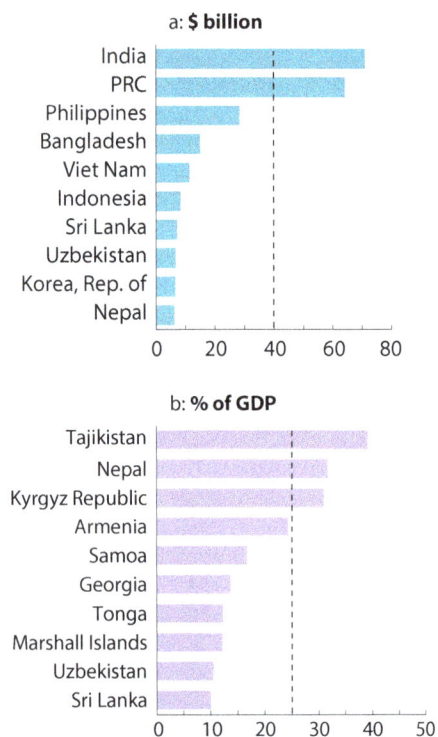

PRC = People's Republic of China.
Source: ADB calculations using *Annual Remittances Data*, World Bank; and *World Economic Outlook April 2015 Database*, International Monetary Fund.

the list with 41.9%, 29.9% and 29.4%, respectively. Remittances contribute significantly to economies in Central Asia, South Asia, and the Pacific. Remittances to Asia mainly come from within Asia (29.4%), Middle East (28.2%) and North America (24.2%) in 2014.[42] South Asia received 53.6% ($62.2 billion) of its remittances inflows from the Middle East. Central Asia received 78.5% ($14.1 billion) from the Russian Federation and the Pacific received 53.3% ($334 million) from Australia and New Zealand. But the high dependency on the remittances also adds vulnerability to external shocks.[43] The growth of remittance inflows is expected to moderate sharply in 2015 due to the protracted global recovery; but is expected to recover in 2016 as prospects improve in advanced economies.

Since 2012, tourism receipts surpassed remittances in Asia, except for South Asia and Central Asia **(Figure 50)**. They rose from $181 billion in 2009 to $288 billion in 2013, equivalent to 1.4% of Asia's GDP. In the Pacific, tourism receipts account for as much as 3.4% of GDP—the largest among subregions. The share of tourism receipts to GDP of the Pacific is 7.4% when Papua New Guinea is excluded.

Remittances and tourism receipts are stabilizing flows to the region. Remittance inflows to Asia have increased steadily since the 1990s **(Figure 51)**. Despite the 1997/98 AFC and 2008/09 GFC, remittances remained stable, especially compared with portfolio investments (debt and equity) and FDI. However, economies with high reliance on remittances for income also tend to experience higher volatility of remittance inflows. These economies should continue to pursue industrialization and economic diversification to make their economies more resilient and provide more job opportunities domestically.

One challenge in increasing remittances to Asian economies is high remittance costs. According to the Remittance Prices Worldwide database, the global average cost of sending $200 in the second quarter of 2015 was 7.7% **(Table 8)**. However, remittance costs have been declining over time, and targeted to be 3% by 2030—which would translate into global savings of over $20 billion annually for migrants

Figure 50: Remittances and Tourism Receipts (2013)

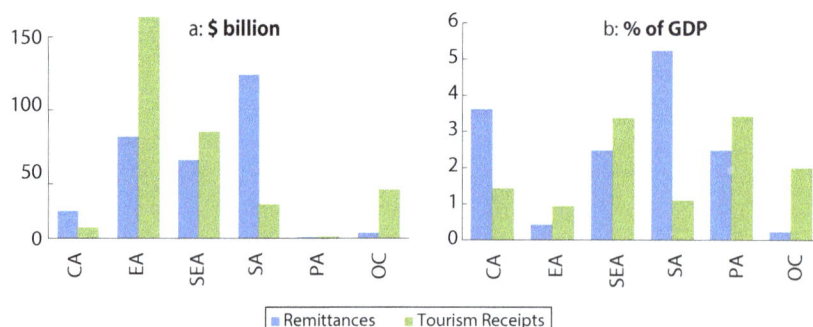

a: $ billion

150
100
50
0

CA   EA   SEA   SA   PA   OC

b: % of GDP

6
5
4
3
2
1
0

CA   EA   SEA   SA   PA   OC

■ Remittances   ■ Tourism Receipts

CA = Central Asia, EA = East Asia, SA = South Asia, SEA = Southeast Asia, PA = The Pacific, OC = Oceania.
Source: ADB calculations using Annual Remittances Data, World Bank; and *World Economic Outlook April 2015 Database,* International Monetary Fund, and World Tourism Organization Data.

---

[42] Based on data from Annual Remittances Data, World Bank.
[43] World Bank. 2015. *Remittances Prices Worldwide.* No. 14. Washington.

and their families. The PRC is the most expensive economy among the G20 to transfer money, with an average cost of 10.4%, while South Asia is the least costly with an average 5.7%. Improvements in technology are helping lower costs. The introduction of online and mobile money transfer systems in developing economies offers far more cost-effective ways of sending money.

Trends in Tourism

Total tourist arrivals in Asia has increased by more than 15%—from around 274 million in 2010 to almost 316 million in 2013. Most tourists went to East Asia—184 million or 74.8% of the total **(Figure 52)**. Southeast Asia came second (96.5 million), followed by Central Asia (15.7 million). Since 2010, Central Asia had the fastest growth, with tourist arrivals doubling in 2013. Arrivals were up 33% in Southeast Asia and 4.5% in East Asia. Tourist arrivals in the Pacific declined slightly since 2010 by 1.9%. More than 77% (246 million) of the total tourist arrivals in Asia came from within the region, 6.2% (19.6 million) from the EU, and 4% (12.7 million) from North America **(Figure 53)**.

Asian tourists traveling within and outside the region reached 317 million in 2013, up from 257 million in 2010 or a 23.3% increase. While most Asian tourists travel within the region, there have been significant increases of Asian tourists travelling outside the region, particularly to Latin America (up 44% since 2010), the EU (up 39%), and North America (up 18%). By origin, the top three subregions were East Asia with 61% of the total (or 193 million), Southeast Asia at 19.7% (62.4 million) and Central Asia at 8.5% (26.8 million). But the number of Asian tourists coming from Central Asia increased most since 2010 (76.3%).

Trends in intraregional and intrasubregional tourism vary by subregion. Southeast Asia had the highest share of intra-Asia tourism—93% (58.3 million) of the subregion's 62.4 million total in 2013. Southeast Asia also had the fastest growing intrasubregional tourism **(Figure 54)**. In 2000, Southeast Asian tourists traveling within Southeast Asia totaled 14.8 million, which almost tripled to 44.3 million in 2013. East Asian tourists traveling within East Asia grew 67% to 130 million from 78 million. Tourist travel between Hong Kong, China and the PRC comprises the majority of East Asia's 193 million outbound tourists in 2013, with 76.9 million tourists from Hong Kong, China heading to the PRC, and 17.1 million from the PRC to Hong Kong, China. Japan and the Republic of Korea are the top two destinations of tourists from the PRC. From January–September 2015, for example, 3.8 million tourists from the PRC and 2.9 million from the Republic of Korea travelled to Japan, partly boosted by weak Japanese yen.[44] During the PRC's National Day holiday week in October 2015, 400,000 tourists travelled from the PRC to Japan.

In Southeast Asia, the top five destinations in 2013 were Malaysia (25.7 million), Thailand (25.5 million), Singapore (15.4 million), Indonesia (8.4 million) and Viet Nam (7.4 million). Recently, however,

---

44   Japan Tourism Marketing Co. Tourism Statistics. http://www.tourism.jp/en/

Figure 51: Financial Inflows to Asia
($ billion, by type)

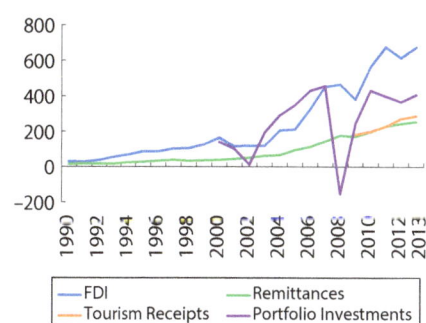

FDI = foreign direct investment.
Note: Portfolio investments (equity plus debt securities).
Source: ADB calculations using data from *Annual Remittances Data*, World Bank; *World Development Indicators* and IMF *Balance of Payments data* from CEIC.

Table 8: Average Cost of Sending Remittances (%, based on benchmark $200 worth of remittance)

Region	Q1 2015	Q2 2015
East Asia and the Pacific	8.1	8.1
Europe and Central Asia	6.1	6.0
Latin America and Caribbean	6.1	6.8
Middle-East and North Africa	8.4	8.2
South Asia	6.0	5.7
Sub-Saharan Africa	10.2	9.7
Global Average	7.7	7.7

Note: Country grouping based on World Bank definition.
Source: World Bank. 2015. *Remittances Prices Worldwide*. Issue No. 14. June. Washington.

Figure 52: Tourist Inflows—Asia
(million, by destination)

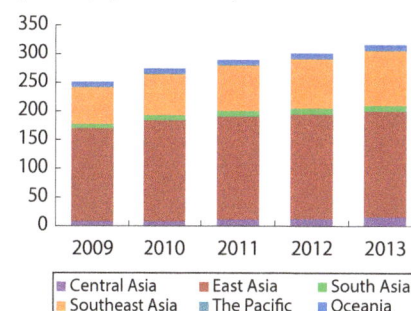

Source: ADB calculations using data from World Tourism Organization.

Figure 53: Tourist Arrivals—Asia
(million, by origin)

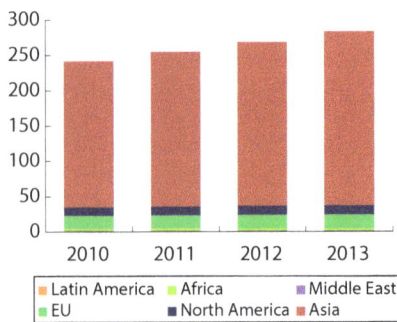

EU = European Union (27 members).
Source: ADB calculations using data from World Tourism Organization.

Figure 54: Tourism Outflows—Asia (million)

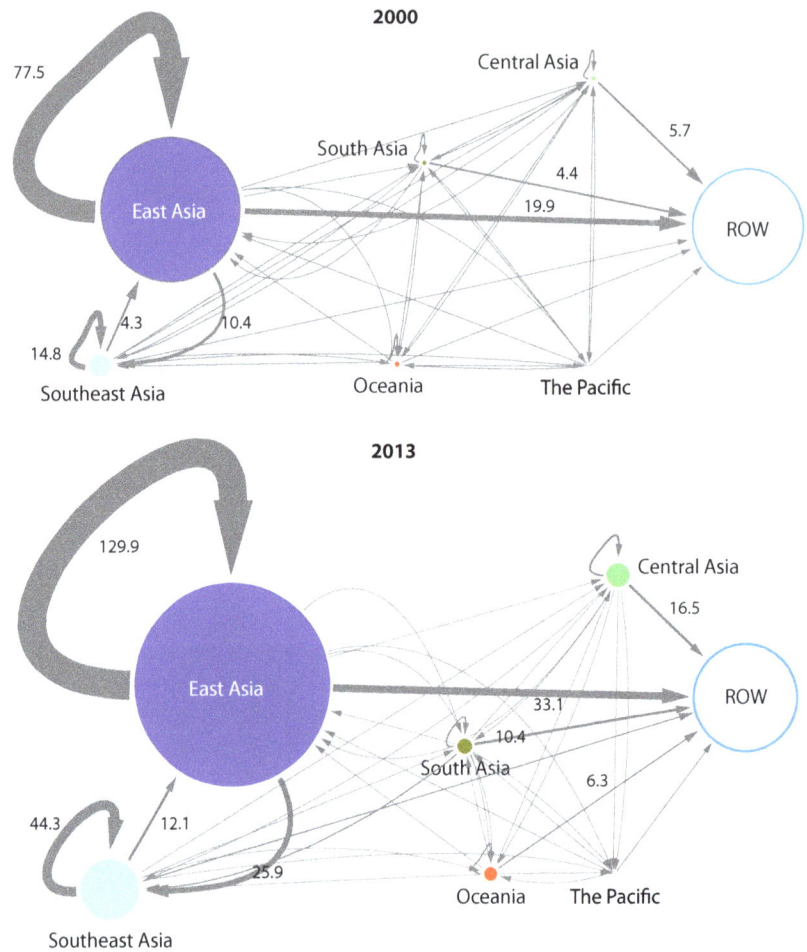

ROW = rest of the world.
Note: Rendered in Cytoscape 3.2.1
Source: ADB calculations using data from World Tourism Organization.

transboundary haze caused by Indonesian forest fires has affected tourism in these economies—especially Indonesia, Singapore and Malaysia. According to the Association of Singapore Attractions, preliminary estimates suggest the number of visitors dropped around 5%-10%, which could translate into a 0.1%-0.4% decline in Singapore's GDP.[45]

Trends in Migration

Generally, the number of outbound tourists from Asia exceeds the number of migrants with significantly varying trends. In 2013, 317 million tourists travelled from Asia compared with a 79.5 million total migrant stock. Within subregions, outbound tourism exceeds migration except in South Asia and the Pacific **(Figure 55)**. In 2013, for instance, East Asia's

[45] According to Chua Hak Bin, economist at Bank of America Merill Lynch, as written in T. Kikuchi. 2015. *Southeast Asia Fighting through the Haze.* Nikkei Asian Review. 3 November.

outbound tourism far exceeded migration (193 million tourists against 13.7 million migrants). In South Asia and the Pacific, however, migration exceeds outbound tourism.[46]

Asian migrants increased from 55.5 million in 2000 to 76 million in 2010 and 79.5 million in 2013.[47] In 2013, Asia accounted for almost 35% of global migrants with 19 million in Europe, 16 million in North America, and 3 million in Oceania.[48] Asian migration is mostly temporary, except to destinations such as the US, Australia, and Canada.[49]

South Asia accounts for the largest pool of migrants from Asia **(Figure 56)**. In 2013, it contributed 35.1 million, or 44% of the total. And they are growing quickly—43% above the 24.2 million in 2000. South Asian intra-subregional migration fell from 11.3 million in 2000 to 10.5 million in 2013. The prospect of increased earnings drives migration from South Asia, especially job opportunities for low-skilled workers in Gulf Cooperation Council members.[50] Migration from South Asia to Southeast Asia has also grown, increasing almost 2.5 times from 500,000 in 2000 to 1.2 million in 2013.

Income and demographic dynamics drive labor migration. Economies with low incomes and young populations (high ratios of 20-34 years old to total population) are generally migrant sources—such as India, Bangladesh, and Afghanistan **(Figure 57)**. Those with high incomes and ageing populations (low shares of working-age population) are mostly recipients—such as Australia, New Zealand, and Japan. Major

Figure 55: Outflows of Migration and Tourism—Asia (2013)

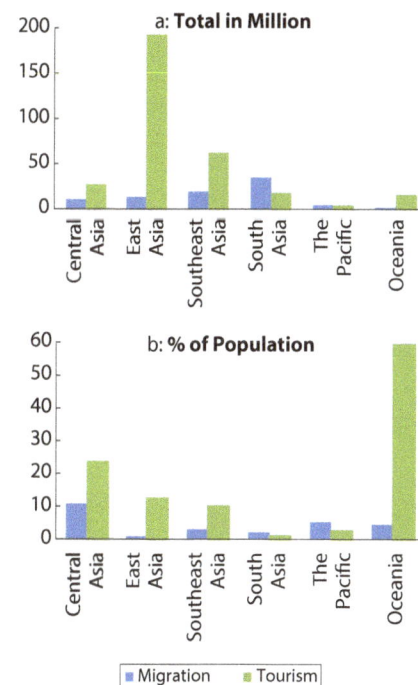

Source: ADB calculations using data from *Trends in International Migrant Stock,* United Nations Department of Economics and Social Affairs; and World Tourism Organization.

Figure 56: Migration—Asia (million)

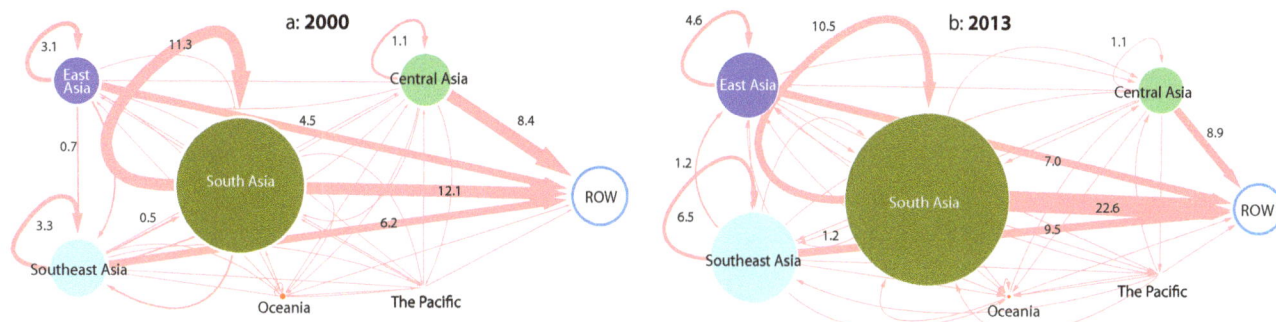

ROW = rest of the world.
Note: Rendered in Cytoscape 3.2.1.
Source: ADB calculations using data from *Trends in International Migrant Stock,* United Nations Department of Economics and Social Affairs.

---

[46] According to the *Pacific Opportunities: Leveraging on Asia's Growth*, majority of migrants from the Pacific are in Australia and New Zealand (about 66% of migrants from Samoa, 74% from Cook Islands, 59% from Fiji) while citizens of other Pacific economies have more limited opportunities to work outside their home economy. See ADB. 2015. *Pacific Opportunities: Leveraging Asia's Growth.* Manila.

[47] An increase of 43% for Asia and 28% for non-Asia since 2000.

[48] Asian Development Bank Institute, International Labor Organization and Organisation for Economic Co-operation and Development. 2015. *Building Human Capital through Labor Migration in Asia.* Japan.

[49] Working as foreigners and leaving the country when the contract is finished. Contracts range from a few months to several years.

[50] United Nations Economic and Social Commission for Asia and the Pacific. 2013. *Interregional Report on Labor Migration and Social Protection.* Technical Paper No. 2.

Figure 57: Outbound Migration, Income, and Working Age Population

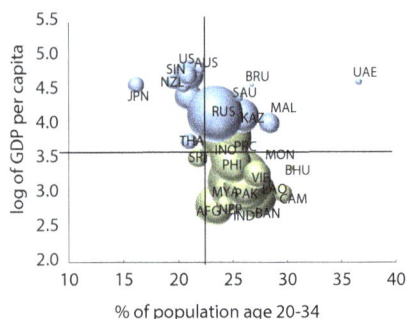

AFG = Afghanistan; AUS = Australia; BAN = Bangladesh; BHU = Bhutan; BRU = Brunei Darussalam; CAM = Cambodia; CAN = Canada; PRC = People's Republic of China; HKG =Hong Kong, China; IND = India; INO = Indonesia; JPN = Japan; KAZ = Kazakhstan; KOR = Republic of Korea; LAO = Lao PDR; MAL = Malaysia; MON = Mongolia; MYA = Myanmar; NEP = Nepal; NZL = New Zealand; PAK = Pakistan; PHI = Philippines; RUS = Russian Federation; SAU = Saudi Arabia; SIN = Singapore; SRI = Sri Lanka; THA = Thailand; UAE = United Arab Emirates; US = United States.

Notes:
(i) Size of bubble corresponds to the number of outbound migrants in 2013.
(ii) Blue bubbles indicate receiving economies (outbound migration is less than inbound).
(iii) Green bubbles indicate source economies (outbound migration is greater than inbound).
(iv) GDP per capita (current $) in 2013; horizontal line in the middle is the middle-income line based on World Bank classification.

Source: ADB calculations using data from *Trends in International Migrant Stock*; United Nations Department of Economic and Social Affairs; and *World Development Indicators*; World Bank.

destinations outside Asia include North America (the US and Canada), the Russian Federation, and Saudi Arabia.

Southeast Asia was second in number of Asian migrants, with 18.8 million in 2013. Intra-ASEAN migration has more than doubled—from 3.3 million in 2000 to 6.5 million in 2013—as ASEAN economic integration deepens and relatively common traditions and languages shared, help reduce migration barriers **(Figure 58)**.[51] While the Mutual Recognition Arrangement of the ASEAN Economic Community for managing labor migration is confined to high-skilled occupations, they account for a very small share of total employment.[52] Rather, intra-ASEAN migration involves mostly low- and medium-skilled workers—and this growing trend will likely continue in the future.

The movement of intra-ASEAN migrant workers is concentrated in a few corridors: (i) from Cambodia, the Lao PDR, and Myanmar to Thailand; (ii) from Indonesia to Malaysia; and (iii) from Malaysia to Singapore. Migration from Viet Nam and Myanmar to Malaysia has also increased. The Philippines has the largest labor migrant stock among ASEAN economies, but Filipino migrants going to other ASEAN economies have dropped substantially since 2000. Most now work in the US and Middle East.

There has been a shift in ASEAN migration—following changes in economic dynamics and the temporary or contractual nature of employment **(Figure 59)**. Since 2000, Brunei Darussalam, Malaysia, Singapore, and Thailand have been labor importers, while Cambodia, Indonesia, the Philippines, and Viet Nam have been labor exporters. In 2000, both the Lao PDR and Myanmar were labor importers. But in 2010 and 2013, they became labor exporters.

[51] G. Sugiyarto. 2015. Internal and International Migration in Southeast Asia. In I. Coxhead, ed. *Handbook of Southeast Asian Economics*. UK: Routledge.

[52] International Labour Organization and Asian Development Bank. 2014. *ASEAN Community 2015: Managing Integration for Better Jobs and Shared Prosperity*. Bangkok: ILO and ADB.

Figure 58: Migration—Southeast Asia (thousands)

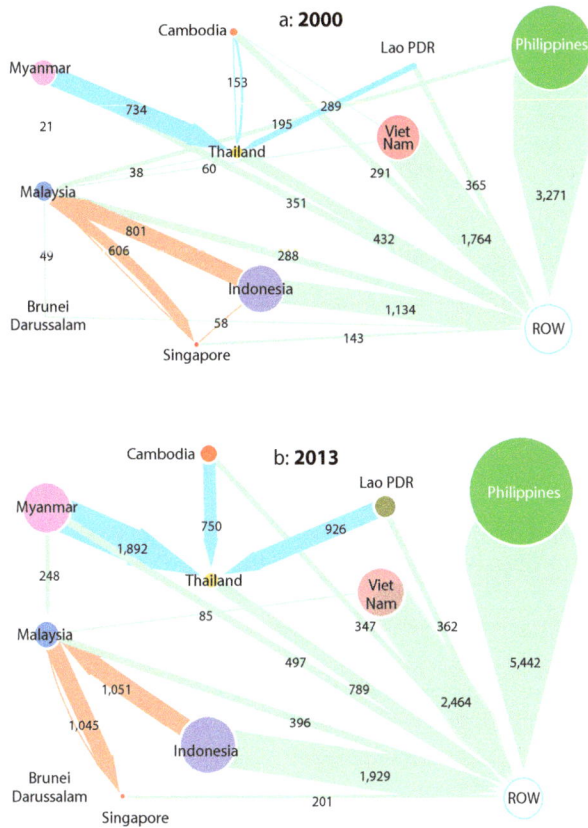

a: 2000

Cambodia
Myanmar
Lao PDR
Philippines
153
734
289
21
195
Viet Nam
Thailand
38
60
291
365
3,271
Malaysia
351
801
606
432
1,764
49
288
Indonesia
Brunei Darussalam
58
1,134
Singapore
143
ROW

b: 2013

Cambodia
Myanmar
Lao PDR
Philippines
750
926
1,892
248
Thailand
85
Viet Nam
347
362
Malaysia
497
1,051
789
5,442
1,045
396
2,464
Indonesia
Brunei Darussalam
1,929
Singapore
201
ROW

ROW = rest of the world.
Note: Includes only migration stock greater than 20,000. Rendered in Cytoscape 3.2.1.
Source: ADB calculations using data from *Trends in International Migrant Stock*, United Nations Department of Economic and Social Affairs.

Figure 59: Net Migration—Southeast Asia (million)

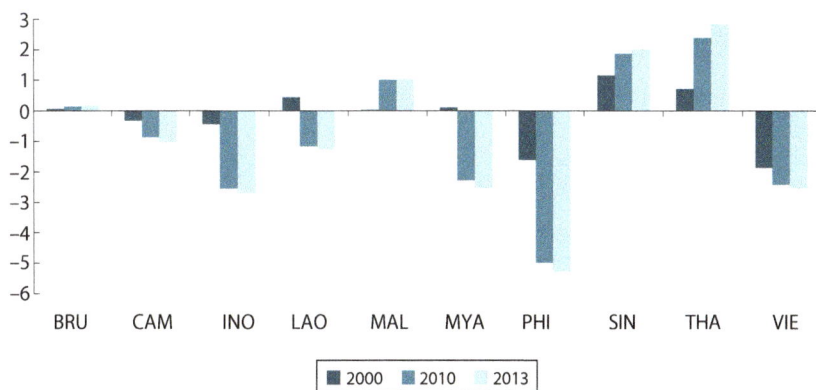

BRU = Brunei Darussalam, CAM = Cambodia, INO = Indonesia, LAO = Lao People's Democratic Republic, MAL = Malaysia, MYA = Myanmar, PHI = Philippines, SIN = Singapore, THA = Thailand, VIE = Viet Nam.
Note: Net migration refers to total inbound migrants less total outbound migrants.
Source: *Trends in International Migrant Stock*, United Nations Department of Economic and Social Affairs.

Updates on Trade Policy

Trans-Pacific Partnership concluded

Considered a platform for closer regional integration in Asia, the Trans-Pacific Partnership (TPP) will set new high standards for trade and investment rules in Asia and around the Pacific rim. The TPP currently has 12 members—representing 37% of global GDP and 28% of world trade. Indonesia, the Philippines, and the Republic of Korea have also expressed interest in joining.[53] TPP negotiations started in March 2010. About 5 years later, on 4 October 2015, ministers of TPP economies announced the conclusion of negotiations.

Following the release of the TPP text on 5 November 2015, the next step is ratification by the respective legislatures of the 12 participating economies. It is generally accepted that this should be done within 2 years. In the case of the US, legislators will have 90 days to study the agreement before Congress votes "yes" or "no"—as President Barack Obama narrowly secured Trade Promotion Authority (TPA) that prevents changes to the agreement itself.

The TPP includes 30 chapters with coverage well beyond traditional FTAs. The TPP covers more comprehensive market access and addresses new and emerging trade and cross-cutting issues compared with its precursor (the Trans-Pacific Strategic Economic Partnership Agreement [TPS-EPA] 2005)—and four other free trade agreements (FTAs) involving TPP members **(Table 9)**. These include those related to development, competitiveness and business facilitation, regulatory coherence, and support for small and medium enterprises (SMEs).

TPP members include developing economies such as Viet Nam, Peru, and Brunei Darussalam. The chapter on development seeks to ensure all TPP members—particularly developing economy members—can obtain full benefits of the TPP and are able to implement commitments. To this end, the development chapter promotes (i) cooperation and capacity building initiatives such as information-sharing and the provision of expertise to help members implement and benefit from the TPP; and (ii) partnerships between public and private sectors, including SMEs, to bring expertise and resources to cooperative ventures with governments in support of development goals.[54]

The competitiveness and business facilitation chapter aims to help the TPP reach its potential to improve the competitiveness of its members and adapt to the ever-increasing competition and complexity inherent in international business. The chapter creates formal mechanisms to review

---

[53] *BBC News.* 2015. Joko Widodo says Indonesia will join TPP free trade deal. 27 October. *Philippines: Official Gazette.* 2015. PH welcomes new Trans Pacific Partnership agreement. 19 October; *Yonhap News.* 2015. [The Republic of] Korea moving toward joining TPP: finance minister. 6 October.

[54] Foreign Affairs, Trade and Development Canada. Trans-Pacific Partnership Development, Cooperation & Capacity Building Chapters. http://www.international.gc.ca/trade-agreements-accords-commerciaux/agr-acc/tpp-ptp/understanding-comprendre/20-development.aspx?lang=eng

Table 9: Coverage Beyond Goods Trade

FTA Coverage	TPP (Negotiations concluded 2015)	Trans-Pacific Strategic EPA (2005)	Japan- Australia (2014)	US- Singapore (2004)	US- [Republic of] Korea (2012)	NAFTA (1994)
Customs Administration and Trade Facilitation	Yes	Yes	Yes	Yes	Yes	Yes
Sanitary and Phyto-sanitary Measures	Yes	Yes	Yes	No	Yes	Yes
Technical Barriers to Trade	Yes	Yes	Yes	Yes	Yes	Yes
Trade Remedies	Yes	Yes	Yes	Yes	Yes	No
Investment	Yes	No	Yes	Yes	Yes	Yes
Services	Yes	Yes	Yes	Yes	Yes	Yes
Financial Services	Yes	No	Yes	Yes	Yes	Yes
Temporary Entry for Business Person	Yes	Yes	Yes	Yes	Yes	Yes
Telecommunications	Yes	No	Yes	Yes	Yes	Yes
Electronic Commerce	Yes	No	Yes	Yes	Yes	No
Government Procurement	Yes	Yes	Yes	Yes	Yes	Yes
Competition Policy	Yes	Yes	Yes	Yes	Yes	Yes
Intellectual Property	Yes	Yes	Yes	Yes	Yes	Yes
Labor	Yes	No	No	Yes	Yes	No
Environment	Yes	No	No	Yes	Yes	No
Cooperation and Capacity Building	Yes	Yes	Yes	No	No	No
Competitiveness and Business Facilitation	Yes	No	No	No	No	No
Development	Yes	No	No	No	No	No
Small and Medium Enterprises	Yes	No	No	No	No	No
Regulatory Coherence	Yes	No	No	No	No	No
Transparency and Anti-corruption	Yes	Yes	Yes	Yes	Yes	Yes
Dispute Settlement	Yes	Yes	Yes	Yes	Yes	Yes

EPA = Economic Partnership Agreement, FTA = Free Trade Agreement, NAFTA = North American Free Trade Agreement, TPP = Trans-Pacific Partnership, US = United States.
Source: ADB staff compilation from official FTA fact sheet (for TPP) and official FTA text (for the rest).

the impact of the TPP on competitiveness with a particular focus on deepening regional supply chains, to assess progress, take advantage of new opportunities, and address any challenges that may emerge once the TPP is in force.[55]

With tariffs down globally, regulatory rules emerge as a major impediment to international trade and gaining access to foreign markets. For instance, regulatory changes without adequate prior notification to foreign companies can severely restrict market opportunities in that country, and can also give unfair advantage to domestic firms. The TPP addresses these trade barriers in its chapter on regulatory coherence—to help ensure an open, fair, and predictable regulatory environment for businesses operating in TPP markets—by encouraging regulatory transparency, impartiality, and coordination across governments. To do this, a committee will be created to give TPP countries, businesses,

---

[55] Office of the United States Trade Representative. Summary of the Trans-Pacific Partnership Agreement. https://ustr.gov/about-us/policy-offices/press-office/press-releases/2015/october/summarytrans-pacific-partnership

and civil society opportunities to report on implementation, share experiences on best practices, and consider potential areas for cooperation.

Recognizing the importance of ensuring SMEs benefit from the TPP, they are given access to information specifically tailored for their use, simplified process for clearing goods through customs, and development of programs to help SMEs to participate in and integrate effectively into global supply chains.[56]

The TPP encourages capital and labor mobility, protects intellectual property and labor and environmental standards, and promotes competition. It may require some members to enact new laws and implement domestic reforms to align with TPP provisions. Its new rules on economic competition could also impact global trade and the region's production network.

Trade in Goods

TPP members agree to eliminate and reduce tariffs and nontariff barriers on industrial goods, as well as other restrictive policies on agricultural products. The preferential access provided through the TPP will increase trade between members—which have a combined market of 800 million people. It was also agreed that most industrial goods tariffs will be eliminated immediately, though tariffs on some products will be eliminated over a longer timeframe. In comparison, the US-Singapore FTA, the US-Republic of Korea FTA, and Japan-Australia Economic Partnership Agreement (JAEPA) liberalized more than 80% of tariff lines (average of tariff lines liberalized by FTA partners) immediately upon entry into force.

The TPP has a single rules-of-origin that applies to all members that determines whether a product originates in the TPP region and is thus eligible for preferential benefits—inputs from other TPP members are treated the same way as if produced in its home country in qualifying for preferential benefits. TPP members also set rules to ensure businesses can easily operate across the TPP region—by creating a common TPP-wide system to verify that goods made in TPP countries meet the rules of origin. Importers will be able to claim preferential tariff treatment so long as documentation supports their claim.[57]

Beyond Goods Trade: Services, Investment, and Intellectual Property

Under the TPP, market access commitments on services and investment provide greater openness and security, enabling businesses to offer services to overseas clients within the TPP region. They should also

---

[56] Foreign Affairs, Trade and Development Canada. Trans-Pacific Partnership Small and Medium-Sized Enterprises Chapter. http://www.international.gc.ca/trade-agreements-accords-commerciaux/agracc/tpp-ptp/understanding-comprendre/22-SME.aspx?lang=eng

[57] Office of the United States Trade Representative. Summary of the Trans-Pacific Partnership Agreement. https://ustr.gov/about-us/policy-offices/press-office/press-releases/2015/october/summary-transpacific-partnership

provide greater confidence to investors who seek to expand operations or investments in other TPP economies. The TPP Agreement establishes a common set of rules on intellectual property protection and enforcement, which aims to encourage investment in new ideas, support creative and innovative industries, address and prevent piracy and counterfeiting, and promote the dissemination of information, knowledge and technology.

Access to TPP markets has been "locked in" for TPP service providers across a range of sectors. It opens access to TPP markets for professional, business, education, environmental, transportation and distribution services. Service exports among TPP countries will benefit from legal protection that could guarantee market access and nondiscriminatory treatment. Market access provides that no TPP country may impose quantitative restrictions on the supply of services (for example, limiting the number of suppliers or number of transactions); or require a specific type of business entity or joint venture. Local presence is also not prerequisite, meaning no country may require a service supplier from another country to establish an office or be resident in its territory. TPP's Cross-border Trade in Services chapter operates on a "negative-list basis", meaning TPP markets are fully open to services suppliers from other TPP countries unless subject to exceptions. In addition, the TPP will also capture future market reforms in services.[58]

The agreement creates a predictable and secure environment for TPP investors. It provides comprehensive, high-quality, modern investment rules that establish a strong, rules-based framework, including basic investment protection, national treatment; most-favored-nation treatment; "minimum standard of treatment" for investments in accordance with customary international legal principles. It prohibits expropriation that is not for public purposes without due process or compensation, prohibits "performance requirements" such as local content or technology localization requirements, and allows free investment-related fund transfers. These provisions are also covered under NAFTA, US-Singapore FTA, and the US-Republic of Korea FTA. JAEPA only accords postestablishment national treatment, while TPS-EPA has no investment chapter.

The TPP investment chapter also contains an investor-state dispute settlement (ISDS) mechanism, which provides investors access to an independent arbitral tribunal to resolve disputes for breaches of investment rules. NAFTA, the US-Singapore FTA and the US-Republic of Korea FTA also include provisions for an ISDS, while JAEPA has none. The ISDS mechanism for TPP members can only be used on matters related to commitments in investment and financial services.

The TPP also includes an IP chapter that creates a common set of regional IP rules. It harmonizes IP standards among TPP members—covering areas such as patents, trademarks, copyrights, industrial designs, and trade secrets, among others. It thus makes it easier for businesses

---

[58] Office of the United States Trade Representative. Summary of the Trans-Pacific Partnership Agreement. https://ustr.gov/about-us/policy-offices/press-office/press-releases/2015/october/summary-transpacific-partnership

Table 10: Comparison of Key Intellectual Property Provisions

Provisions \ FTAs	TRIPS	TPP (Negotiations concluded 2015)	Trans-Pacific Strategic EPA (2005)	Japan-Australia (2014)	US-Singapore (2004)	US-[Republic of] Korea (2012)	NAFTA (1994)
Copyright							
Term of protection (number of years)	50	70	50	50	70	70	50
Technological protection measures (TPM)	No	Yes	No	Yes	Yes	Yes	No
Data protection (number of years)							
Pharmaceutical drugs	No	5	No	No	5	5	5
Agricultural chemicals	No	10	No	No	10	10	5

EPA = Economic Partnership Agreement, FTA = Free Trade Agreement, NAFTA = North American Free Trade Agreement, TPP = Trans-Pacific Partnership, TRIPS = Trade-Related Aspects of Intellectual Property Rights, US = United States.
Source: ADB staff compilation from official FTA fact sheet (for TPP) and official FTA text (for the rest).

to search, register, and protect IP rights in new markets—an area of particular significance for small businesses.[59]

IP chapters in the five surveyed FTAs have already gone beyond the multilateral IP protection standards established in the World Trade Organization's (WTO) Trade-Related Aspects of Intellectual Property Rights (TRIPS) Agreement. TPP further raises the bar by incorporating international best practices. It extends copyright term protection to 70 years—similar to the "gold standard" IP provisions of US-Singapore FTA and the US-Republic of Korea FTA. NAFTA, JAEPA and TPS-EPA build on the existing TRIPS commitment of 50-year term protection **(Table 10)**.

While JAEPA, the US-Singapore FTA, and the US-Republic of Korea FTA already have remedies against circumvention of effective technological measures to protect copyrights, the TPP requires members to provide stronger technological protection measures (TPMs)—digital 'locks' that protect copyrights—by introducing a new requirement to provide civil and criminal remedies against people breaking TPMs. It also includes obligations to prevent selling devices and services that enable breaking of TPMs.

On data protection, the TPP is also consistent with the "gold standard" provisions of the US-Singapore FTA and the US-Republic of Korea FTA, which accord 5- and 10-year data protection to new pharmaceutical products and agricultural chemicals, respectively. It also requires 5-year data protection for small molecule pharmaceuticals or biologics. Data protection is key to IP protection as it sets a timeframe that generic manufacturers must wait before they can use data provided by manufacturers of new pharmaceutical products to advance approval of generic versions.

[59] New Zealand Ministry of Foreign Affairs and Trade. 2015. *Trans-Pacific Partnership Intellectual Property Fact Sheet.* http://www.tpp.mfat.govt.nz/assets/docs/TPP_factsheet_Intellectual-Property.PDF

Lastly, the TPP includes strong enforcement systems—including civil procedures, provisional measures, border measures, and criminal procedures and penalties for commercial-scale trademark counterfeiting, copyright or related rights piracy, among others.

Likely TPP Impact

Sizeable income gains are expected to accrue to TPP members mainly from new trade and investment. According to one estimate (Petri, Plummer and Zhai 2014) the TPP would yield annual income of $285 billion for the 12 TPP members, equivalent to 0.9% of their total GDP.[60] The agreement will enhance investor confidence, increase competition and cooperation and thus lead to faster productivity growth and greater innovation—even perhaps improved political relations.

While the TPP creates new opportunities for trade and investment, there remains the possibility of potential trade and investment diversion, depending on rules-of-origin requirements across sectors, and potential harm to regional and global value chains—as the TPP currently excludes the PRC, the Republic of Korea, and other important members of existing Asian production networks. Nevertheless, overall welfare increase effect will far exceed negative effect. It would have a much larger positive impact if Asia's large trade partners were to join—such as the PRC, the Republic of Korea, Indonesia, and Thailand.

For individual economies, Viet Nam is expected to reap the largest income growth. The US is Viet Nam's biggest trade partner, yet the two countries do not have an FTA. The tariff reductions by the US through the TPP will make Vietnamese exports—in particular exports of labor-intensive products—much more competitive than goods from non-TPP members. While Viet Nam is generally seen to benefit from the TPP, its estimated 1,000 state-owned enterprises (SOEs) will be most affected by provisions aimed at levelling the playing field between SOEs and private companies, though reforms are already underway.

For Japan, government estimates from 2013 suggest the TPP could drive up the country by 0.66%, or around ¥3.2 trillion, which amounts to a full year's worth of extra growth.[61] Japan's gains will come from increased exports of manufacturing goods such as automobiles and machineries, but will also be due to larger inward foreign investment afforded by the liberalization of Japan's service and other investment sectors.[62]

Australia and New Zealand could gain in exporting agricultural and dairy products. For example, the TPP eliminates tariffs on more than $4.3 billion of Australia's dutiable exports of agricultural goods. A further $2.1 billion of Australia's dutiable exports will receive significant

---

[60] P. Petri, M. Plummer, and F. Zhai. 2014. The TPP, [the People's Republic of] China and the FTAAP: The Case For Convergence. In G. Tang and P.A. Petri, eds. *New Directions in Asia-Pacific Economic Integration*. Honolulu: East-West Center.

[61] *The Japan Times News*. 2013. Abe declares Japan will join TPP free-trade process. 16 March.

[62] P. Petri and M. Plummer. 2012. The Trans-Pacific Partnership and Asia-Pacific Integration: Policy Implications. *Peterson Institute for International Economics Policy Brief*. No. PB12-16.

preferential access through new quotas and tariff reductions. [63] The overall impact on New Zealand's economy, once fully implemented, amounts to an annual increase of at least 0.9% of New Zealand's real GDP, or NZ$2.7 billion, by 2030. [64]

Based on the estimates of Petri, Plummer, and Zhai (2014), the US is expected to reap $76.6 billion of income gains or 0.4% increase in GDP. [65] Manufacturing will experience a minor drop, while agriculture and mining combined will see little impact. However, services are projected to reap huge welfare gains, offsetting the negative impact on manufacturing. [66] The United States International Trade Commission (US ITC) is expected to deliver its analysis on economic impact of TPP in mid-May 2016. [67]

For Canada, gains from tariff elimination and improved market access for Canadian agriculture under the TPP would be especially significant in Japanese, Malaysian, and Vietnamese markets—markets where Canada faces high tariffs and no prior preferential access.

Although Singapore is already an open economy, the trade pact will still boost trade and investment links between Singapore and key markets in the region and globally, including Latin America. For instance, Singapore firms in some sectors can bid for government contracts in other TPP countries and take larger stakes in foreign firms operating in key sectors abroad. Still, additional benefits to Singapore, which already has 21 FTAs and economic partnership agreements, might be incremental.

TPP members should reap significant gains from increased trade and investment flows. Meanwhile, countries outside the trade deal could incur losses one way or another in terms of both current and new opportunities for trade and investments.

For the Republic of Korea, although it is unlikely to see a significant degree of trade diversion or any marked increase in transaction costs due to its trade agreements with most TPP members—the US, Viet Nam, Malaysia, and other ASEAN members—domestic manufacturers could lose some competitive edge they gained from existing FTAs, particularly with the US. This could encourage manufacturers from the Republic of Korea to move production lines and investments into countries like Viet Nam, a bilateral FTA partner and TPP member.

---

[63] Australian Government Department of Foreign Affairs and Trade. Trans-Pacific Partnership Outcomes at a Glance. http://dfat.gov.au/trade/agreements/tpp/outcomes-documents/Pages/outcomes-at-aglance.aspx

[64] New Zealand Ministry of Foreign Affairs and Trade. 2015. *Economic Modelling on Estimated Effect of TPP on New Zealand Economy.* https://www.tpp.mfat.govt.nz/assets/docs/TPP%20-%20CGE%20Analysis%20of%20Impact%20on%20New%20Zealand,%20explanatory%20cover%20note.pdf

[65] P. Petri, M. Plummer, and F. Zhai. 2014. The TPP, [the People's Republic of] China and the FTAAP: The Case For Convergence. In G. Tang and P.A. Petri, eds. *New Directions in Asia-Pacific Economic Integration.* Honolulu: East-West Center.

[66] Ibid.

[67] United States International Trade Commission. 2015. USITC begins assessment of the Trans-Pacific Partnership agreement. 17 November. http://www.usitc.gov/press_room/news_release/2015/er1117ll524.htm

The PRC's nonmembership in TPP also retains the possibility of trade diversion, as the PRC is a net exporter to TPP economies—with exports to these economies accounting for almost 35% of its total exports. The PRC is expected to face direct competition from some TPP members that compete with the PRC's low cost production. This could possibly increase investments in low-cost, labor-intensive products—such as textiles and footwear—to TPP members like Malaysia and Viet Nam.

India's absence from the TPP might not be highly costly. Petri, Plummer, and Zhai (2014) estimate the costs to India would be $2.7 billion, or 0.1% lower annual income growth. Nevertheless, these costs could be greater than suggested due to the dynamic nature of the TPP as membership increases over time.[68]

If the TPP is ratified and implemented effectively, there is no doubt it will have a significant impact on both members and nonmembers. There are also intangible effects of renewed momentum toward global economic integration. The TPP should revive momentum in other trade talks and will help reshape the regional and global trade architecture. The fact that negotiations have been concluded is expected to pressure other groups to lift their game, such as the ASEAN+6 Regional Comprehensive Economic Partnership (RCEP).

In the longer term, the real impact of the TPP will depend on whether other economies in the Asia-Pacific region—especially large trading nations such as the PRC and the Republic of Korea—seek to join. If the TPP's open accession clause succeeds, then it could become a building block toward a Free Trade Area of the Asia-Pacific (FTAAP), for instance, which brings together the remaining ASEAN, RCEP, and Asia Pacific Economic Cooperation (APEC) members under one umbrella.

Recent Trends of Free Trade Agreements

The number of newly effective FTAs in Asia has been modest. So far, there have been three waves toward trade integration. **Figure 60** shows the historical trend of FTAs that became effective each year, based on WTO notification. The first wave occurred in Europe in the 1960s and 1970s, following the launch of European Community (EC) in 1958 and European Free Trade Association (EFTA) in 1960. This wave did not grow, partly because economies wanted to join the EC rather than set up their own FTAs. The second wave began in the 1990s with the North and South America at the forefront. NAFTA (1995) and South America's Mercado Común del Sur (MERCOSUR)—or southern common market (1991) are examples.

Asia became centerstage during the third wave of FTAs **(Figure 61)**. The PRC and ASEAN agreed to establish an FTA within 10 years at their November 2001 summit, which triggered an avalanche of Asian FTAs, with many economies starting negotiations. Japan and the Republic of Korea began negotiating FTAs with ASEAN and soon after the PRC. It is

Figure 60: Number of Newly Effective FTAs—World

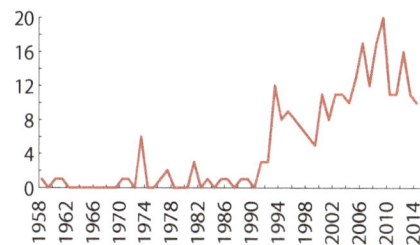

FTA = free trade agreement.
Source: *Regional Trade Agreements Information System (RTA-IS) Database,* World Trade Organization.

---

[68] See footnote no. 65.

Figure 61: Number of Signed FTAs—Asia (cumulative)

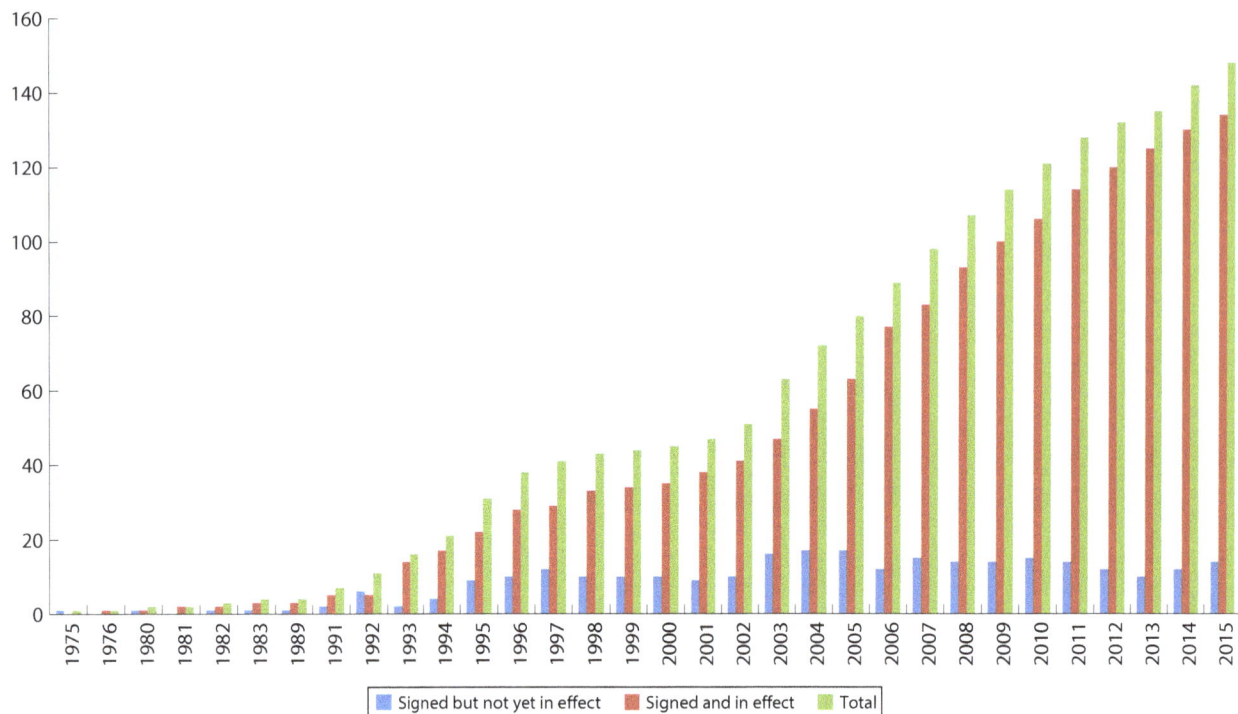

Signed but not yet in effect | Signed and in effect | Total

FTA = free trade agreement.
Note: Includes bilateral and plurilateral FTAs with at least one of ADB's 48 regional members as signatory. 2015 covers January to August. Signed but not yet in effect refers to FTAs where the parties sign the agreement after negotiations have been completed, but the agreement has yet to become effective. Signed and in effect refers to FTAs where provisions become effective, after legislative or executive ratification.
Source: *Asia Regional Integration Center FTA Database,* ADB.

interesting that the domino effect in Asia differed from Europe's in the 1960s–1970s. Asian economies have been proposing their own bilateral FTAs, which led to the proliferation of bilateral agreements. The different type of domino effect between Asia and Europe was partly because Asia did not have a regional FTA with an open accession clause.[69]

Recently, the number of FTAs newly signed yearly has declined **(Figure 62)**. Only around 10 new FTAs were signed yearly between 2012 and 2014. This coincides with more active multilateral negotiations through regional trade talks such as the TPP and RCEP. However, the number of FTAs signed may increase in 2015–2016—a potential fourth wave of FTAs. If the number of FTAs proposed and signed are compared, there is about a 1-2 year lag—the time needed to conclude negotiations.[70] Thus, a 2-year moving average of the number of proposed FTAs with a 1-year lag is a good leading indicator for the number of FTAs signed each year. Using this approach, there is a possibility the number of Asian FTAs will rise again in the near future. At least those signed over the next

---

[69] Asia-Pacific Trade Agreement (APTA) has an accession clause, and in fact the PRC joined in 2005. But APTA is open only for developing members of the United Nations Economic and Social Commission for Asia and the Pacific (UNESCAP).

[70] The number of proposals peaked in 2004–2005. But the number of agreements signed peaked in 2006. Likewise, the number of proposals declined in 2008 for a short period—reflected in the decline in signed FTAs in 2009–2010.

Figure 62: Number of FTAs Proposed and Signed Each Year—Asia

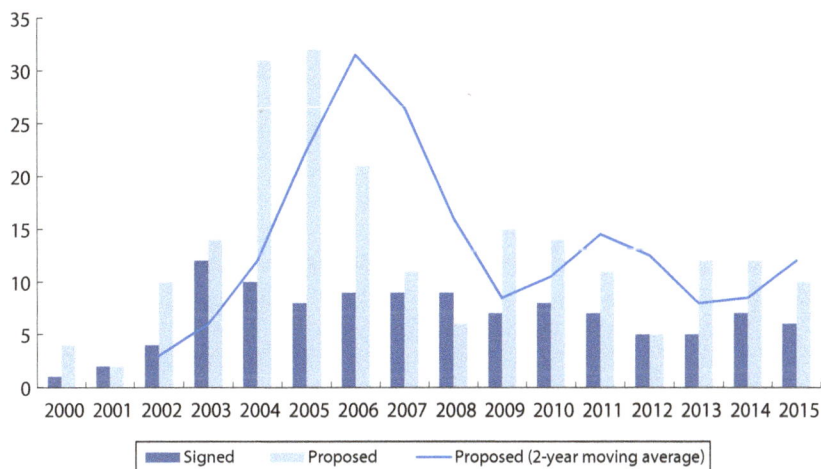

FTA = free trade agreement.
Note: Includes bilateral and plurilateral FTAs with at least one of ADB's 48 regional members as signatory. 2015 covers January to August. Signed includes FTAs that are (i) signed but not yet in effect and (ii) signed in effect. Proposed includes FTAs that are (i) proposed (i.e. the parties consider an FTA; governments or relevant ministries issue a joint statement on its desirability or establish a joint study group/joint task force to conduct feasibility studies); (ii) framework agreement signed/under negotiation (i.e. the parties, through relevant ministries, negotiate the contents of a framework agreement that serves as a framework for future negotiations); and (iii) under negotiation (i.e. the parties, through relevant ministries, declare the official launch of negotiations, or start the first round of negotiations).
Source: *Asia Regional Integration Center FTA Database*, ADB.

Table 11: List of Recently Proposed FTAs in Asia

2012	2013	2014	2015*
PRC-Colombia	India-Customs Union (of Russian Federation, Belarus, and	ASEAN-Hong Kong, China	EEU-Iran
Philippines-Taipei,China	Kazakhstan)	Indonesia-Peru	India-Iran
Thailand-Canada	Indonesia-Chile	Pakistan-US	Japan-Sri Lanka
Viet Nam-Ukraine	Japan-EU	Peru-India	Philippines-Canada
	Japan-Turkey	Philippines-Australia	Philippines-Chile
	Myanmar-US	Philippines-EU	Philippines-Mexico
	Pakistan-Thailand	Philippines-EFTA	PRC-Maldives
	Pakistan-Republic of Korea	PRC-EU	PRC-Georgia
	PRC-Japan-Republic of Korea	PRC-Sri Lanka	PRC-Israel
	RCEP	New Zealand-EU	Thailand-Jordan
	Thailand-EU	Singapore-Turkey	
	Thailand- Colombia	Taipei,China-India	

*Until August.
ASEAN=Association of Southeast Asian Nations, PRC=People's Republic of China, EEU=Eurasian Economic Union, EFTA=European Free Trade Association, EU=European Union, FTA = free trade agreement, RCEP= Regional Comprehensive Economic Partnership, US = United States.
Source: *Asia Regional Integration Center FTA Database*, ADB.

few years will not decline significantly. This is due to the relatively large number of FTAs proposed in 2013 and 2014.

Given recently proposed FTAs (2012–2015), two interesting observations can be made **(Table 11)**. First, the majority of proposals came from economies outside the TPP. These include the PRC (8), the Philippines (9), Thailand (7), India (4), and Pakistan (3). Second, it appears some FTAs are motivated by the launch of the Transatlantic Trade and Investment Partnership (TTIP) negotiations, the proposed mega-

Figure 63: Cumulative Bilateral FDI Before and After Implementation of FTA (FTAs implemented since 2008)

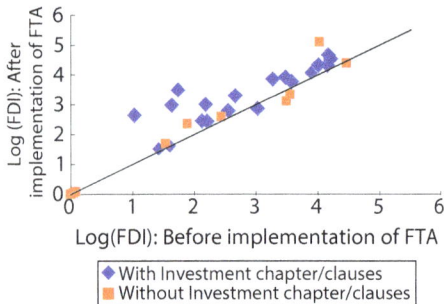

FDI = foreign direct investment, FTA = free trade agreement.
Note: Points above (below) the 45 degree line show FTAs which have higher (lower) cumulative FDI flows after the implementation of the FTAs compared to the values prior to their implementation. Equal number of years before and after the implementation of FTAs was used.
Source: ADB calculations using data from United Nations Conference on Trade and Development (UNCTAD) and national sources.

agreement between Europe and the US. In fact, five of the proposed FTAs are between the European Union (EU) and Asian economies (the PRC, Japan, New Zealand, the Philippines, and Thailand).

A growing number of FTAs in Asia include an investment chapter to facilitate two-way investment flows. Indeed, of the 37 FTAs in effect from 2008 to 2012, 24 FTAs (65%) contain investment clauses that accord varying degrees of investment liberalization and protection in specific sectors. Of these FTAs, 21 have separate investment chapters with six FTAs covering all basic investment liberalization and protection measures. As mentioned, these include national treatment; most-favored-nation treatment; "minimum standard of treatment" for investments in accordance with customary international legal principles; prohibition of expropriation not for public purpose without due process or without compensation; prohibition on "performance requirements" such as local content or technology localization requirements; and free transfer of funds related to an investment.

The impact of FTAs with investment provisions on FDI flows requires more analysis, but a simple scatterplot offers a useful glimpse **(Figure 63)**. Most economies having FTAs with investment provisions saw an increase in FDI flows once implemented.

Beyond Trade Liberalization: Trade Facilitation and Capacity Building

In general, scholarly and policy discussions on the WTO and FTAs tend to focus on liberalization. There is no doubt that tariff liberalization or market access has been the center of the trade agenda. In contrast, trade facilitation measures that reduce nontariff barriers tend to be overlooked. The assistance for capacity building was off the agenda for a long time. However, the situation is gradually changing, and trade facilitation and capacity building are finally attracting attention from policy makers involved with both the WTO and FTAs.

Trade Facilitation and Capacity Building under Asia-Pacific FTAs

Despite low tariffs, trade transactions remained complicated. Thus the focus of Asian FTAs today is not so much tariff reduction but trade facilitation. In fact, recent studies find that FTAs have a positive trade impact on products ineligible for FTA preference, which implies that nontariff items under FTAs—especially trade facilitation—plays an important role.[71] Various trade facilitation items are included in FTAs although those fall under various sections.

Many FTAs in Asia have chapters on technical cooperation where (developed) parties provide tailor-made capacity building assistance

---

[71] For details, see K. Hayakawa, T. Ito and F. Kimura. Forthcoming. Trade Creation Effects of Regional Trade Agreements: Tariff Reduction versus Nontariff Barrier Removal. *Review of Development Economics*.

to their partner, sometimes binding. FTAs signed by Japan and Australia tend to have an exclusive chapter on economic and technical cooperation, including capacity building. Importantly, capacity building is usually included in the trade facilitation provisions under FTAs as well. The importance of capacity building cannot be overemphasized as a direct tangible benefit for developing economies that have FTAs with developed economies.

Trade Facilitation and Capacity Building under WTO TFA

The WTO's Trade Facilitation Agreement (TFA)—agreed at the Bali WTO ministerial meeting in December 2013—suggests two important things for future WTO negotiations. First, the WTO should go beyond trade liberalization to have a true positive impact on trade. The WTO TFA—despite slow progress on the overall Doha Round negotiations—recognizes that trade facilitation measures could benefit all countries involved. A study conducted by the OECD suggests that successful TFA implementation would have a large impact on trade.[72] Still, many TFA provisions are not binding, meaning political will is critical in promoting trade facilitation.[73]

In the forthcoming 10th WTO Minsterial conference in Nairobi, Keyna in December 2015, the ratification and the implementation of the TFA is one of the agenda following the agreement reached at the Bali Meeting in 2013. As of November 2015, 52 economies out of 161 WTO members have ratified the TFA.[74]

Second, trade facilitation and capacity building are closely related under the TFA. Under the TFA, developing economies can decide when to implement commitments and also can ask assistance from other economies—especially advanced economies—to implement the agreement. The direct linkage between implementation of trade facilitation reform and assistance is expected to have trade impact beyond the technical legal discussions. Also, the TFA includes financial assistance along with technical assistance.

Progress of Trade Facilitation in Asia[75]

The broad definition of trade facilitation (TF) covers the overall environment in which trade transactions occur, including infrastructure connectivity, procedures, and trade finance.[76] Developing Asia has

[72] E. Moïsé, T. Orliac and P. Minor. 2011. Trade Facilitation Indicators: The Impact on Trade Costs. *OECD Trade Policy Working Papers*. No. 118. Paris: OECD Publishing.

[73] S. Hamanaka. 2014. WTO Agreement on Trade Facilitation: Assessing the Level of Ambition and Likely Impacts. *Global Trade and Customs Journal*. 9 (7/8).

[74] WTO Trade Facilitation Agreement Facility. 2015. *List of Ratifications*. http://www.tfafacility.org/sites/default/files/ratifications_list_1.pdf

[75] This section was drawn mainly from ADB. Forthcoming. *Trade Facilitation Progress in Asia: Performance Benchmarking and Policy Implications*. Manila: ADB.

[76] For the citation on the narrow and broad World Bank definitions on trade facilitation, see P. Sourdin and R. Pomfret. 2012. *Trade Facilitation: Defining, Measuring, Explaining and Reducing the Cost of International Trade. The* UK: Edward Elgar Publishing Limited. p. 5.

significantly advanced on trade facilitation over the last several decades, both in infrastructure hardware and software. A total of 48,000 kilometers of regional transport corridors along major supply chains have been improved. From 1992 to 2014, developing Asia together with ADB and its partners have mobilized $38.4 billion for 186 regional transport and trade facilitation investment projects under three subregional programs—the Central Asia Regional Economic Cooperation (CAREC), the Greater Mekong Subregion (GMS), and South Asia Subregional Economic Cooperation (SASEC).

ADB's Trade Finance Program (TFP) also helps fill market gaps in developing Asia by providing guarantees and loans to banks to support trade. Backed by ADB's AAA credit rating, the program works with over 200 partner banks to provide companies with the financial support needed for import and export activities. Since 2009, the TFP has supported 6,140 SMEs in 9,118 transactions valued at $19.97 billion in a wide range of sectors—from commodities and capital goods to medical supplies and consumer goods in the region's most challenging markets.

After the WTO Bali meeting—and the necessary procedural actions taken since—the WTO TFA is moving toward implementation. The World Customs Organization (WCO) immediately took action. It launched the Mercator Programme, which assists economies implement the TFA using WCO instruments and tools—such as the International Convention on the Simplification and Harmonization of Customs Procedures, commonly known as the Revised Kyoto Convention (RKC). The Mercator Programme supports TFA implementation through (i) technical assistance and capacity building, (ii) harmonized implementation based on WCO's global standards, and (iii) effective coordination among all stakeholders.

Figure 64: Level of Accession to the Revised Kyoto Convention—Asia and World

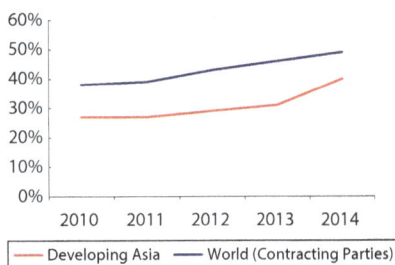

Note: Developing Asia refers to ADB's 45 developing regional members.
Source: Koide, H. 2015. Trade Facilitation Progress in Asia: Performance Benchmarking and Policy Implications. Presented at Regional Conference on Time-Release Studies. Tokyo. 6-8 October.

During the last 5 years, developing Asia has actively implemented customs modernization and trade facilitation reforms. As a result, for example, it has improved its accession level to the RKC by 14 percentage points—from 26% in 2010 to 40% in 2014 **(Figure 64)**. However, while the level of accession among developing Asian economies has improved, it remained below the world average of 50% in 2014. As most of the WTO TFA provisions are implemented though the RKC, RKC accession provides the key foundation for customs modernization and improvement in line with the global trade facilitation agenda.

The OECD trade facilitation indicators (TFIs) are in line with the global trade facilitation agenda—such as the WTO TFA and WCO Mercator Programme and RKC.[77] The TFIs were constructed based on 11 policy areas being negotiated under the auspices of the WTO to estimate the impact of these policies on trade volumes and trade costs. Latest data on the OECD TFI shows Asia performed second best among regions with an average score of 1.27—behind Europe (non-OECD) and Central Asia (1.47), and slightly better than the world average (the average of non-

---

[77]   See (i) E. Moïsé, T. Orliac and P. Minor. 2011. Trade Facilitation Indicators: The Impact on Trade Costs. *OECD Trade Policy Papers*. No. 118. Paris: OECD Publishing; and (ii) E. Moïsé and S. Sorescu. 2013. Trade Facilitation Indicators: The Potential Impact of Trade Facilitation on Developing Countries' Trade. *OECD Trade Policy Papers*. No. 144. Paris: OECD Publishing.

Figure 65: Trade Facilitation Performance (2013)

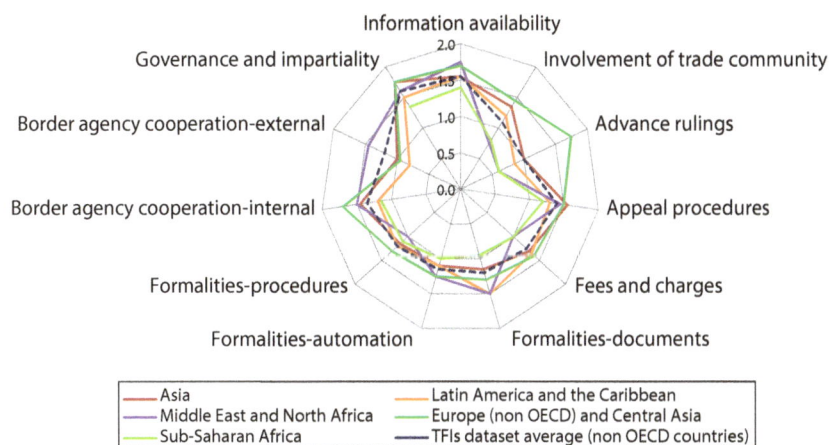

OECD = Organization for Economic Co-operation and Development.
Note: Country groupings are based on OECD definition. Asia consists of Bangladesh, Bhutan, Brunei Darussalam, Cambodia, the PRC, Fiji, India, Indonesia, Malaysia, Mongolia, Nepal, Pakistan, Papua New Guinea, the Philippines, Singapore, Sri Lanka, Thailand, and Viet Nam. Europe (non-OECD) and Central Asia consists of Albania, Armenia, Azerbaijan, Belarus, Bosnia and Herzegovina, Bulgaria, Croatia, Cyprus, Georgia, Kazakhstan, the Kyrgyz Republic, Latvia, Lithuania, FYR Macedonia, Malta, Moldova, Montenegro, Romania, Russian Federation, Serbia, and Ukraine. Advance Ruling – Prior statements by a customs administration to requesting traders concerning the classification, origin, valuation method, and the like, applied to specific goods at the time of importation, as well as the rules and process applied to such statements. Appeal Procedures – Possibility and modalities to appeal administrative decisions by border agencies. Border agency cooperation: External – Cooperation with neighboring and third countries. Border agency cooperation: Internal – Cooperation between/among various border agencies of a country; delegation of border control authority to customs authorities. Fees and Charges – Disciplines on the fees and charges imposed on imports and exports. Formalities: Automation – Electronic exchange of data, automated border procedures, and the use of risk management. Formalities: Documents – Simplification of trade documents, harmonization in accordance with international standards, and acceptance of copies. Formalities: Procedures – Streamlining of border controls, single submission points for all required documentation (single windows), postclearance audits, and authorized economic operator schemes. Governance and Impartiality – Customs structures and functions, accountability, and ethics policy. Information Availability – Publication of trade information, including on the internet; and enquiry points. Involvement of the Trade Community – Consultations with traders.
Source: *Trade Facilitation Indicators*, OECD.

OECD countries, 1.24), Latin America and the Caribbean (1.23), Middle East and North Africa (1.23), and further Sub-Saharan Africa (1.08) **(Figure 65)**.[78] Among the 11 indicators, Asia's performance has been above the world average in terms of involvement of trade community, appeal procedures, and governance and impartiality, while it lags in external border agency cooperation.

For the three Asian subregional programs cited, the OECD TFI shows large disparities on advance rulings and internal border agency cooperation, and to a lesser extent, fees and charges **(Figure 66)**. Overall, the CAREC program performed best with an average score of 1.35, especially on advance rulings and fees and charges. The average score of the GMS and SASEC programs are comparable—1.28 for GMS and 1.25 for SASEC. The performance of each indicator in these regions also shows similar trends, except for internal border agency cooperation for which SASEC performed better than the GMS by a large margin.

---

[78] Following the regional classification by OECD, "Asia" and "Europe (non-OECD) and Central Asia" are used instead of Developing Asia. Each of these regions includes several countries in the subject subregions.

Figure 66: Trade Facilitation Performance—CAREC, GMS, and SASEC
(2013)

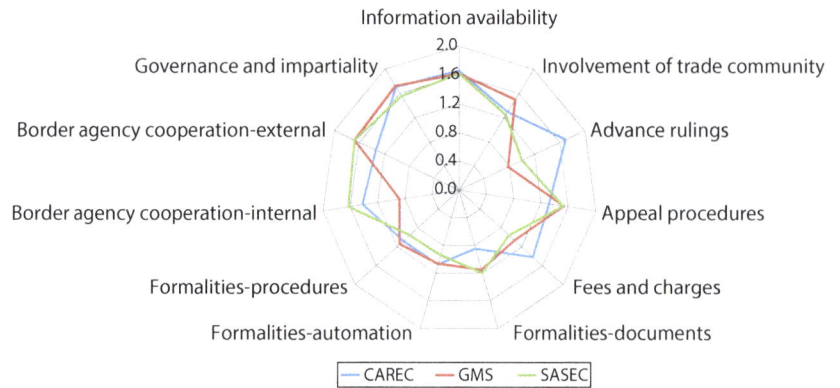

CAREC = Central Asia Regional Economic Cooperation, GMS = Greater Mekong Subregion, SASEC = South Asia Subregional Economic Cooperation.
Note: Based on simple average per subregion. CAREC includes Azerbaijan, Kazakhstan, Kyrgyz Republic, Mongolia, Pakistan, and the People's Republic of China (PRC). GMS includes Cambodia, Thailand, the PRC, and Viet Nam. SASEC includes Bangladesh, India, Nepal, and Sri Lanka. Border agency cooperation-external covers the following countries: GMS–Thailand; CAREC–Azerbaijan, Kyrgyz Republic, Mongolia; SASEC–Bangladesh.
Source: *Trade Facilitation Indicators*. OECD.

Benchmarking and measuring TF progress is gaining importance. However, the results should lead to actual implementation of necessary TF reforms and actions. Asian economies need to carefully select a direct TF impact measurement methodology with the goal of having long-term ownership and sustaining the methodology, while reducing external financial support. A cost-effective and flexible method—such as Time Release Study (TRS) surveys, which can cover a border or corridor—is useful in measuring changes in time required for trade (one of the major outcomes of implementing TF measures). Efforts to sustain the conduct of TF measurement surveys through TRS trainer workshops are important to collect comparable time series data at low cost, considering the limited budgets of both developing Asia governments and development partners.

Periodic, systematic, and cost-effective benchmarking of TF progress will provide useful information for policy makers. For example, the evidence-based OECD method provides a convenient assessment tool as it covers all aspects of the TFA major reform agenda. It also helps identify areas where further improvement is needed—by visualizing assessment results and comparing them with regional or global averages. These diagnoses can be a basis for planning TF policies and programs and filling gaps based on global best practices—bearing in mind the importance of implementing TF measures holistically rather than taking them in isolation.

International trade flows are complicated by requirements of private industries, increased security threats, and trade of illicit goods (prohibited and dangerous goods that could pose hazard to the general public). Hence, the challenge is to facilitate legitimate trade without compromising trade security. Thus, developing Asia should continue to undertake policies and conduct capacity-building programs on both trade facilitation and countering security threats and illicit trade. Coordinated border management among various trade and customs-related agencies—local and international—is key, given the increasing complexity, volume, and speed of global and regional trade. This way, developing Asia can draw useful insights from the successful interagency work conducted by the Port Control Units under the Container Control Programme of the WCO and the United Nations Office on Drugs and Crime.[79]

Trade Remedies

With the progress of freer trade and free trade policies—such as FTAs and unilateral and mutual trade facilitation measures, statutory, and regulatory trade barriers have eased significantly globally. On the flip side of freer trade lies more frequent trade remedies being projected as legitimate trade policy tools to protect domestic industries and businesses. From a political economy standpoint, while contributing to safeguard domestic business interests against unjust trade behavior of exporters, sometimes vested interests overtake the logic of fair trade. At times, this translates into political lobbying of affected domestic industries and government administrative tactics that serve these vested interests. Nevertheless, the incidence of trade remedies will likely continue to increase without more effective administrative tools at the economy level amid greater international free trade structures. After all, these measures should contribute to restoring fair trade by curbing unfair trade behaviors.

Asia is no exception. A total of 1,294 trade intervention measures have been imposed on Asian economies from January 2010 to May 2014. Among these, 517 have come from Asia itself, while 777 have come from the rest of the world. Both dwarf the number of measures implemented by Asia outside the region.

Of these 1,294 intervention measures, 443 are trade remedial actions—178 of these implemented intraregionally. Anti-dumping, countervailing, and other safeguard measures fall under this category. Ninety percent or 397 are antidumping duties **(Figure 67)**. Looking into cases filed with the WTO over the same period, 65% of the 52 trade remedial measures involve Asia either as a complainant or respondent **(Table 12)**. However, only 8% that targeted Asia have been appealed to the WTO.

The incidence of new trade intervention has grown significantly—a 153% increase in May 2013–May 2014 compared to January–April 2013 **(Figure 68)**. More intraregional trade remedial measures have been triggered recently.

---

[79] For further details, see United Nations Office on Drugs and Crime and World Customs Organization. 2014. Container Control Programme Annual Report 2014. http://www.wcoomd.org/en/topics/enforcement-and-compliance/activities-and-programmes/drugs-programme/~/media/WCO/Public/Global/PDF/Topics/Enforcement%20and%20Compli-ance/Activities%20and%20Programmes/Drugs%20and%20Precursor%20Chemicals/CCP/CCP_Annual_Report_2014-150309_WEB.ashx

Figure 67: Number of Trade Remedial Measures Affecting Asia
(by type)

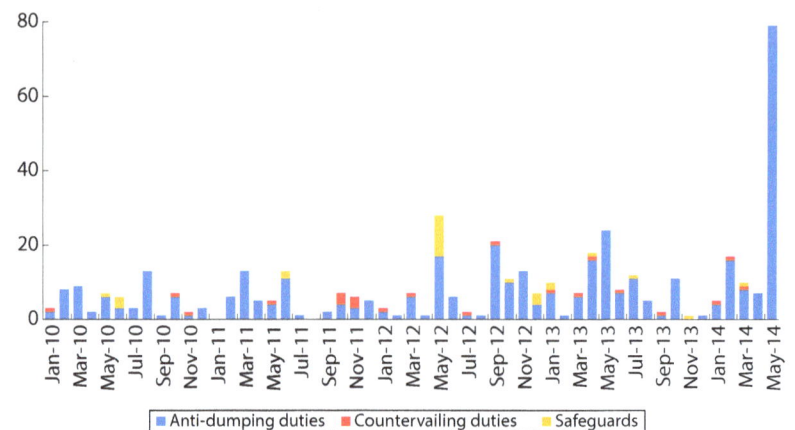

Source: ADB calculations using data from Global Trade Alert.

Table 12: Trade Remedial Measures and WTO Cases (Jan 2010–May 2014)

Agreement	World Total	Asia[1] Total	Asia (Complainant) ROW (Respondent)	ROW (Complainant) Asia (Respondent)	Asia (Complainant) Asia (Respondent)
Anti-dumping (Article VI of GATT 1994)					
No. of measures implemented	513	427	233	31	163
No. of cases	23	17	9	6	2
	(4%)	(0.4%)			
Subsidies and Countervailing Measures					
No. of measures implemented	33	28	22	5	1
No. of cases	19	14	6	7	1
	(57%)	(61%)			
Safeguards					
No. of measures implemented	38	30	14	3	13
No. of cases	10	3	3	0	0
	(26%)	(10%)			
Total[2]					
No. of measures implemented	571	478	265	35	178
No. of cases	52	34	18	13	3
	(9%)	(7%)			

ROW = rest of the world, WTO = World Trade Organization.
[1]Asia as implementing/affected region, which is equivalent to global number of trade remedy measures less ROW-ROW (not shown in table).
[2]Some measures are combinations of 2 or 3 agreements.
Source: ADB calculations using data from Global Trade Alert and WTO.

Figure 68: Newly Initiated Trade Interventions Measures Involving Asia

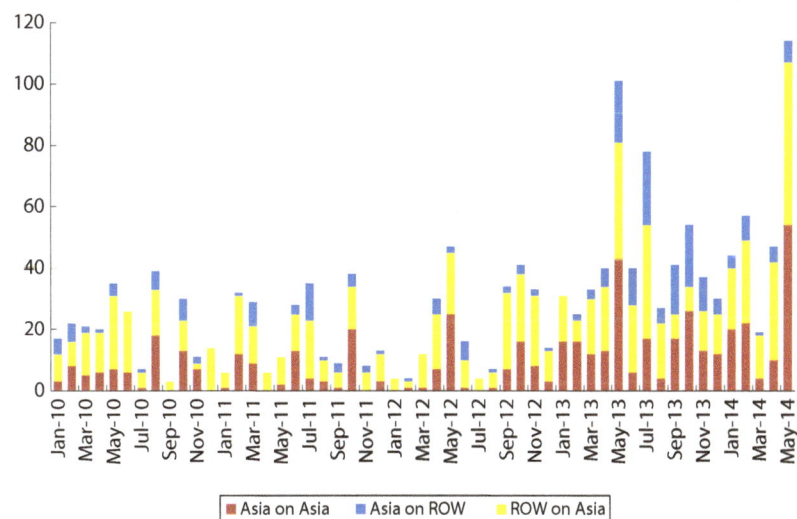

ROW = rest of the world.
Note: Legend convention XX on YY means XX = implementing region, and YY = affected region. For example, Asia on Asia in the number of measures imposed by Asian economies on Asian economies.
Source: ADB calculations using data from Global Trade Alert.

Table 13: Number of Trade Remedial Measures Affecting Asia
(Jan 2010–May 2014, by top affected sectors)

Sector No.	Sector Name	Implemented by ROW	Implemented by Asia	Total
34	Basic chemicals	27	65	92
41	Basic metals	38	31	69
42	Fabricated metal products, except machinery and equipment	39	11	50
36	Rubber and plastics	24	12	36
37	Glass and glass products and other non-glass metallic products	20	12	32

ROW = rest of the world.
Source: ADB calculations using data from Global Trade Alert.

The high frequency of trade remedial measures against Asian economies follows a period when global as well as Asian trade growth has begun to taper, such as in 2012. Research often points to growing trade intervention as one of the underlying sources of tepid international trade growth.[80] Barring any presumptions on potential causality, the high incidence of remedial measures against Asia will not support trade growth. Trade remedial measures on Asia have been implemented mostly on basic chemicals (CPC v2 sector no. 34) at 20% of the total from January 2010 to May 2014 **(Table 13)**. This is particularly true for measures imposed by Asian economies intraregionally. Trade remedial measures from the rest of the world to Asia have mostly been implemented on fabricated metal products, except machinery and equipment (CPC v2. sector no. 42).

80   C. Constantinescu, A. Mattoo, and M. Ruta. 2015. The Global Trade Slowdown: Cyclical or Structural? *IMF Working Papers*. WP/15/6. Washington: IMF.

Figure 69: London Metal Exchange Metals Index (end-of-period, in thousands)

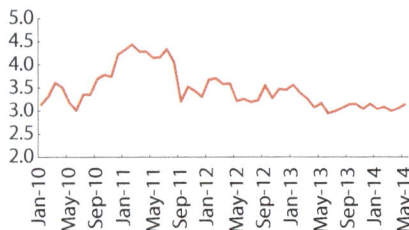

Note: The London Metal Exchange (LMEX) Index is based on the closing prices of six primary metals: copper, aluminum, lead, tin, zinc and nickel. It has a base value of 1,000 starting in 1984.
Source: Bloomberg.

Figure 70: Share in Global Trade of Basic Chemicals (%)

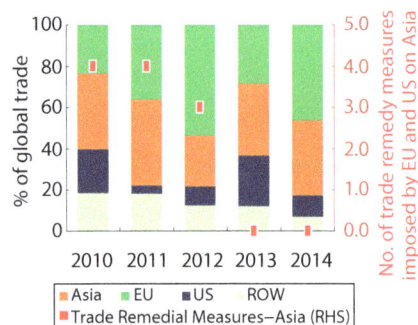

EU = European Union (27 members), US = United States, RHS = right-hand scale, ROW = rest of the world.
Note: Asia does not include Taipei,China as data unavailable.
Source: ADB calculations using data from United Nations Commodity Trade Database and Global Trade Alert.

Table 14: Number of Implementers of Trade Remedial Measures—Top Affected Asian Economies (Jan 2010–May 2014)

Economy	Number of implementers from		
	ROW	Asia	Total
PRC	211	112	323
Korea, Rep. of	30	47	77
Taipei,China	25	34	59

PRC = People's Republic of China, ROW = rest of the world.
Source: ADB calculations using data from Global Trade Alert.

The highest incidence of trade remedial measures on Asian basic metal producers from the rest of the world have followed falling global metal prices since 2012 **(Figure 69)**. **Figure 70** shows how the incidence of trade remedial measures against Asia from ROW and Asia's global trade share in basic chemicals have fared over time.

The PRC has been the most frequent target of trade remedial measures in Asia **(Table 14)**. The sectors hit with the highest number of measures implemented against the PRC; the Republic of Korea; and Taipei,China are basic chemicals and basic metals. The European Commission, Brazil, South Africa, and Turkey are the economies outside the region that have implemented the most number of trade remedial measures, while India, Thailand, Indonesia, and Australia implemented the most number of measures intraregionally.

The Republic of Korea's basic chemicals trade has declined in value—from $61 billion in 2012 to $30 billion in 2013 and further to $86 million in 2014. Likewise, its market share (as % of global trade in basic chemicals) also declined—from 8.2% in 2012 to 4.8% in 2013, and to just 0.01% in 2014. In contrast, the PRC's global share in total basic chemicals trade increased from 4.5% in 2012 to 13.6% in 2013 and to 13.9% in 2014, despite having been the target of frequent remedial measures.

SPECIAL CHAPTER: HOW CAN SPECIAL ECONOMIC ZONES CATALYZE ECONOMIC DEVELOPMENT?

2

Special Chapter: How Can Special Economic Zones Catalyze Economic Development?

In Asia, economies just starting to industrialize have used special economic zones (SEZs) as a way to initiate or expand export-oriented manufacturing—and to promote structural change more broadly through linkages and demonstration effects. They take their cues mainly from successful East Asian economies that began virtuous growth spirals in the late 1960s and early 1970s. Within 3 decades, they had become upper middle or high-income economies. Although a host of developing economies pursued industrialization in parallel with East Asia, in most cases their objective was to manufacture home grown substitutes for imported products. Tariff barriers sheltered their industries, which serviced small domestic markets. Protection and small scale left productivity low, with high unit costs and no pressure to upgrade technology or innovate. East Asia also began with import substitution, but quickly saw the advantage exports held as a means of accelerating growth while bringing in foreign exchange revenues. However, they approached trade liberalization cautiously and tried to separate the domestic market from the traded goods sector. SEZs—insulated from the rest of the economy—offered a convenient vehicle for testing export-led strategies and incentives to produce for the global market.

By the 1960s, the concept of zones for processing exports was already in the air and evidence was accumulating from a few trials. With the General Agreement on Tariffs and Trade (GATT) initiating trade negotiations—improving prospects for international trade—several East Asian economies jumped on the trade bandwagon and established export processing zones (EPZs). The early mover advantages attracted the attention of other developing economies. By the 1970s, zones of various kinds were multiplying, but with mixed results. Nevertheless, their popularity increased over the years with the "miracle of Shenzhen" serving as beacon.[81] They have become a development policy fixture even as import-substitution fell out of favor with most economies adopting market and trade liberalization.

---

[81] Other noteworthy success stories include Penang–one of the earliest of the modern zones– Mauritius, Costa Rica and the multitude of EPZs in the Dominican Republic. Not all agree that the latter promoted growth. See R. Kaplinsky. 1993. Export Processing Zones in the Dominican Republic: Transforming Manufactures into Commodities. *World Development*. 21(11). pp. 1851–1865; and L. Willmore. 1995. Export Processing Zones in the Dominican Republic: A Comment on Kaplinsky. *World Development*. 23 (3). pp. 529–535. Schrank (2008) maintains that the attitudes of local elites affected the contribution of the zones in the Dominican Republic. Doubts have been expressed also regarding the Haiti EPZ. Also see Shamsie (2010).

With world trade slowing, manufacturing as a share of gross domestic product (GDP) stabilizing or shrinking (in developed and developing economies alike), and barriers to trade and domestic competition steadily whittling away, the efficacy of SEZs or EPZs as drivers of exports, policy reform and growth is under scrutiny.[82] Moreover, many export subsidies and incentives offered by zones will expire at the end of 2015.[83] Policy makers continuing to pin their faith on the catalytic effect of zones need to answer the question: Can zones serve as cost effective drivers of economic growth and development?

The purpose of this chapter is to assess the contribution of SEZs to export-led industrialization in developing Asia. Based on an analysis of their past efficacy in a global context at various stages of development, the chapter also aims to define the conditions, incentives, and underlying strategies that maximize the developmental impact of SEZs over the coming decades. The chapter is divided into seven sections. The first section spells out the reasons why SEZs have grown ubiquitous in developing economies and defines the growth enhancing benefits expected. The second section describes the variety of zone-types, discusses how modalities and ownership arrangements evolved, and indicates why a specific class of zones is favored as economies ascend the development ladder. The third section examines what drives SEZ success. The fourth section discusses how SEZs are linked to country development strategies and institutions. The fifth section reviews empirical evidence on the economic gains from SEZs—are resources channeled into SEZs allocated efficiently, and do they effectively promote trade, FDI, and growth?

The sixth section draws on cross-country experience to distil preconditions and policies associated with zone success. Finally, the seventh looks to the future and explores the role of SEZs in a world of accelerating technological change—change that affects production techniques and the advantages conferred by low labor costs, global value chain (GVC) development, the onshoring of certain new manufacturing

[82]   C. Constantinescu, A. Mattoo and M. Ruta. 2014. Slow Trade. *IMF Finance and Development.* 51(4); D. Rodrik. 2015. Premature Deindustrialization. *National Bureau of Economic Research (NBER) Working Papers.* No. 20935. Massachusetts: NBER.

[83]   J.J. Waters. 2013. Achieving World Trade Organization Compliance for Export Processing Zones While Maintaining Economic Competitiveness for Developing Countries. *Duke Law Journal.* 63 (2). pp.481-524; S. Creskoff and P. Walkenhorst. 2009. Implications of WTO Disciplines for Special Economic Zones in Developing Countries. *World Bank Policy Research Working Papers.* No. 4892. Washington: World Bank.

activities, the growing importance of services in trade, the role of urban development, and possibly, a persistent "new normal" of slower global GDP and trade growth. Annex A discusses some salient aspects of country experiences based on brief country case studies of Bangladesh, Cambodia, and the People's Republic of China (PRC).

The Rise of the Zones: Origin, Objectives, and Diffusion

The very first economic zone was established in New York in 1937 with the passing of the Free Trade Zone Act by the United States (US) Congress in 1934.[84] Puerto Rico was second in 1942 in an effort to industrialize the territory by luring in US firms. A steady trickle of new zones appeared beginning in 1959—with the Shannon Free Zone in Ireland and others mostly in Western Europe amid the industrial revival after the World War II. Soon developing economies tried their hand. India was arguably the first with the creation of a processing zone at Kandla Port in 1965. Taipei,China's Kaohsiung Harbor was set up in 1966. The success, particularly of Taipei,China's EPZ, attracted widespread attention—and imitation. By 1978, zones of various stripes had sprouted across 22 economies, including Malaysia, the Philippines, Singapore, and the Republic of Korea.[85] Since then, scores of zones have been established annually across the developing world as one country after another seeks to emulate the industrial achievements of the PRC and other East Asian economies' use of zones to catalyze exports and industrialization generally. From an estimated 500 zones in 1995, there are now some 4,300 zones in more than 130 economies, employing more than 68 million workers directly—and possibly twice as many if indirect jobs are included (Moberg 2015). Two-thirds of those directly employed are women. By 2005, almost a fifth of exports from developing and emerging economies were sourced from zones —although data on exports tends to be scanty and of limited reliability. Their popularity with policy makers almost irrespective of past performance—in low-income economies such as Myanmar and Rwanda and high income ones such as Qatar and Japan—suggests zones could continue proliferating.[86]

While zones can take different forms (see "Varieties of Zones: Modalities, Ownership, and Evolution", p. 69), developing economies created them with several objectives. The earliest Asian zones (and Mexico's Maquiladoras), which were export-oriented enterprises enjoying specific tax and duty exemptions, arose in the context of a relatively closed economy and with the purpose of circumventing trade restrictions.

---

84   Zone-like entities appeared in Europe during the 12th century. They took the form of free cities and ports. Zones closer to the ones that were created in the 20th century were first established in Gibraltar (1704), in Singapore (1819), and in Hong Kong, China and Macau, China (1842-1845). See FIAS (2008) and Aggarwal (2010, 2012).

85   K. Li. 1995. *The Evolution of Policy behind [Taipei,China's] Development Success.* Singapore: World Scientific. The ILO counted 79 zones in 1975.

86   *The Economist.* 2015. Special Economic Zones, Not so Special. 4 April.; L. Moberg. 2015. The Political Economy of Special Economic Zones. *Journal of Institutional Economics.* 11(1). pp. 167-190.

They were strategically located adjacent to transport hubs using access to land and cheap unskilled local labor to process or assemble export products.[87] Employment, albeit on a modest scale, was one objective they fulfilled. In addition, the zones helped economies build a workforce for modern industry, to nurture skills, and to institute workplace rules. The zones also served to widen the manufacturing base and enabled economies largely dependent on primary product exports to establish and diversify a manufacturing foothold in global markets. Although downstream assembly and processing added little value, earning foreign exchange was a primary consideration (Cheesman 2012). Starting in the 1960s, global trade in manufactures was gaining momentum and Western companies—especially from the US—came under pressure from Japanese imports. They began to relocate some of their labor-intensive manufacturing activities overseas to cut costs. EPZs, shorn off tariff barriers, were seen as ideal platforms for products at a mature stage in the life cycle.[88]

Once policy makers found that suitably tailored zones with ready trade access could attract FDI, which brought not just capital but also technology and soft skills that were in short supply throughout Asia, the appeal of zones intensified. This happened well before multinational corporations (MNCs) and policy makers ever thought of production networks and GVCs. But by the 1970s and 1980s, economies already intent on rapid industrialization realized that manufactured exports offered a path toward rapid growth. Skittish foreign investors also felt secure with ring-fenced, preferential treatment, and property protection in the absence of well-functioning markets.

The creation of zones proved to be an experiment that paid handsome dividends for early movers with a focus on industrialization because of three parallel, fortuitous developments: (i) trade liberalization spearheaded by the US and Western Europe, which widened opportunities for developing economies[89]; (ii) the "second unbundling" and worldwide dispersion of downstream production—that grew in tandem with the increased capacity of MNCs to manage production[90], sourcing, product integration, and logistics across multiple locations; and (iii) advances in transport and logistics—including containerization,

---

[87]   In the PRC, SEZs paved the way to land policy reforms. The successful introduction of land markets in Shenzhen demonstrated that land use rights should not only be transferable, but also be transferred through market competition.

[88]   Vernon (1966) introduced the concept of a product life cycle in a path breaking paper. See R. Vernon. 1966. International Investment and International Trade in the Product Cycle. *Quarterly Journal of Economics.* 80 (2). pp. 190-207.

[89]   International Monetary Fund (IMF). 2001. Global Trade Liberalization and the Developing Countries. *IMF Issue Briefs.* 8 November. https://www.imf.org/external/np/exr/ib/2001/110801. htm

[90]   The offshoring of production and the emergence of global value chains that now orchestrate 80 percent of world trade is discussed by the following reports: R. Baldwin. 2011. Trade and Industrialisation After Globalisation's 2nd Unbundling: How Building And Joining A Supply Chain Are Different And Why It Matters. *NBER Working Papers.* No. 17716. Massachusetts: NBER; IMF. 2013. *Trade Interconnectedness: The World with Global Value Chains.* http://www. imf.org/external/np/pp/eng/2013/082613.pdf; World Economic Forum. 2012. *The Shifting Geography of Global Value Chains: Implications for Developing Countries and Trade Policy.* http:// www3.weforum.org/docs/WEF_GAC_GlobalTradeSystem_Report_2012.pdf; J. Amador and F. di Mauro, eds. 2015. *The Age of Global Value Chains: Maps and Policy Issues.* The UK: CEPR Press.

new and more powerful diesel engines, better design of large container ships, and a revolution in air transport.[91] Combined, they reduced both production and shipping costs and sped up the movement of goods. The GVCs created in the wake of the second unbundling offered opportunities for these early movers to consolidate supplier relationships and capture choice segments of the evolving value chain.

Once the utility of zones was established, the more enterprising Asian economies raised their sights and began to use them as test beds for incentive policies and structural reforms that—if successful—could be spread economy-wide and thus overcome certain development constraints. They began making attempts to integrate zones with the rest of the economy and maximize spillovers from industrial technologies and practices employed in zones—particularly by MNCs. These spillovers plus input-output (I-O) links with other parts of the economy helped stimulate development and economic growth overall. More ambitious still were—and continue to be—initiating industrial transformation by attracting higher technology to the zones and planting the seeds of a knowledge economy so as to catch up with the advanced economies. Thus, at later stages of development, governments see SEZs as innovative clusters of domestic and foreign firms actively participating in GVCs and helping sustain growth over the longer term.[92]

In fact, economic zones are associated with creating distortions in an economy. The rationale was that large, nationwide economic benefits from this experiment far outweigh the fiscal and other economic costs incurred by temporary distortion of price and incentive mechanisms within the enclave.

However, economic zones do have their costs and all too often governments have been swayed by the lure of benefits and ignore the fiscal costs incurred in providing infrastructure, land, subsidized utility services, tax incentives, and in some instances, access to easy, below market rate credit.[93] There is also the problem—sometimes the likelihood—of land grabbing by central or subnational governments for SEZs, a source of conflict in some economies. Related is the absence of proper procedures and oversight. SEZs sometimes have been used as conduits for money laundering and smuggling goods into domestic markets. Furthermore, worker exploitation and environmental degradation can become serious problems. SEZs in some economies exempt firms from paying minimum wages and are lax in enforcing environmental and safety rules to lower costs and attract FDI. This has increased tension between management and labor in several Asian economies. For example, in Bangladesh, SEZs previously shielded investors from activist trade unions. This changed following a slew of serious accidents and ensuing international outcry. Zone authorities now work with owners, the International Labour Organisation (ILO),

91   World Trade Organization. 2008. *WTO Report: Trade in a Globalizing World.* Geneva: Hummels (2007) emphasizes speed rather than the decline in transport costs.

92   On the expected benefits from zones, see also FIAS (2008), and Zeng (2010).

93   The Economist (2015) observes that "Africa is littered with white elephants. India has hundreds that failed to get going, including more than 60 in Maharashtra state alone in just the past few years." See *The Economist.* 2015. Special Economic Zones, Not so Special. 4 April.

government, and foreign buyers to allow space for trade union activities and to protect worker rights, safety, wages and benefits. Nonetheless, working conditions in SEZs across Asia remain a matter of contention. Even as governments move to eliminate abuses, they also must be wary over excessively tightening labor laws. Given the pace and direction of technological change, rigid laws could drive an exodus of foreign firms and/or shift to more capital-intensive production that would affect long-run labor demand (Aggarwal 2012).

Varieties of Zones: Modalities, Ownership, and Evolution

The concept of SEZs evolved as they multiplied in numbers, creating a variety of zones with differing objectives, markets, and activities. The core definition of a zone—as well as its regulatory guidelines and standards—are stated in the Revised Kyoto Convention of the World Customs Organization (WCO), relating to the treatment of imports and exports of free zones within defined territorial limits. These include minimal documentation and issues covered by national legislation (FIAS 2008). SEZs cover a wide spectrum and take a variety of forms, including free zones, free trade zones, free ports, foreign trade zones, export processing zones, free export zones, trade and economic cooperation zones, economic processing zones, and economic technological development areas (Baissac 2011).

This chapter defines SEZs as "clearly defined geographically, with a single management or administration and separate customs area (often duty free), where streamlined business procedures are applied, and where physically located firms qualify for more liberal and effective rules than those in the national territory (covering, for example, investment conditions, international trade and customs, tariffs, and taxation)" (ADB 2014a). Similarly, Baissac (2011) states that SEZs share two structural characteristics: (i) they are formally delimited portions of the national territory; and (ii) they are legal spaces with a set of investment, trade, and operating rules that are more liberal and administratively efficient than those prevailing in the rest of the national territory. The administration of the zone regime usually requires a dedicated governance structure, whether centralized or decentralized. The attributes of this structure vary according to the nature of the zone regime, the prevalent administrative culture, the number of existing zones, the role of the private sector in developing and operating zones, and other factors. In addition, zones are usually provided with a physical infrastructure supporting the activities of the firms and economic agents operating within them.

In practice, this broad definition of zones has plenty of variations, mostly centered on the type of activity a zone engages in. For instance, free zones typically allow for duty- and tax-free imports of raw materials and intermediate goods—and in many cases include capital equipment (FIAS 2008). Free trade zones, also known as commercial free zones and free commercial zones, are small, fenced-in, duty-free areas located in most ports of entry around the world. They offer warehousing, storage, and distribution facilities for trade transshipment, and re-export operations. EPZs are industrial estates giving special incentives and facilities for manufacturing and related activities aimed mostly at export markets. Free ports typically encompass much larger areas and provide a much broader set of incentives and benefits. They accommodate all types of activities, including tourism and retail sales, and allow people to reside on site.

Most zones began as enclaves with some gradually mutating as economies develop—in response to changing comparative advantage, institutional deepening, and also to the global trading environment **(Table 15)**. Access to a generous set of incentives and privileges was tightly controlled, while qualifying firms typically had to be 80–100% export-oriented and engaged in specified manufacturing. Some examples are the Kandla EPZ in India, Bataan EPZ in the Philippines, and Masan EPZ in the Republic of Korea. These were intended primarily to promote exports, create jobs, and secondarily to transfer technology through backward linkages.

The rapid pace of globalization and trade liberalization is responsible for a change in the perceived function of zones. Increasingly, the focus is on two-way trade and zonal characteristics that facilitate the liberalization and modernization of the host economy. This resulted in policies that in many cases give primacy to cross-border trade and integration with GVCs—as with SEZs in Cambodia, Kazakhstan, Myanmar, Thailand, and the PRC. In economies or regions at a more advanced stage of development—such as the Republic of Korea and coastal regions in the PRC—the SEZ's role has expanded to include provision of logistics.

Asian economies and others in Africa and Latin America have experimented with various types of SEZs, frequently of the enclave type—although some carried weightier policy ambitions.[94] In the PRC, however, the development of SEZs from the outset has been an integral part of the country's economic opening and reform process. SEZs have almost always sought to attract manufacturing—though recent trends favor services (as in the PRC and the Republic of Korea). Most Asian SEZs are a combination of a stand-alone area (Cambodia) and cluster or agglomeration (as in the PRC, India, and Bangladesh). In many instances, they remain weakly connected to the rest of the economy. However, the long term objective is usually to meld the two together.

---

[94] According to Leong (2013), "There are different types of special economic zones: customs-bonded warehouses, customs-bonded factories, export processing zones, special economic zones and free trade zones, in ascending order of comprehensiveness and area." Other zones are industrial parks, enterprise zones and free ports (Zeng 2011). Citing Zeng, "As used in [the People's Republic of] China, however, the term *SEZ* refers to a complex of related economic activities and services rather than to a unifunctional entity (Wong 1987)." The People's Republic of China includes open coastal cities, economic and technological development zones (ETDZs), and high-tech industrial development zones (HTDZs) in its definition of zones. The PRC also distinguishes between comprehensive SEZs and those principally for export processing. Bangladesh has set up country-specific EPZs like the [Republic of] Korean Export Processing Zone (KEPZ) and is considering setting up an SEZ for Japan and one for the PRC.

Ownership Characteristics

SEZs vary by ownership type. They can be purely public, private, or can be shared between public sector and private partners (see Table 15). Through the 1970s, SEZs were exclusively in the domain of the public sector. Governments took responsibility for planning financing, defining and administering regulations, offering incentives, working with investors, and managing real estate—including buildings, rent, and facility maintenance (Farole 2011). By the late 1980s and 1990s, this model came under pressure from both push and pull factors. The main push factors were (i) the drive for macroeconomic stability and the resulting need for budgetary and fiscal discipline—it became too expensive for many economies to shoulder the full costs of establishing and running zones, and (ii) the need to regenerate lackluster or failing free zones in some economies. This prompted governments to seek private sector participation, resulting in a steady increase in privately owned, developed, and operated zones. Across developing and transition economies in the 1980s, less than 25% of zones worldwide were privately owned, compared with 62% in 2007 (FIAS 2008).

Table 15: Evolution of Various Types of SEZs—Selected Asian Economies[1]

Economy	By linkage to domestic and global economy				By Modality		
	Enclave	GVC	Logistics/ services	Border Areas	Private[2] (%)	Public[2] (%)	Total[3] (no. of zones)
Bangladesh	●				11	89	8*
Cambodia	●			●	100	0	14*
India	●	●	●		74	26	615*
Kazakhstan	●		●	●	0	100	10
Malaysia	●	●		●	23	77	530
Myanmar	●			●	–	–	3*
Pakistan	●				0	100	8*
Philippines	●	●			92	8	460*
PRC	●	●	●	●	12	88	1,515*
Korea, Rep. of	●	●	●		10	90	102
Sri Lanka	●				6	94	14
Thailand	●	●		●	84	16	110
Viet Nam	●	●			89	11	411

– = unavailable, GVC = global value chain, SEZ = special economic zones, * = includes zones that have a public-private partnership component.

[1] Based on operational and planned SEZs.
[2] Figures under Private and Public column refer to the percentage of private (public) zones against the total. Data as of 2008. Figures for Cambodia based on recent data from government website.
[3] Based on most recent data from government websites.

Source: Baumgartner et al. (2013), Chai and Im (2009), Chen (1993), Cling et al. (2007), World Bank Facility for Investment Climate Advisory Services (2008), Farole ed. (2011), Farole and Akinci (2011), Furby (2005), IBEF (undated), Jayanthakumaran (2003), Kaplinsky (1993), Memon (2010), Sarsembayeva (2012), Sivalingam (1994), Varma (2013), Viswadia (2013), Warr (1989), Wang (2013), Won (1993), national sources.

Another factor responsible for the spread of private zones was that private developers could make the development and operation profitable (FIAS 2008). In fact, the first wave of private zones—in the Caribbean and Central America in the 1980s and in Southeast Asia (the Philippines and Thailand) in the 1990s—was done without much forward planning or government support. As such, while private SEZs were welcomed for operational efficiency, they were at times criticized for compromising socioeconomic development because governments failed to clearly specify performance criteria, undertake complementary investments, evaluate results, and take quick remedial actions. New zones frequently made significant demands on public infrastructure and amenities, and outpaced government ability to boost infrastructure and other services. In the Philippines and Viet Nam, private developers built external infrastructure (access roads and utility connections) in addition to financing onsite infrastructure and facilities (internal roads, utilities, common facilities, and factory buildings). In Asia, some examples of privately developed and operated SEZs are Andhra Pradesh in India, the upcoming Meghna Economic Zone in Bangladesh, Port Klang Free Zone in Malaysia, and AG&P Special Economic Zone in the Philippines.

In recent years, the advent of public-private partnerships (PPPs) has accelerated zone development. PPP-based SEZs have mushroomed, motivated by potential synergies between government provision of public infrastructure, land and financing and the private sector's strength in the less politicized management structure and superior business models. Since the 1990s, innovative PPPs have blurred the line between what is strictly public and strictly private SEZs. Cooperation and division of labor—rather than competition—has become the preferred model. The 1992 Subic Bay project in the Philippines was one of the first large SEZs based on extensive cooperation and public and private investment. It became a template for other SEZs, including Panama's Pacifico SEZ and the Aqaba SEZ in Jordan (Baissac 2011). These wide-area SEZs combine traditional manufacturing with services, residential living, accompanying amenities, tourism, and environmental protection.

Government participation in PPPs may include (i) public provision of offsite infrastructure and facilities (utility connections, roads), as an incentive for private funding of onsite infrastructure and facilities; (ii) assembly of land parcels with secure title and development rights by government for lease to private zone development groups; (iii) defining better land use or ownership laws and regulations along with enforceable zoning and land use plans; and (iv) build-operate-transfer and build-own-operate approaches to onsite and offsite zone infrastructure and facilities, with government guarantees and/or financial support. Purely private zones have emerged in Cambodia and Thailand, while purely public and PPP-based are found in the PRC and Bangladesh, respectively.

Evolution of SEZ Development

Given the wide diversity in stages of development across economies, Asia's adoption of SEZs can be viewed as an evolutionary process involving various objectives. These include export promotion, attracting FDI, establishing globalized manufacturing, advancements in logistics and services, and increasingly, recognition of SEZ's role as instruments for increasing regional cooperation and integration (RCI). RCI goes beyond transnational infrastructure and trade reform, requiring and taking advantage of policy coordination, labor mobility, skill development, and transfer of technology.

First-stage enclave-type zones can play an important role in generating employment and foreign exchange revenues, setting the stage for further economic development (Aggarwal 2012). In their initial phase, zones are typically an enclave-type EPZ focusing on employment and skills upgrading through attracting FDI, particularly in export-oriented labor-intensive manufacturing over a limited range of goods. SEZs in Cambodia for example remain relatively small (and quite new—the legal framework was established in 2005). They are traditional EPZs, with nearly all workers employed as low-skilled production operators in garments, electronics, electrical products, and household furnishings. Low labor costs initially attracted firms to Cambodia's SEZs and, in some cases, along with favorable tariff treatment from the European Union (EU) and the US (Warr and Menon 2015). Similarly, EPZs in Bangladesh are small industrial enclaves where nearly all workers are low-skilled, mostly in garments. SEZs benefit from labor cost advantage—workers in Bangladesh's formal garment's subsector are among the lowest paid worldwide, with starting wages around just $30 per month (Shakir and Farole 2011).

As SEZs advance, the second-stage zones help diversify the production base of the economy by strengthening linkage with domestic economy— for example, Malaysia and Thailand moved from assembling imported inputs to increasing sales of their own branded merchandise in domestic and global markets. They then began to market their own branded merchandise in domestic and global markets. Second-generation SEZs have benefited from MNCs moving increasingly complex economic activity offshore. These have taken root in more developed economies with larger pools of skills, which permit the adoption of more sophisticated technologies.

These SEZs can in turn induce further capacity building and skill accumulation. For instance, in 1987, Malaysia adopted a new industrial strategy where successful EPZs would serve as growth poles. The EPZs were to increasingly integrate with the rest of the economy and source more inputs domestically from new foreign-owned plants and joint ventures—compared to traditional EPZs where the main domestic linkage was employment. As these linkages developed, Malaysian machine shops supplying inputs to EPZ-based semiconductor companies acquired new skills and competencies (Lester 1982). MNCs have also prioritized investments that enhance the skills and technical expertise of their staff, allowing Malaysians to assume leading managerial and technical positions. MNC demand for skilled workers and managers led to the creation of the Penang Skills Development Centre in 1989 in the Bayan Lepas Free Industrial Zone.[95] This more advanced stage of SEZs arises when zones can give birth to productivity augmenting networked clusters of firms.

Forming clusters can attract MNCs as they help supply intermediate inputs. Clustering also has potential vertical spillover effects. Providers of customized business development services, research institutions, information technology (IT) vendors, consultants and other logistics-related organizations support cluster development by providing innovative solutions, cutting costs, and creating external economic activities. Clustering firms within SEZs also expands cooperation between companies, workers, management, equipment suppliers, technological institutes and marketing firms. This interactive learning helps in making production more efficient, and a fruitful source of process and product innovation (Enright 2001, Lundvall 2002).

In more technologically-advanced setting of third-stage zones, SEZs can facilitate their nationwide impact by introducing certain reforms in such areas as labor market and services sector, improving productivity, promoting innovation, and strengthening skills development—as seen in the PRC; the Republic of Korea; and Taipei,China. They in turn become important contributors to further technological upgrading and spillovers. For example, in 1998, the PRC began establishing National High-tech Industrial Development Zones (HIDZs) under the 'Torch Plan' to promote domestic research and development (R&D). These HIDZs promote new local, high-technology industries for both domestic and overseas markets, and are based on the PRC's indigenous scientific and technological strengths. There are currently 219 national and 30 provincial State Council-approved HIDZs, mainly located near economic and technological development zones (ETDZs).

Thus, while the most important contribution of first-generation zones is generating employment and foreign exchange reserves, second-generation zones contribute to human capital upgrading and export diversification. Third-generation SEZs are important contributors to technology advancement, transfer, and spillover effects, along with diversification into services. Overall, SEZ benefits are not uniform across zones or economies. They are conditioned upon the type of activity they attract and their evolution. The industrial composition of SEZs, their linkages with the rest of the economy, and sophistication of production determine their contribution to technological catch-up and growth. Moreover, the broader regional contribution of SEZs depends on developing transport and I-O links that can create industrial corridors and increase trade substantially across the region's economies.

The raison d'etre behind SEZs has come a long way. In the 1960s through the 1980s, zones enabled economies still wedded to protectionist import-substitution polices to explore alternative policies and to boost economic

---

95   Penang Skills Development Centre. History. http://psdc.org.my/html/default. aspx?ID=9&PID=155

performance. EPZs opened a narrow window. They were intended to promote exports, create jobs, and initiate technology transfer. Rapid globalization and trade liberalization has broadened the policy outlook on zones, their development objectives and performance expectations. Increasingly, zones are viewed as a key mechanism to promote two-way trade and facilitate liberalization and modernization—through technological advancement and innovation. The new emphasis is to integrate zones into the domestic and regional economy as well. The attempts at integration are reflected in SEZ policy packages, approaches to physical development, and governance structures, among others.

Success Outcomes and Drivers of SEZ Performance

Recent research by Acemoglu et al. (2004, 2008) has further highlighted the close relationship between institutions and economic development.[96] Institutions are comprised of formal and informal rules—many germinated decades or centuries ago. Institutions evolve slowly and cannot be easily hurried by policies, a considerable challenge for decision makers anxious to accelerate economic growth. In economies with institutions resistant to dismantling barriers to trade and foreign investment, SEZs offer an instrument to create opportunities in an area largely insulated from the pressure of domestic institutions. Where institutions are inimical to opening the economy and are truly a drag on growth, zones are a way of evading resistance to change. They demonstrate that an 'institution-lite,' legally bounded environment is more conducive to export-oriented industrialization supported by FDI. Where they succeed, the policies and institutions tested in SEZs can be used to advocate reforms and reduce domestic institutional impediments to economic openness. These reforms include economic liberalization, introducing market mechanisms, and land ownership or leasing reform. So under certain circumstances, SEZs do not just spur industrialization and trade in a segregated corner of the economy, they speed up the reform process and drive institutional change.

Once domestic institutions are primed for deeper liberalization, authorities begin to favor a larger role for SEZs. First is a transition away from export-oriented enclaves, and the greater importance of linkages—technological spillovers to the rest of the economy and skill development through SEZs. Foreign investment also gains importance and expectations rise. In more advanced stages, economies use successful SEZ policies and institutions to pursue economic openness and integration into vertical specialization. Further on, when institutional resistance to the kind of market-led development piloted in the zones has largely dissipated, economies view the role of zones as test beds for new products and services—such as logistics, green technologies,

---

[96] D. Acemoglu, S. Johnson, and J. A. Robinson. 2004. Institutions as the Fundamental Cause of Long-Run Growth. *NBER Working Papers.* No. 10481. Cambridge, MA: NBER; D. Acemoglu and J. Robinson. 2008. The Role of Institutions in Growth and Development. *Commission on Growth and Development Working Papers.* No. 10. Washington, D.C.: IBRD/World Bank.

as vehicles for regional integration, and better integration into GVCs. SEZs are useful in exploring policies, institutions and activities that could buttress the path toward becoming an advanced modern economy.

Policy makers can justify the creation and institutional elaboration of SEZs on two grounds **(Table 16)**:

(i)   a static institutional approach; and/or
(ii) an evolutionary institutional change or developmental approach.

The static institutional approach distinguishes between 'good' and 'bad' institutions. Good institutions promote economic growth by protecting property rights and providing economic freedom (especially for profit-oriented business). SEZs offer platforms to test 'good' institutions relatively quickly and without disturbing the wider economy. Once applied across an economy, SEZs lose relevance. They thus stand as a 'second best tool'. This view is supported by orthodox and heterodox approaches.

The orthodox approach views SEZs as enclaves that promote trade and growth—in a tariff-distorted economy—by removing impediments to free markets. SEZs allow duty-free access to raw materials in an export production enclave to offset the bias created by high tariffs. An EPZ enclave allows an economy to keep (protectionist) domestic policies. Employment generation has positive income effects, but there are few—if any—indirect effects of SEZs without backward or forward links with the rest of the economy.

The heterodox approach views SEZs as promoting export-based industrialization under an open regime. The heterodox school emerged in the 1980s underlining the state's role in economic development. Using the 'developmental state theory' (Amsden 1989, 2001; Wade 1990), 'neo institutionalism', and drawing on East Asia's experience, it argues that developing economies face a chronic lack of capable institutional actors—thus creating 'production and market failures'. This hampers efficient resource allocation, production, and motivates government intervention. This heterodox approach sees SEZs as a tool for overcoming these institutional constraints. Even if developing economies embrace 'export-oriented industrialization' (EOI) as the lynchpin of their developmental strategy, continuing strategic interventions can more effectively tackle production and market failures.

The central premise of the evolutionary or developmental approach is that SEZs are a strategic government initiative that addresses institutional failures and sequence enabling conditions for economic growth at each stage of development. There are two broad but nonmutually exclusive approaches to establishing SEZs: vertically specialized industrialization (VSI) promotion and agglomeration. The VSI approach views SEZs as a tool of smart industrial policy where SEZs require continuous upgrading to create higher value added products and services. The agglomeration approach views SEZs as essentially a geographically

Table 16: Analytical Framework on SEZ Outcomes and Success Factors

Theoretical approach	Development outcomes	Success factors
Static institutional approach		
1. Orthodox approach • Overcoming tariff distortions and promoting exports	Direct effects • Trade promotion • Foreign exchange earnings • Employment generation • Income generation • Transition to a free economy Indirect effects • Indirect income generation through demand created for domestic products	• Fiscal incentives • Nonfiscal relaxations including labor laws • Abundant labor • Low wages • Cheap land and utilities • Proximity to sea or airport • Enclave nature
2. Heterodox approach • Attracting offshoring and promoting industrialization	Direct effect: Attracting FDI Indirect Effects • FDI generated spillover effects • Technology transfer • Skills development • Technology spillovers • Catalytic effect on exports	• International economic situation, and multilateral and bilateral agreements Macroclimate • Macro policy framework, exchange rate policies, market size, trade policy tools, resource availability, political and economic stability Mesoclimate • Regional economic infrastructure, export infrastructure, availability of labor, labor laws of the region, and regional governance Microclimate • Legal framework, incentive package, zone infrastructure and zone administration
Evolutionary institutional approach		
1. Small industrialization: Vertically specialized industrialization (VSI) • Getting domestic firms into GVCs and moving up value chains or into high-technology value chains	Direct effects • Getting domestic firms—in particular SMEs—into GVCs • Industry targeting Indirect Effects • Building competitiveness and productive capacities of local producers • Access to a global pool of new technologies, skills, capital, and markets • Learning by exporting	Static • The traditional business climatic factors Dynamic • Strong linkages with the rest of the economy • Targeted industrialization in the wider economy • Evolutionary approach in the design of SEZs • Strong commitment and political will
2. Agglomeration approach • Develop SEZs as a tool to promote agglomeration economies, which draw on the regional advantages. SEZs in this case become the growth pole	Direct effects • Cluster-induced industrialization • Cluster targeting Indirect Effects • Economies of scale • Efficiency enhancing • Re-allocation of resources • Knowledge and innovation spillover effects • Catalytic effects of trade gains • Spatial restructuring and urbanization	Static • Traditional business climate factors • Large size of SEZs • Carefully selected locations appropriate for cluster development (Porterian clusters) Dynamic • Systematic development of SEZs as growth poles

Table 16 continued

Theoretical approach	Development outcomes	Success factors
3. SEZs as a tool for border development and regional integration • Development of border areas by promoting economic activity and making peripheries part of the core	**Direct effects** • Utilization of resources at the border • Exploiting resource complementarity at the border • Low utility costs • Expansion of markets and economies of scale **Indirect effects** • Regional integration • Peace and stability	**Macroclimate** • Political cooperation removing trade and investment barriers **Mesoclimate** • Regional connectivity • Trade facilitation • Regional governance • Regional financial • Regional institutions • Social capital • Regional institutions **Microclimate** • Good investment climate • Fiscal incentives

FDI = foreign direct investment, GVC = global value chain, SEZ = special economic zone, SME = small and medium-sized enterprise.
Source: A. Aggarwal. 2015. *Special Economic Zones: A Conceptual Framework for Success Drivers and Development Outcomes*. Background paper for the Asian Development Bank for the Asian Economic Integration Report 2015 Special Chapter. Manila. December.

concentrated government-promoted collection of internationally competitive enterprises. SEZs are equipped with efficient infrastructure, quality services, a favorable business environment, few regulatory restrictions, and a minimum of red tape. They are set up to generate a circular and cumulative growth process that requires two-way linkages between SEZs and the wider economy. Taken together, both approaches require creating a good climate within and around SEZs—and a parallel upgrading of the domestic economy that reinforces upgrading of SEZs.

Viewed against this analytical framework, the PRC and the Republic of Korea stand out as having developed their SEZs and the larger economy away from labor-intensive toward skill- and technology-intensive production (see Annex B for more detailed country studies on the PRC, Bangladesh, and Cambodia). Malaysia also succeeded in developing its electrical and electronics industry, and along with the Philippines succeeded in attracting FDI and generating exports. Both, however, have had limited success in moving up the value chains. This is similar to Bangladesh, which attracted FDI in garments and generated new trade, but has had limited success in upgrading and diversifying SEZ exports.

Other economies have had more limited success. Low income economies tend to have more enclave-type SEZs of the orthodox or heterodox type consistent with their level of development. Cambodia and Myanmar in Southeast Asia and Mongolia in East Asia, Pakistan in South Asia and most Central Asian economies fall under this category. Many of their zones are operating below capacity, because the business enabling environment is weak and firms operating in these zones have been unable to move up the industrial value chain.

Experiences are diverse. In East Asia, the Republic of Korea; the PRC; Hong Kong, China; and Taipei,China have built impressive and sustained growth based on outward orientation and strong development state models since the early 1970s. For instance, as of 2007, SEZs (including all types of industrial parks and zones) in the PRC accounted for about 22% of GDP, 46% of FDI, 60% of exports, and generated more than 30 million jobs (Zhang 2012). In the Republic of Korea, SEZs in 2007 accounted for 28% of FDI, 11% of exports, with 13,000 employed.[97] SEZs have played a crucial role in industrializing these economies, where SEZs have been credited with technology spillover, increases in national productivity, and structural transformation. Hong Kong, China was transformed into a high performing economy by its free port status, while the PRC, the Republic of Korea and Taipei,China arguably have had the most successful experience in the world, with manufacturing-type SEZs. These were launched when their economic structure was still dominated by primary economic activity while pursuing the inward looking policies. Mongolia is known for its liberal trade regime, but has not demonstrated steady growth partly due to its overreliance on minerals.

Generally speaking, the Republic of Korea initially used a heterodox approach and Taipei,China an orthodox approach. But they quickly moved to the VSI approach where the state played a crucial role in targeting industries and strengthening domestic firms' production capabilities using targeted credit, subsidies, incentive packages, and import protection to expand output, productivity, export competitiveness, and economic growth (Amsden 1989, Evans 1995, Wade 1990). While Taipei,China used EPZs as platform for strengthening SMEs by integrating them into GVCs and upgrading firms within them, the Republic of Korea focused more on attracting FDI in EPZs for manufacturing technologies and stimulating growth of large companies. The PRC complemented the VSI with the agglomeration approach. It promoted domestic firms' production capabilities by facilitating alliances directly with foreign firms and by creating a myriad of specialized zones with varying degrees of technological sophistication. Lately, it has been promoting overseas SEZs to help its firms upgrade them through learning by doing.

These experiences show how government SEZ strategies play an important role in dramatic industrial transformation. Creating highly well-endowed SEZs is a necessary condition to generate SEZ activity. But achieving SEZ-induced industrial diversification quickly requires a strong focus on domestic firms' competitiveness and continuously strengthening their capacity. The evolutionary SEZ approach places them at the core of national industrial strategy. Their development outcome depends on how successful policy makers are in addressing the challenges of moving up these chains. Synchronization between policy approaches and understanding success factors and development outcomes are critical.

In Southeast Asia, Brunei Darussalam has an FTZ in the hinterlands of Muara Port (since 1994), while Singapore, a free port, has promoted five FTZs. Malaysia was the first ASEAN country to adopt an EPZ program in 1971. It was followed by the Philippines (1972), Indonesia (1973), and Thailand (1978). All adopted zones to kick start export-

---

[97] Based on employment and exports for five Free Trade Zones (FTZ) and investment for nine FTZs.

oriented industrialization while still pursuing import substitution using an orthodox approach—having phenomenal success in generating direct benefits. Overall, SEZs have undoubtedly significantly affected growth and industrial diversification. In 2006, SEZs in Malaysia accounted for 72% of FDI, 83% of exports, and 5% of employment. They have been credited with developing a vibrant electrical and electronics (E&E) sector. In 2011, SEZs in the Philippines accounted for 15% of FDI, 73% of exports, and 2% of employment. However, the primary effects in some economies remain 'direct' effects. Spillover effects are still some way far from being fully realized. Policy interventions in Malaysia have indeed encouraged development beyond production capabilities (Jomo 2001), and its attempt at strategic industrial policy did have some success in certain sectors (Akyüz, Chang, and Kozul-Wright 1998). The Philippines has been able to attract FDI in its zones, but still needs to enhance benefits of technological spillovers and agglomeration—especially since enacting its more comprehensive 1995 SEZ policy. In general, the success in ASEAN has been relatively limited from a lack of linkages to the wider economy. There is a risk that the footloose investment these economies attract might move to other economies which have natural advantage in these activities. This calls for strong state support in boosting domestic capabilities. Liberal invitational strategies can stimulate early manufacturing, but they are insufficient in sustaining rapid growth and structural change toward higher value-added activities unless domestic firms operate in an environment that boosts their capabilities.

The CLMV are relatively new ASEAN members and late industrializers. Although Viet Nam had a head start and enjoys relatively higher per capita income and industrialization, as a group they remain primarily agriculture-based and transition economies characterized by low incomes, high unemployment, high poverty incidence, insufficient infrastructure, and weak institutions. Most CLMV economies have been developing SEZs as part of a broader industrial cluster development strategy. The distinction between different industrial parks is blurred. Following the PRC's success, the CLMV (plus Thailand) are focusing on generating agglomeration economies. To date, Viet Nam has been quite successful in its massive industrialization drive. According to *The Trade Policy Review 2013*, the proportion of industrial output generated in industrial zones and EPZs rose from 8% in 1996 to 32% in 2010. By December 2012, they had attracted 5,074 domestic and 4,509 FDI projects, employing 2.1 million workers. These zones benefitted from companies relocating from the PRC and other Southeast Asian economies where labor costs have been rising. Further, most new zones are being developed with regional participation, deepening RCI in the region.

In Myanmar, the government enacted a revised SEZ Law in 2014. Currently, three zones are under development. The Thilawa project opened in September 2015, developed by Myanmar and Japanese investors (Myanmar owning 51% and Japan 49%). The Lao PDR has two SEZs and eight specific economic zones. The Savan-Seno special economic zone in Savannakhet province has attracted several international companies including Aeroworks, Toyota, and KP Breau. They have been useful in overcoming institutional barriers and providing a good investment climate for intensifying industrialization more quickly. To become effective, however, they need to keep moving up value chains and refine competitive edge.

In South Asia, Bangladesh, India, Pakistan, and Sri Lanka have a long record of promoting SEZs. Recently, Bhutan, the Maldives and Nepal also plan to create SEZs. While Nepal has identified seven locations, Bhutan is developing three SEZs. In Nepal, SEZs are still in the development stage, after establishing an EPZ in 2006 (FIAS 2008). The Maldives adopted an SEZ law in September 2014. Afghanistan has also shown interest in SEZs, but the macroeconomic environment may affect the government's plans.

Overall, Bangladesh and Sri Lanka continue to reap static SEZ benefits, in particular employment generation and FDI inflows—based on orthodox and heterodox approaches. As of June 2012, eight EPZs in Bangladesh provided employment to over 3.4 million workers and accounted for 17.1% of total exports (BEPZA 2012). In Sri Lanka, zones employed 127,123 workers in 2012 (Karunaratne and Abayasekara 2013) and in 2008 accounted for over 38% of total exports. They have been instrumental in attracting FDI with over 80% of zone investment coming from FDI. However, with growth and rising wages in the wider economy, the competitive advantage of labor-intensive production cannot be sustained in the long run unless incentives remain attractive. Pakistan is already marketing its EPZs by offering 'industry friendly' labor laws. India's experience has been somewhat different. It followed a different trajectory. With industrial capabilities generated during the import substitution period, it holds huge potential to diversify industry through VSI using SEZs as a platform. Outward investment flows have accelerated—with faster outward investments than the inward flows in some years. SEZs could be instrumental in providing a platform for investors to contribute domestic investment and diversify the industrial sector.

Central Asia is rich in natural resources with agriculture and minerals dominating in Kazakhstan, the Kyrgyz Republic, Tajikistan, Turkmenistan and Uzbekistan. They can further be divided into oil- and gas-exporting economies (Kazakhstan, Turkmenistan, and Uzbekistan) and non-oil-exporting economies (the Kyrgyz Republic and Tajikistan). Previously high energy prices and investments in oil and gas, including petrochemicals, were the main growth engines for the first group. Migrant worker remittances have been instrumental for the Kyrgyz Republic (in addition to gold and tourism) and Tajikistan (together with agriculture and foreign aid). Despite recent strong growth, essentially based on commodity prices, these economies must diversify their economic structures with more emphasis on FDI. To restructure their economies and help transit from directive to market systems, these economies have all set up SEZs using the heterodox approach. They report a total of 27 SEZs, with 10 in Kazakhstan, seven in Turkmenistan, five in the Kyrgyz Republic, two in Uzbekistan, and three in Tajikistan. However, some continue having difficulties in enhancing benefits from their SEZ experiments.

The contribution of a zone to the national economy and its attractiveness to investors—foreign and domestic—depends on tailoring incentives and enabling institutions to specific circumstances and objectives.

Cost competitiveness and profitability can be enhanced through factor endowment and incentives. Nevertheless, there are six key factors for success:

(i) Fiscal incentives may be needed to attract SEZ investment. These include duty-free imports of raw and intermediate inputs, along with capital goods and income tax exemptions. These may directly reduce the costs of producing and exporting. However, empirical evidence raises questions as to the value of tax incentives—economies feel compelled to offer them as they are expected, but other institutional factors exert much greater pull.

(ii) Nonfiscal incentives expedite decision-making, streamline day-to-day operations and help create an enabling environment. An investor-friendly customs regime for instance, implies that entrepreneurs are free from routine cargo inspections (both imports and exports). By relaxing labor standards, governments can help reduce labor market rigidities that may affect labor productivity. But they can also create future problems as lax workplace standards can discourage buyers. Institutional efficiency—dependable judicial systems, adequate security—and employing international best practices (as in Singapore and Dubai, for example) are instrumental in attracting investors.

(iii) Cheap factory sites, subsidized land rents, built-up factory spaces, low electricity and other utility charges are instrumental in keeping costs low.

(iv) Abundant low wage labor supply is critical, in particular, for initial stage of SEZs.

(v) A strategic—preferably coastal—location and multimodal connectivity with major trading destinations are crucial to SEZ success. Generally, strategically located zones give investors easy gateways to international trade. The proximity of PRC SEZs to seaports and airports of Hong Kong, China and Taipei,China was vital to SEZ success in their initial stages (World Bank 2009). Dubai's Jebel Ali Free Zone is well served by capacious and efficient port and airport facilities with excellent connections.

(vi) Under the orthodox approach, it can help if SEZs are insulated from the oft-dysfunctional institutions prevalent in the wider economy. They become 'economic enclaves' where export manufacturing occurs under virtually free trade regimes.

Under the heterodox approach, government focus, macroeconomic stability, level of industrialization, trade policies and legal institutions take on greater importance. So too does the depth of labor markets and quality of available skills. Moreover, cluster formation and the creation of regional corridors calls for improving the regional economic and export infrastructure that strengthens connectivity.

Improving the business climate reduces both direct and indirect transaction costs. Authorities should pay greater attention to administrative and trade facilitation, and to relaxing the regulatory regime and increasing transparency. Generally, it is much easier to resolve infrastructure and governance issues within a limited geographical area than to tackle them countrywide (Watson 2001 and Mondol 2000)— enhancing investor confidence.

The potential for upgrading value chains under the evolutionary approach depends on entrepreneurial initiative and innovation as well as the capabilities and services an SEZ offers. Increasing participation in GVCs requires efficient logistics, low barriers in importing intermediate goods, reliable energy, and sufficient labor supply with the right skills. Once SEZ firms join a GVC, increasing value-added in either direction (toward sourcing and R&D or toward sales, distribution and marketing) requires a range of services at competitive quality and price. This is particularly crucial for local SMEs, unable to mobilize these services otherwise.

Ultimately, how well an SEZ performs depends on the international environment. Incentives, infrastructure and the enabling environment can create the preconditions. But international demand is crucial. The higher the growth in world GDP, trade and FDI flows, the more attractive SEZs become. Their performance is also influenced by multilateral and regional free trade agreements (FTAs). Evidence suggests FTAs influence both intra-and extra-regional trade and FDI flows (Aggarwal 2010).

Needless to say, government strategies greatly influence the success or failure of SEZs **(Box 4)**. Overly ambitious goals relative to an economy's conditions can hinder success. In Kazakhstan for instance, Seaport Aktau and Astana account for over 83% of goods produced in 10 SEZs (Nevmatulina 2013). While Seaport Aktau is an FTZ trade and logistics zone, Astana is the Kazakhstan capital and can be compared with the PRC's city-like SEZs. Other zones have yet to take off. More importantly, production and innovation zones have not progressed much. In the total production of goods and services, the share of SEZs remains miniscule at 0.003%. Further, SEZs have created a mere 9,000 jobs since 2001 (Nevmatulina 2013). There appears to be a mismatch between factor endowment and policy approach. While the emphasis has been on skill- and technology-intensive SEZs, technical skills, management expertise, and marketing skills are all in short supply. Many large investors rely on foreign workers and engineers to fill the void.

Other SEZs have also been constrained by the lack of skilled labor. In Malaysia, for instance, in the mid-1990s the government introduced an ambitious program to induce a structural shift from low to high value-added production. But by the 2000s, manufacturing started to plateau. It slowed before shifting to high value-added activities. Rasiah et al. (2015) attribute this to a combination of poor policy coordination

Box 4: Why Some Special Economic Zones Fail

The flipside of success drivers and factors are also potential factors for less successful or failed special economic zones (SEZs). There are several that stand out:

Wrong positioning. Vision and position defines SEZ goals and strategies. Over-ambition and unenthusiastic pursuit are two mistakes often found in developing SEZs. They usually stem from unrealistic assessments of existing conditions and potential by the host city. Apart from the obvious unrealistic aspiration of a third- or fourth-tier city to be a national or regional economic center, some positioning problems are imperceptible as conditions for economic development change. For instance, many SEZs in Asia list new emerging industries such as telecommunications, computers and software, new materials such as those used in energy supply and advanced equipment manufacturing, or biopharmaceuticals as a key part of their industrial plan. These aspirations can be successful under a clear strategy on industrial and technological development—or they become wishful thinking. Wrong positioning also includes overlooking competitive and/or comparative advantages, which may lead to suboptimal development.

The result can be SEZs paying substantial costs as development and growth stagnates with low return from investment.

Industrial islands. SEZs should not be designed as industrial islands, without plans linking business and commerce and—more importantly—building the amenities needed to make the zone livable. It is a paradox that industrial or manufacturing-led parks are being developed in modern urban economies, in which services are of increasing importance. An industrial park built without living areas cannot attract high-skilled labor—such as the People's Republic of China's (PRC) Airbus Park in Tianjin. This limits production and growth.

Rent-seeking and policy competition. SEZs use preferential policies, which may lead to policy competition between them. For example, in 2000, to attract firms and investment, some cities close to Shanghai announced an 'X+1' plan for policy support, meaning these cities offered one additional form of policy support in addition to the policy support offered by Shanghai (X). In response, Shanghai expanded the planning area of the Economic and Technological Development Zones (ETDZ) from 67 square kilometers to 173 square kilometers to compete for firms. In the meantime, if policy support imposes no costs or obligations on firms, it can make firms seek rents and be footloose.

Land uses. Governments may claim large amounts of land for setting up SEZs. As an incentive, land is usually provided for development and charged below market price. In some cases, large tracts of arable land are utilized, forcing many farmers off their land and increasing the compensation cost of land. This has been a salient issue for SEZs in India, where prime agricultural land was at times utilized for zones. In the PRC, 55% of the development park area in 2003 was claimed from arable land (Li 2004). In other cases only a small fraction of the land allotted is actually utilized by SEZs.

Lack of localized strategy. Attracting foreign direct investment (FDI) is one of the main aims of most SEZs, especially in the initial stages. Over reliance on FDI is risky given its sensitivity to labor and land costs. Some SEZs however do not have effective plans to develop local production capacity by making the best use of opportunity and spillover effects of FDI on technological promotion and upgrading industrial value chains. Technological spillover is often less in foreign companies than domestic ones. This is perhaps because foreign companies are reluctant to build research & development (R&D) departments overseas, afraid of divulging technological secrets, or face a shortage of local talent, and given poor amenities for expatriate staff. For instance, it could be quite difficult to find adequate international schools nearby. Relying on foreign companies—rather than developing locally embedded production networks—can result in very few connections among SEZ firms (Liu 2006; Yang, Cai, and Fu 2012).

and monitoring, counterproductive labor market practices, and human resource constraints. Firms resorted to importing foreign unskilled labor to sustain operations, which reduced the pressure to upgrade (Rasiah 1995, Henderson and Phillips 2007). In Indonesia, the shortage of good quality human resource development programs in Batam EPZ has undermined the ability of the zones to upgrade skills, improve working conditions and productivity to become a dynamic and internationally competitive platform (Shivathiran, undated). EPZs' working conditions, labor relations and human resource development are areas which require further improvement in many regional economies. Lower labor standards remain an attractive feature, yet they constrain productivity growth and movement up the value chains (Kam and Kee 2009). The Kyrgyz Republic also faces a shortage of skilled labor as many migrate to neighboring economies, while in Cambodia adequate labor literacy constrains FDI (see Annex B for country case studies on Cambodia, Bangladesh, and the PRC).

Good governance, streamlined regulations, and SEZ autonomy are crucial factors. Early on, India's development strategy was focused on import substitution. It set up SEZs to overcome its anti-export bias, starting with Asia's first SEZ in Kandla in 1965. This was followed by six more EPZs by the late 1980s. All were geographically closed small industrial estates located in port areas (except for the Noida EPZ). With EPZs viewed merely as a tool for offering fiscal incentives for export promotion, the program lacked any supportive legislation or administrative framework (Aggarwal 2004, Kundra 2000). Operationally, an inward looking trade policy with numerous controls and regulations worked against EPZ success (Kundra 2000). The zones were subject to controls and regulations to prevent misuse of incentives by firms. The policies were rigid, incentive packages and facilities unattractive. Zone authorities had limited powers. There was no single window facility within the zone. Entrepreneurs had to acquire individual clearances from various state and central government departments. Day-to-day operations were subjected to rigorous controls. Custom procedures for bonding, bank guarantees, and movement of goods were tight with little help offered in FDI policy. The lack of SEZ success in 1965–2005 led India to a comprehensive SEZ law in 2005 to overcome institutional weaknesses, boost industry, and encourage SEZ investment.[98] In Cambodia, most zones operated below capacity, partly due to bureaucratic delays—the time taken in import and export clearance, application processing, company registration, and high informal costs for import or export documents (Batith 2009). In some economies, firms inside zones face multiple layers or conflicting regulations—tantamount to "noodle bowls"—from central and provincial governments—a lack of coordination—leading to high compliance costs in doing business.

Corruption and rent-seeking also leads to poor performance. Kazakhstan, for instance, introduced its first SEZ law in the 1990s with nine SEZs created. However, these SEZs were ineffective and had to be scrapped by 2000 due to corruption, mistakes in spatial planning, lack of transparency,

---

[98] Under the Act, the scope of SEZs was expanded to include services, manufacturing, trading and re-engineering. The share of SEZs in total national exports (both merchandise and services) increased from a mere 3.2% in 2005–2006 to around 17% by 2011–2012.

shortcomings in the regulatory and legal frameworks, and poor site selection (Nevmatulina 2013, Karzhaubayeva 2013).

The limited success experienced by SEZs usually comes from many factors. Pakistan faced great challenges in establishing SEZs for various reasons. It set up one EPZ in Karachi in 1981. However, by 1990, employment in the zone was just 2,000 (Schrank 2001). A study assessing the performance of SEZs in Pakistan finds political instability and lack of state support and local partnerships at the macro level; lack of export facilities at the meso level; and a weak package of incentives; an inadequate legal framework; and absence of a single window clearance facilities at the microlevel behind the poor performance (Akhtar 2003).[99]

The Kyrgyz Republic also had little success with free economic zones (FEZs). Despite numerous attempts to amend legislation, no significant progress has been made. Statutory acts on FEZs need to be updated and improved to achieve the results expected from an economic zone. The incentive system is quite weak with partial concessions on various taxes. Weak infrastructure and poor connectivity are other major concerns. With the Kyrgyz Republic on the New Silk Road route, its status as transit economy requires flexible rules for moving goods (Uulu undated). The theoretical rationale—and causal reasoning—behind the roles to be assigned to SEZs need to be clearly specified within an economy's broader development strategy.

Development Strategy and Institutions

Linkage to development strategy

SEZs can become a major engine for national development— through backward and forward linkages which accelerate structural transformation nationally—raising productivity and income. Zones begin as arenas for employment and new investment. To be development catalysts rather than enclaves for absorbing underemployed workers, zones need to be linked to the domestic economy, provide significant opportunities for domestic participation, knowledge-sharing, innovation, and skills development. Several success stories demonstrate the effective use of SEZs as policy tools to increase employment and exports, attract FDI, and improve economic growth supported by various factors—fiscal incentives, skills upgrading, access to infrastructure, location, among others. However, the debate among researchers and policy makers continues because not all SEZs succeed (GIZ 2014). FIAS (2008) notes that maximizing EPZ benefits depends on how much they are integrated with their host economies and with the overall trade and investment reform agenda. In particular, when zones are designed to pilot legal and regulatory reforms within a planned policy framework, they are more

---

[99] Apart from traditional EPZs, in 2012, the economy passed SEZ laws and set up SEZs in Khairpur, Sindh for agro-processing industries, which is targeted to attract date processing and packaging plants.

likely to reach development objectives. Farole (2011) also states that institutionally and strategically, successful zone programs have been an integrated component of a long-term national growth (trade and industry) policy framework. In addition, policy instruments must be flexible enough to adjust to the evolving needs of the country. In the future, SEZs should remain a viable tool for developing economies, especially when reform initiatives are ex ante part of the overall strategy.

Table 17 shows the extent to which economies in the region incorporated SEZs into development strategies. Group 1 comprises those that incorporate SEZ policy into their national development strategy. Group 2 refers to those economies that use SEZs as a tool to develop specific industries (usually manufacturing). Group 3 are those that use SEZs as a peripheral policy—it is not clearly aligned with development strategy or industrial policy.

In the PRC, SEZs have been integrated into development and spatial planning as part of its "reform and opening" policy, with growth through export-based industrialization policy and Coastal Area Development Policy, among others. SEZs were initially set up as experimental, controlled enclaves to encourage development of technology, knowledge, and management. Four zones—Shenzhen, Zhuhai, Xiamen, and Shantou, which were initiated by "special foreign economic policies" in 1979, were experiments in managing market liberalization and attracting FDI. Emboldened by this success, the government gradually increased the number of SEZs (Aggarwal 2012). From the 1980s onward, hundreds of national, provincial and municipal economic and technological development zones (ETDZs) were established. National High-tech Industrial Development Zones (HIDZs) were set up from 1998. These are concentrated zones aimed at promoting new local, high-tech industries oriented toward both domestic and overseas markets, based on the PRC's indigenous scientific and technological strengths. By 2007, 54 HIDZs hosted about half of the national high-tech firms and science and technology incubators, registering some 50,000 invention patents—more than 70% were registered by domestic firms. Over the 15 years since their formation, HIDZs account for half of the PRC's high-tech gross industrial output and one-third of its high-tech exports. In addition, ETDZs are responsible for another one-third of the country's high-tech industrial output and exports (Zeng 2011).[100]

In the Republic of Korea, SEZs were pursued aggressively to lift industrial growth that slowed after the 1980s. SEZ development was fully synchronized with industrial spread and growth within the framework of the national medium-term economic development plan. SEZs helped the transition from labor-intensive to higher value-added production. In the initial phase, only foreign (including majority-owned local) firms were allowed to operate in 'free export zones.' They were largely involved in labor-intensive processes—textiles, footwear, and electronics parts. Subsequently, policies were amended to allow outsourcing

---

[100] D.Z. Zeng. 2011. [The People's Republic of] China's Special Economic Zones and Industrial Clusters: Success and Challenges. *World Bank: Let's Talk Development.* 27 April. http://blogs. worldbank.org/developmenttalk/china-s-special-economic-zones-and-industrial-clusters-success-and-challenges

Table 17: Asia's Special Economic Zone Experience (by country group on development strategy)

Development Strategy	Country Examples	Development Constraints[1]	Government Strategy	Benefits
Group 1: SEZ as part of the National Development Strategy	Bangladesh	Weak economic base led by jute industry; loss of jobs as the global jute industry faced long-term decline; weak governance as bureaucrats given discretionary authority in enforcing laws encouraged rent-seeking	Structural shift toward a more liberalized mechanism for trade and investment through - Foreign Investment Act and - Bangladesh Export Processing Zone Authority (BEPZA), which addressed land issues and administrative and logistical obstacles	SEZs accounted for 8% of total investment (foreign and domestic) and 17% of national exports in 2013; SEZs credited with development of garments industry
	PRC	Cost and risk associated with wholesale policy shift from closed economy to open door policy; disabling legal framework on property rights, tax incentives and land reform; rigidities in the labor market	SEZs as test-bed for new policies and institutions for PRC transition to a market economy: - Innovative methods to attract FDI and enhance exports - Market competition in transfer of land use rights - Land use planning and zoning systems to meet market needs - Expanded scope of FDI to cover infrastructure development	SEZs accounted for about half of national foreign direct investment (FDI), 44% of exports, 6.3% of employment in 2012[2]; SEZs credited with technology spillover, national productivity increases, industrial clustering, structural transformation
	Indonesia (2009–present)	High cost of finance hindering private investment—especially SMEs; skills shortages in some industries; inadequate national and subnational infrastructure, where poor transport networks and inadequate electricity supply considered most critical	- Government enacted the Special Economic Zones Law in 2009 establishing SEZs as centers of economic activity to enhance business competitiveness and encourage value-added processing and exports - SEZs to be situated in strategic positions—close to trade and/or maritime routes, to be supported by a business clusters or key sectors and linked to well-developed external infrastructure	SEZs starting to be operational in 2015
	Korea, Rep. of	Massive imports of foreign capital goods to acquire foreign technology led to foreign exchange shortage; highly restrictive FDI; industrial growth slowdown	Shift from import substitution to export promotion - Heavy and chemical industry development - FDI promotion for capital formation and technology transfer - Export drive to overcome the constraint in domestic demand	SEZs accounted for 28% of FDI, 11% of exports in 2007, with 13,000 employed[3]; SEZs credited with technology spillover, national productivity increases, structural transformation
	Malaysia	Encouraged import-substitution industries ending Penang's free port status; mounting job loss with unemployment rate around 7.3 % and a more critical 14.5% in Penang	Shift to industrialization through - Proposal to develop Free Trade Zones (FTZs) leading to creation of Free Trade Zone Act - Establish first FTZ in Bayan Lepas, Penang which began development of electrical goods and electronics cluster of zones	SEZs accounted for 72% of FDI, 83% of exports, 5% of employment in 2006; SEZs credited with technology spillover, development of electrical and electronics (E&E) sector, link with supporting industries, structural transformation
	Philippines	Balance of Payments (BOP) crisis led to the erosion of the manufacturing base (1962); adoption of export-oriented industrialization strategy through a series of measures faced opposition by local entrepreneurs	Facilitate investment in manufacturing and compensate for infrastructural deficiencies through - Amendment of the free port plan and creation of Export Processing Zone Authority (EPZA) - Laws and various incentive schemes (relating to EPZs) to provide basic guarantees to investors	SEZs accounted for 15% of FDI, 49% of exports, 2% of employment in 2011; SEZs credited with product diversification

Table 17 continued

Development Strategy	Country Examples	Development Constraints[1]	Government Strategy	Benefits
	India (2005 onward)	Very slow employment expansion; total investment remained abysmally small; relatively low FDI levels	Launch of new SEZ scheme through - A comprehensive SEZ Act to provide a significant push to investment in SEZs - Extended scope of SEZs to include services, manufacturing, trading, re-engineering, and re-conditioning	SEZs accounted for 26% of exports and 4% of employment in 2014
	Viet Nam	Transition to industrialization under socialist regime	Industrialization through development zones leading to - Industrial estates, EPZs and high-technology parks - Formalization of SEZ creation through the launch of Socio-Economic Development Strategies 2001–2010	SEZs accounted for 49% of FDI in 2014 and 4% of employment in 2013
Group 2: SEZ as an Industrial Policy	Cambodia	High unemployment rate; underdeveloped infrastructure with high cost of basic utilities; political instability; weak legal environment and judicial institutions; corruption	Legal framework for SEZ led to - Setup of the first SEZ, Neang Kok Koh Kong SEZ - Setup of second SEZ, Manhattan SEZ, the largest SEZ employing 28,000 workers	Employment of about 68,000 in 2014; gains in FDI, exports; SEZs have more diversified production base than domestic tariff area (DTA)
	Kazakhstan	Dependence on oil and gas exports (performance of commodity prices); cost and risks associated with transition from the directive to market system	Help shift to a market system through - SEZ laws which created nine initially ineffective SEZs - Creation of a new Act on four types of SEZs - Setup of 10 free economic zones to upgrade industrial prowess—seven production SEZs, two trade and logistics zones, one metallurgy and textile zone	About 6,000 of SEZ employment in 2013
	Sri Lanka	Anti-export bias followed under the import substitution policy	Liberalized trade and investment through - Changes in exchange rate, tariffs and quotas, tax holidays, fiscal incentives and relaxed FDI policy - Setup of first SEZ in Katunayake with improved investment climate, good site connectivity, developed infrastructure and services	SEZs accounted for 67% of exports in 2005 and 2% of employment in 2007; some evidence of backward linkages
	Thailand	High protection rate and incentives giving rise to industries heavily dependent on imports with little linkage with the rest of the economy	Outward-oriented policy framework initiated through - Regional trade networks with GMS - Setup of Special Border Economic Zones to streamline and formalize trade in a border area	SEZs accounted for 15% of FDI, 6% of exports, 13% of employment in 2006; SEZs credited with some product diversification

Table 17 continued

Development Strategy	Country Examples	Development Constraints[1]	Government Strategy	Benefits
Group 3: SEZ as part of an Administrative Objective	India (1965–2005)	Severe foreign exchange shortage due to failure in agriculture, mounting imports, and two border conflicts (early 1960s)	Export promotion through - Fiscal incentives - Setup of Asia's first EPZ in Kandla to overcome anti-export bias followed by six more EPZs, all geographically closed small industrial estates in port areas	SEZs accounted for 5% of exports and 0.2% of employment in 2000 (and rose to 26% and 4.2%, respectively, in 2014)
	Indonesia (1973–2009)	Heavily regulated import substitution regime; extensive foreign exchange controls; foreign capital flight resulting in economic stagnation; highly restrictive FDI policy	Policy reversal toward FDI and export promotion through - Setup of Kawasan Berikat Nasantara (KBN) and Batam, Bintan, and Karimun (BBK) SEZs - Framework Agreement on Economic Cooperation with Singapore to develop islands into SEZs - Official declaration of BBK as FTZ without taxes, customs and excise duties	In Batam Island SEZ, investments totaled $13.1 billion—36% came from foreign investors; total workforce increased from 16,336 in 1990 to 243,857 in 2007; regional GDP reached IDR29.22 trillion in 2007, growing at 7.5% per year

GMS = Greater Mekong Subregion, PRC = People's Republic of China, SEZ = special economic zone.

[1] Development constraints for each country refer to the period corresponding to the first generation of SEZ development.

[2] The PRC includes three types of development zones (DZ)—five comprehensive SEZ, Economic and Technological DZs, and High-tech Industrial DZ. Export processing zones and industrial parks are not included.

[3] For the Republic of Korea, employment and export data refer to five Free Trade Zones (FTZ), and investment in nine FTZs.

Sources: ADB Country Diagnostic Studies; CEIC; ILO Database on Export Processing Zones (2007); national sources.

production processes outside zones. In the 1980s, domestic firms were also allowed to invest in free export zones. Following the 1987 political transformation to democracy, labor rights saw disputes proliferating. Local wages increased steeply and the country started losing competitive advantage on labor-intensive products. This led the government to restructure economic activity and to incentivize a concentration of capital- and technology-intensive products in EPZs. In the mid-2000s, the government introduced logistics-oriented duty free zones to improve competitiveness of the logistics industry through higher value-added from transshipping, distribution, repackaging, multiple-country consolidation, processing, and manufacturing. In 2002, the government legislated an "Act on the Designation and Management of Free Economic Zones" to help attract more FDI, particularly in services and R&D, to become a financial, logistics, and business hub of Northeast Asia, and to test corporate deregulation—intended to help revive the sluggish domestic economy. [The Republic of] Korea Free Economic Zones (KFEZ) are designed to strengthen national competition for business and promote balanced regional development—by improving living conditions and the FDI business climate. Six FEZs have been designated with a distinct growth model adopted for each—focused for example on logistics or high-technology manufacturing.

In 1971, Malaysia passed the Free Trade Zone Act to create EPZs; these were especially attractive to foreign investors (Sivalingam 1994). It called for zones to be developed and managed by state governments. The first was set up near the Bayan Lepas airport in Penang in 1972, and signaled the start of the development of electrical and electronics (E&E) industry cluster in Malaysia (Chai and Im 2009). By 1975, eight zones were operating, and others soon joined. EPZs became the primary drivers of manufactured exports as large waves of foreign investors—particularly from the US—relocated E&E assembly and processing plants in Malaysia in the 1970s. E&E grew rapidly during both the 1970s and 1980s in export earnings, employment and FDI, becoming the main growth engine in the economy. These were also supported by the country's long-term development strategy. In 1987, the country adopted a new industrialization policy and attempted to integrate EPZs by facilitating backward linkages of SEZs with the rest of the economy.

In the mid-1990s, the government introduced a program to induce a structural shift from low to high value-added activities. By 2000, however, manufacturing began to plateau. It slowed before shifting to high value-added production. Rasiah et al. (2015) attribute this to a combination of poor policy, coordination and monitoring, counterproductive labor market practices, and human resource constraints. By 2009, nevertheless, E&E accounted for 55.1% of total manufactured exports, 90% in electronics. FDI in E&E has had multiplier effects on the national economy. In the beginning, semiconductor factories focused on simple assembly operations. But over the years the industry expanded and moved up the value chain, producing advanced semiconductor packages like flip chips, organic land grid array packages, field programmable gate arrays and multi-lead chips. Today the E&E industry has evolved to the point where several MNCs increased investment to turn their Malaysian operations into centers of R&D, design, brand development, procurement, distribution, and customer services.

To encourage FDI despite an import-substitution regime, the Philippines established EPZs—the Bataan Processing Zone (BEPZ) was the first, established in 1971, along with the Foreign Trade Zone Authority (FTZA). Three more export processing zones followed: the Cavite Export Processing Zone in Rosario; the Mactan Export Processing Zone in Cebu; and the Baguio City Export Processing Zone. The share of EPZs in attracting FDI and in merchandise exports grew considerably. Early EPZ performance helped fuel interest in establishing mainly private financed zones. However, expansion was horizontal rather than vertical. The Special Economic Zone Act of 1995 created 'eco zones' to be managed by the new Philippine Economic Zone Authority (PEZA), and expanded incentives offered to foreign investors—shifting focus away from government-developed EPZs to private industrial zones. PEZA data show steady increases in investments, exports, and employment; although there remains a lack of vertical expansion—as the country increasingly relies on low- to medium-end services (Aldaba 2013).

SEZs have also been used as instruments to advance governance and institutional reform. In the PRC, SEZs (especially the first several) successfully tested the market economy and new institutions, and became role models for the rest of the country to follow. Innovative methods like one-stop service were first tested in SEZs before being adopted elsewhere. Most incentives given SEZs at the beginning of the reform era have now become common policies across the PRC. SEZs also played a role in land policy reforms. The success of land market reforms in Shenzhen sent a strong message that land use rights should not be just transferable, but be transferred through market competition. The initial success boosted the confidence of legislative reformers nationally. In parallel with land transfer reforms, the Shenzhen SEZ also led the PRC to adopt Western concepts and practices of market-directed land use planning and zoning.

Because linkages and the transactions through SEZs are both tangible and nontangible—infrastructure connectivity, spatial transfer of information, people, materials, administrative and communication links—a locational pattern and strategy that accelerates SEZ integration into the regional economy is important. Hence, successful integration of SEZs in an economy's development strategy should be considered in the context of a balanced development strategy. In Bangladesh, only two of eight EPZs have successfully contributed to national economic growth—Chittagong EPZ (CEPZ) and Dhaka EPZ (DEPZ). Both lie within two corridors linking Bangladesh and Northeast India—Samdrup Jongkhar–Shillong–Sylhet–Dhaka–Kolkata corridor and Agartala–Akhaura–Chittagong corridor (ADB 2014b). Economic activity is highly concentrated in the two EPZs—Dhaka, as capital, and Chittagong, part of a larger trade corridor. As of fiscal year 2014–2015, CEPZ and DEPZ monopolize the majority of benefits accruing EPZs—the CEPZ has the highest share of investment (38%), employment (45%), and exports (47%). DEPZ follows in investment share (32%), employment (21%), and exports (40%).

In contrast, Malaysia's EPZs contribute to more balanced economic growth. Key industries and industrial parks have been established in Selangor State with prominent SEZs located on the coast and economic corridors—the Iskandar Development Zone, Sabah Development Corridor, East Coast Economic Corridor, and the Northern Corridor Economic Region.

Institutions

SEZ contributions to economic development and integration into overall development strategy should be understood in the context of a zone's overall institution and governance setting. The importance of a strong institutional framework and governance cannot be overstated in discussing the success of SEZs and their developmental impact.

Establishing SEZs pose several risks to the government and investors if mismanaged or governed inadequately. One risk is returns on investment in infrastructure—and returns on concessions. As mentioned, SEZs come with the costs of providing infrastructure, land, subsidized utility services, and access to below market rate credit. Tax incentives to attract foreign investors are another major cost. However, administrative discretion in managing incentives can increase the risk of corruption and rent-seeking. There is strong evidence that questions the effectiveness of certain tax incentives for investment in tax free zones due to the lack of transparency and clarity of provisions, administration and governance of tax incentives (OECD 2013). These risks justify an effective institutional setting to support the zone operations—ideally free from institutional constraints prevalent in the rest of the country.

A good representation of the supporting institutional framework is the relevant law enacted in establishing SEZs. In most economies—where the rule of law and governance remains a challenge—the importance of an effective legal framework is crucial. A well-developed and comprehensive legal framework with stable, transparent and unambiguous rules is a critical foundation for any successful SEZ program. While this may not be sufficient for the success of SEZs, the absence of good laws and regulations almost inevitably leads to failure in the zone program as well as in ensuring broader nationwide impact of SEZs.

SEZ laws in many cases specify the purpose of SEZ policy in the context of national development strategies and plans, and regulate their governing structure and operating procedures to provide transparent guidance to investors. They also set the primary framework for various incentives, including tax and land incentives. In this sense, well defined SEZ laws could be a proxy not only for good institutional settings but good business environment and incentive mechanisms—tailored to the country's development strategy and industrial policy.[101]

Apart from a well-developed legal framework, an independent governing body effectively supporting zone operation is critical. The SEZ authority should meet the needs of investors involving a wide range of activities that spread over various ministerial domains, including customs, land use and zoning, taxation, business registration and licensing, immigration, and environmental, labor, and social compliance. Further, the regulator's authority should extend both nationally and in SEZs but also local authorities, particularly regarding land use planning and licensing. The authority should be adequately empowered through the SEZ law. The governing authority can also offer one-stop services to both developers and investors. While many economies have made significant progress in ensuring effective administrative delivery to SEZ units, they remain hampered by weak institutional authority and lack of proper coordination. The governing authority should be able to execute a mechanism that ensures accountability and prompt redress of complaints and grievances. Depending on the relevance for each country, the distribution of governing power may allow local officials more decision-making authority in the management and administration of zones. As such, an SEZ

---

[101] For instance, the Philippines' Special Economic Zone Act of 1995 specifically links SEZ strategy with its national development plan: "The strategy and priority of development of each ECOZONE established... shall be formulated by the PEZA, in coordination with the Department of Trade and Industry and the National Economic and Development Authority; Provided, That such development strategy is consistent with the priorities of the national government as outlined in the medium-term development plan (Chapter III, Section 21)." In PRC, the "The Regulations on Special Economic Zones in Guangdong Province" promulgated in 1980 acted as the centerpiece legislation on SEZs (Fenwick 1982). Approved by the National People's Congress for implementation, it followed the economic strategy of opening up and attracting FDI in very broad terms. While EPZs in other countries were focused largely on laborintensive industrial production, Article 4 of the SEZ Regulations invites foreign capital to participate in "all items of industry, agriculture, livestock breeding, fish breeding and poultry farming, tourism, housing and construction, [and] research and manufacture." It also provided a basic legislative framework upon which other areas would set up SEZs. In the Republic of Korea, the central purpose of establishing free economic zones is closely aligned with national objectives of economic competitiveness, transparency, and a fair, free and open market economic system as stated in its Free Economic Zone Act: "The purpose of this Act is to facilitate foreign investment, strengthen national competitiveness and seek balanced development among regions, by improving the business environment for foreign-invested enterprises and living conditions for foreigners through the designation and management of free economic zones (Article 1)."

authority may be established at national and/or provincial levels. The PEZA, the BEPZA and the Republic of Korea's regional Free Economic Zone Authority are a few examples.

A detailed economic analysis testing the impact of SEZ law and authority as proxies for institutional settings and governance structures, respectively, is explored in next section.

Economic Impact of SEZs

Early studies of SEZs were largely descriptive and concerned with the macroeconomic effects on employment, exports, and foreign exchange earnings (Aggarwal 2012). However, as SEZs multiplied, a few empirical studies analyzed SEZ-induced effects using econometric analysis, including ones using a cost-benefit approach. These attempted to gauge the effects of SEZs at national, city, and firm levels. As mentioned throughout, anecdotal evidence documents that SEZ success in terms of volume of exports, FDI, etc., depends on the integration of SEZ strategy to the overall national development plan and institutional framework. While no econometric studies were found, this section attempts to estimate the effect of the presence of SEZs, their laws, and authorities on national level economic performances. We also examine firm performances which characterize cross-country variances.

Effects of SEZs: Growth, Exports and FDI

Past nationwide studies of SEZs have yielded mixed evidence of their effects on exports, FDI, and output. While there are some successes, in the majority of cases, zones appear to have increased exports only marginally (Gibbon et al. 2008). In one of the earliest studies, Johansson and Nilsson (1997) estimated the impact of SEZs on the export performance of 11 developing economies for the period 1980–1992. They found that on average SEZs exerted a positive influence, although cross-country effects varied. Their analysis of Malaysia, for example, revealed that in addition to the exports generated by FDI in the zones, the EPZs also helped catalyze exports from the rest of the country as well by introducing export knowhow.

Tyler and Negrete (2009) adopted the endogenous growth model framework to analyze how SEZs affected growth using cross-country data for the period 1961–1999. The dummy variable representing SEZs was positive and significant after controlling for other factors representing cyclical variations, institutions and structural policies, macroeconomic and stabilization policies, and external conditions. In a more recent study, Leong (2013) investigated the role of SEZs in liberalizing economies in the PRC and India and raising growth rates. The shift to a more liberalized economy is identified using SEZ variables as instrumental variables. The results indicate that exports and FDI growth have positive and statistically significant effects on economic growth—a 1% increase in exports raises national income by 0.44%. The presence of SEZs augments growth, but increasing the number of SEZs has negligible effect. It is the pace of economic liberalization that appears to be the key to faster economic growth.

Exports and FDI performance are the usual benchmarks used in gauging SEZ impact nationally or regionally. Different policy objectives embedded in SEZ experiments such as job creation and economic growth and development along the spectrum of different SEZ development stages are all associated with exports and FDI performance one way or another. Hence, attempts to assess the effect of SEZs on these two variables at the global as well as regional level were done with focus on Asia. Further, given that the success and nationwide impact of SEZs are significantly affected by institutional framework and governance structure, it was tested whether the presence of SEZ laws and an autonomous SEZ authority have a bearing on an economy's economic performance, as proxied by FDI and exports.

The effect of SEZs on exports was estimated using a gravity model based on bilateral exports data of manufactured goods **(Box 5)**. This is estimated through a Random-Effects Generalized Least Squares regression with country fixed effects for both exporters and importers.

The results of the base model, after controlling for the impact of economic size, geographic, cultural, and economic proximity, show that globally, the presence of SEZs has a slightly negative effect on exports

Box 5: Measuring the Effects of Special Economic Zones on Trade

To test the quantitative effect of the establishment of special economic zones (SEZs) on exports, we use a dynamic gravity model, which is staple in measuring trade flows in the international trade literature. We construct the model as follows:

$$\ln X_{ijt} = \beta_0 + \beta_1 Y_{it} + \beta_2 Y_{jt} + \sum_{i=1}^{N} \delta_i F_i + \sum_{j=1}^{M} \delta_j F_j + \beta_3 \tau_{ijt} + \beta_4 SEZ_{it} + v$$

Where Y_{it} and Y_{jt} refer to log of GDP of exporter country i and importer country j, respectively, at time t. The set of exporter country dummies F_i and importer country dummies F_j account for unobserved country effects that can enhance or deter trade. The second to the last term τ_{ij} captures the observed trade costs such as distance, shared border, common language, among others. The SEZ variable is added

to account for the export effects the SEZs in the exporter country i generate.

Exports of manufacturing goods from 1990–2014 of 169 economies with information on the existence of SEZ was used in the regression, including 42 economies in Asia, 31 in Latin America, 49 in Africa, 26 in European Union (EU), 13 in the Middle East, and 2 in North America. Only 119 economies with SEZs are included in the regressions related to SEZ institutions (independent SEZ authority and SEZ law). For each region, dummy variables conditional on SEZ were constructed to capture the effect of SEZs compared to economies without SEZs. For testing SEZ authority and SEZ law, regional dummy variables were constructed in a way to measure the impact of those institutions among economies with SEZ.

Table 18: Gravity Model Estimation Results: Impact of SEZs on Exports—World

[Dependent variable: Log (Exports)]

Variables	Coefficients
Log (Distance)	-1.61**
	(0.02)
Colonial relationship dummy	0.85**
	(0.10)
Common language dummy	0.93**
	(0.03)
Contiguity dummy	1.19**
	(0.10)
Log (GDP of exporter)	0.42**
	(0.02)
Log (GDP of importer)	0.67**
	(0.01)
SEZ existence dummy	-0.08**
	(0.03)
Constant	-2.24
R-Squared (overall)	0.75
Sample size	389,426

** = significant at 5%.
Standard errors in parentheses.
Notes:
(i) Country-fixed effects were estimated but are not shown for brevity.
(ii) Estimated using Random-Effects Generalized Least Squares.
(iii) Period coverage is 1990–2014.
(iv) SEZ existence dummy is defined as: 1 for economies with SEZs, 0 otherwise; see Annex A for details.
(v) Includes 169 economies covering six regions (Africa, Asia, European Union, Latin America, Middle East, North America) with information on the existence of SEZs.
Source: ADB calculations using data from *UN Commodity Trade Database,* CEPII, and national sources.

(Table 18). This might attest to the observation that many zones worldwide have not performed well and show mixed results. By region, the presence of SEZs in North America and EU positively affects overall export performance, while in Latin America and Africa SEZ presence has a negative effect **(Table 19)**. In the EU, economies with SEZs export 34% more than economies in the EU without SEZs. African and Latin America economies with SEZs have exports lower by 40% and 41%, respectively, compared with economies in these regions without SEZs. These results are statistically significant. For Asia and Middle East, the SEZ variable is not statistically significant.

The results indicate that the level of exports of economies with SEZs in Asia is not significantly different from exports of economies without SEZs. We also test if increasing the number of SEZs has any positive impact on the economies's export performance in Asia. For this, we use the log of number of SEZs per sq. km. to normalize country size which differs across economies. Economies included are Bangladesh, Cambodia, the PRC, India, Kazakhstan, the Philippines and Sri Lanka which have available data on annual number of SEZs from 1990 to 2014. The result shows a positive and significant coefficient for the normalized number of SEZs. This indicates that a 10% increase in the number of SEZs increases an economy's manufacturing exports by 1.1% **(Table 20)**.

The effect of SEZ institutions on exports is also estimated **(Table 21)**. The results show that in Asia, the presence of an independent SEZ authority and SEZ law both have positive effect on exports. Within Asian economies with SEZs, those with SEZ law export 40% more than those without SEZ law; and economies with independent SEZ authorities in Asia export more by about 27%. These results are statistically significant.

Similar to Asia, among economies with SEZs, those with law in the EU and Middle East export significantly higher than those without SEZ law. On the presence of an independent SEZ authority, aside from Asia, only economies in EU export significantly more than economies without SEZ authority. The presence of SEZ authority in Latin America and Africa negatively affects exports of these regions.

The impact of SEZs on FDI is estimated alongside the impact of global push and country specific pull factors of FDI, using a two-step Generalized Method of Moments (GMM) estimation technique **(Box 6)**. Using FDI (in natural logarithm) as the dependent variable, running the regression of the SEZ variable, along with the global push and country pull factors, yields significant results for the impact of SEZ existence **(Table 22)**.

The GMM regression results show that the existence of SEZ has a significant and positive impact on FDI globally as well as regionally except for developing Europe. Globally, SEZ existence is estimated to lead to 89% higher FDI for an economy. However, when time dummy is included, most of the significant results disappear. Nevertheless, the results of regressions for developing Asia are robust and still significant at 10% level.

Table 19: Gravity Model Estimation Results: Impact of SEZs on Exports—Asia versus Other Regions

[Dependent variable: Log (Exports)]

Regions	SEZ Existence Dummy
Asia	0.03
	(0.05)
Africa	-0.40**
	(0.05)
European Union	0.34**
	(0.04)
Latin America	-0.41**
	(0.09)
Middle East	0.06
	(0.07)
North America	1.88**
	(0.13)

** = significant at 5%. Standard errors in parentheses.
Notes:
(i) Country-fixed effects were estimated but are not shown for brevity.
(ii) Gravity model was orsestimated for each region using Random-Effects Generalized Least Squares. Standard errors are heteroskedasticity robust.
(iii) Period coverage for all regions is 1990-2014.
(iv) SEZ existence dummy is defined as: 1 for economies with SEZs, 0 otherwise; see Annex A for details.
(v) The base of the regional dummies is non-SEZ economies within the same region. The coefficient is interpreted as the percentage increase (decrease) in exports of economies in the region that have SEZs compared with economies within the same region that do not have SEZs.
(vi) Includes 169 economies covering the six regions with information on the existence of SEZ.
Source: ADB calculations using data from *UN Commodity Trade Database,* CEPII, and national sources.

Table 20: Gravity Model Estimation Results: Alternative Specification Asia

[Dependent variable: Log (Exports)]

Variables	Coefficients
Log (Distance)	-1.98**
	(0.19)
Colonial relationship dummy	0.66
	(0.57)
Common language dummy	0.43**
	(0.17)
Contiguity dummy	1.08**
	(0.40)
Log (GDP of exporter)	0.74**
	(0.06)
Log (GDP of importer)	0.67**
	(0.06)
SEZ variable: Log (Number of SEZs per sq. km)	0.11**
	(0.02)
Constant	-3.32
R-Squared (overall)	0.80
Sample size	21,115

** = significant at 5%. Standard errors in parentheses.
Notes:
(i) Country-fixed effects were estimated but are not shown for brevity.
(ii) Gravity model was estimated using Random-Effects Generalized Least Squares. Standard errors are heteroskedasticity robust.
(iii) Includes the following Asian economies as exporters: Bangladesh, Cambodia, India, Kazakhstan, the PRC, the Philippines, and Sri Lanka which have available time-series data on number of SEZs established..
Source: ADB calculations using data from *UN Commodity Trade Database,* CEPII, and national sources.

Table 21: Gravity Model Estimation Results: Impact of SEZ Institutions on Exports—Asia versus Other Regions

[Dependent variable: Log (Exports)]

Regions	SEZ Law dummy	SEZ Authority dummy
Asia	0.40**	0.27**
	(0.04)	(0.06)
Africa	-0.43**	-0.49**
	(0.05)	(0.07)
European Union	0.16**	0.11**
	(0.04)	(0.04)
Latin America	-0.08	-0.79**
	(0.08)	(0.20)
Middle East	0.37**	-0.08
	(0.07)	(0.09)
Sample size	300,901	300,901

** = significant at 5%. Standard errors in parentheses.
Notes:
(i) Country-fixed effects were estimated but are not shown for brevity.
(ii) Gravity model was estimated using Random-Effects Generalized Least Squares. Standard errors are heteroskedasticity robust .
(iii) Period coverage for all regions is 1990-2014.
(iv) SEZ variable is defined as: SEZ Law dummy – for economies with SEZ-related law, ordination, or presidential decrees, 0 otherwise; SEZ Authority– for economies with an independent SEZ authority either at the national or provincial level, 0 otherwise; see Annex A for details.
(v) The base of the regional dummies is non-SEZ economies within the same region. The coefficient is interpreted as the percentage increase (decrease) in exports of economies in the region that have SEZs compared with economies within the same region that do not have SEZs.
(vi) Covers 119 exporter economies with SEZs and information on Law and Authority.
Source: ADB calculations using data from *UN Commodity Trade Database,* CEPII, and national sources.

This shows the existence of SEZ in developing Asia leads to higher FDI level by 82.4%, compared to other developing Asian economies without SEZ.

The effect of the existence of SEZ law and SEZ authority on FDI is also estimated. The GMM estimation shows insignificant results for the relationship of the existence of SEZ law and FDI level when tested for all developing and emerging market economies, including developing Asia. It shows, however, that the presence of an SEZ law for economies with SEZ in Latin America, leads to a higher FDI level by 39.4%, compared to economies with SEZs but without an SEZ law in the same region.

Box 6: Measuring the Effects of Special Economic Zones on Attracting FDI

A two-step Generalized Method of Moments (GMM) estimation technique is used to measure the effects of global and push factors on foreign direct investment (FDI) inflows in the base model.[1] The GMM estimator is preferred to fixed effects estimation methods for dynamic panel models with endogenous regressors. In GMM model, the given equation is as follows:

$$fdi_{t,i} = \beta_0 + \beta_1 fdi_{t-1,i} + \beta_2 X_t + \beta_3 Y_{t,i} + u_i + v_{t,i}$$

where X_t denotes the global push factors, and $Y_{t,i}$ indicates the time-varying country-pull factors, for country i.

The global push factors are growth in capital exporting countries—G7—which are the main sources of FDI for emerging market and developing economies, growth rate of advanced economies, international liquidity, and global risk environment.[2] Country pull factors include variables on host countries' size, and macroeconomic and policy environment. A time dummy variable is included to reflect crisis periods, specifically for Asian financial crisis (1998), and global financial crisis (2007, 2008 and 2011).

A dummy variable is also included for i) the existence of special economic zone (SEZ), ii) existence of SEZ law and iii) existence of SEZ authority as the SEZ policy variable for separate regressions.

---

[1]   Based on the model by E. Arbatli. 2011. Economic Policies and FDI Inflows to Emerging Market Economies. *IMF Working Papers.* No. 192. Washington: IMF. We modify the model by (i) using FDI level as the dependent variable, rather than the FDI as % of GDP, and by (ii) using crisis periods as time dummies.

[2]   See IMF. World Economic Outlook. Database—WEO Groups and Aggregates Information. https://www.imf.org/external/pubs/ft/weo/2015/02/weodata/groups.htm

The GMM estimation indicates insignificant results for the impact of SEZ authority on FDI level when tested for all developing and emerging market, economies except for Middle East. For the Middle East, the presence of an SEZ authority for economies with SEZ indicates a higher FDI level by 61.4%, compared to those without an SEZ authority **(Table 23)**.

Globally, SEZs seem to have more positive effect in inducing FDIs than promoting exports. This is particularly true for Asia. In the meantime, SEZ's impact on exports varies across regions. While it is positive for advanced economies such as those in EU and North America, it is negative for developing economies in Africa and Latin America. Underlying reasons behind this difference warrants further studies.

The impact of SEZ institutions is more evident for the performance of exports across the regions although the impact widely varies across regions. For Asia, the impacts of SEZ institutions are significant and positive. However, the impacts of SEZ institutions are rather subdued in FDI. FDI performance might depend on a much broader set of institutional as well as policy factors which characterizes the overall investment climate of the host economies.

Table 22: GMM Model Estimation Results: Impact of SEZ on FDI—Developing Economies
[Dependent Variable: Log(FDI)]

Variables	All		Developing Asia		Africa		Developing Europe		Latin America		Middle East	
Lag of dependent variable	0.463*** (4.05)	0.550*** (5.25)	0.446*** (3.80)	0.533*** (5.53)	0.533*** (5.55)	0.579*** (6.12)	0.531*** (5.66)	0.529*** (5.18)	0.490*** (4.30)	0.560*** (5.58)	0.501*** (4.65)	0.574*** (5.91)
Global push factors												
G7 GDP growth rate	-0.0596* (-1.67)	-0.0261 (-0.71)	-0.0483 (-1.11)	-0.0272 (-0.70)	-0.0557 (-1.47)	-0.0382 (-0.80)	-0.0299 (-1.07)	-0.0537 (-1.08)	-0.0602 (-1.64)	-0.0285 (-0.72)	-0.0484 (-1.58)	-0.0323 (-0.64)
G7 real interest rate	0.00622 (0.27)	-0.0290 (-1.29)	0.0148 (0.62)	-0.0169 (-0.70)	-0.0206 (-0.97)	-0.0336 (-1.63)	-0.0208 (-1.12)	-0.0273 (-1.31)	0.00401 (0.17)	-0.0263 (-1.15)	-0.000429 (-0.02)	-0.0296 (-1.52)
Log(VIX)	-0.107 (-0.87)	-0.255 (0.0261)	-0.103 (-0.74)	-0.302** (-2.13)	-0.136 (-1.04)	-0.291** (-2.00)	-0.0724 (-0.64)	-0.279* (-1.78)	-0.155 (-1.44)	-0.299** (-2.32)	-0.116 (-1.08)	-0.284* (-1.92)
Country pull factors												
Inflation	1.735*** (4.25)	0.955** (1.97)	1.840*** (4.53)	1.193** (2.51)	1.685*** (4.38)	0.819* (1.85)	1.601*** (4.10)	0.692* (1.77)	1.823*** (4.46)	1.42** (2.27)	1.702*** (4.30)	0.841* (1.85)
Log(GDP)	0.0258 (0.14)	0.279* (1.83)	-0.0565 (-0.27)	0.146 (0.89)	0.124 (0.51)	0.309 (1.50)	0.280 (1.28)	0.429** (2.19)	-0.0243 (-0.14)	0.223 (1.39)	0.0602 (0.36)	0.289* (1.89)
Average tariff rate (manufacturing goods)	-0.0172* (-1.85)	-0.0124** (-2.32)	-0.0199* (-1.66)	-0.0151** (-2.47)	-0.0107 (-1.60)	-0.00909* (-1.66)	-0.0119* (-1.92)	-0.0120* (-1.91)	-0.0169* (-1.70)	-0.0128** (-2.15)	-0.0165** (-1.99)	-0.0105* (-1.83)
Corporate tax rate	-0.00835 (-0.94)	-0.00953 (-1.41)	-0.00980 (-0.79)	-0.00809 (-1.03)	-0.00322 (-0.27)	-0.00969 (-0.94)	-0.0106 (-1.04)	-0.0166 (-1.56)	-0.00270 (-0.29)	-0.00741 (-0.94)	-0.00389 (-0.45)	-0.0101 (-1.36)
SEZ existence dummy	0.893*** (2.62)	0.291 (0.90)	1.860** (2.08)	0.824* (1.71)	0.467* (1.68)	0.205 (0.93)	0.251 (0.65)	-0.0331 (-0.10)	1.248** (2.23)	0.462 (1.25)	1.243** (2.22)	0.605 (1.32)
Constant	3.272 (0.82)	-2.531 (-0.74)	4.459 (0.96)	0.317 (0.08)	-3.256 (-0.75)	0.350 (0.07)	-5.730 (-1.27)	-3.061 (-0.61)	3.997 (1.09)	-1.282 (-0.35)	1.854 (0.49)	-3.001 (-0.98)
Observations	876	876	903	903	903	903	903	903	903	903	903	903
Economies	95	95	98	98	98	98	98	98	98	98	98	98
Time Dummy	No	Yes	No	Yes	No	Yes	No	Yes	No	Yes	No	Yes
Instruments	54	58	56	60	56	60	56	60	56	60	56	60
Arellano-Bond test for AR (2)	0.259	0.140	0.271	0.178	0.280	0.166	0.256	0.162	0.275	0.177	0.268	0.163
Hansen Test	0.327	0.409	0.341	0.290	0.314	0.433	0.205	0.765	0.348	0.336	0.325	0.386

t-statistics in parentheses. * = significant at 10%, ** = significant at 5%, *** = significant at 1%, GMM = Generalized Method of Moments.

Notes:
(i) Standard errors are heteroskedasticity robust.
(ii) Period coverage for all models is 1990–2013.
(iii) SEZ existence dummy: 1 for economies with SEZs, 0 otherwise; see Annex A for details.
(iv) The base of the regional dummies is non-SEZ economies within the same region. The coefficient is interpreted as the percentage increase (decrease) in FDI levels of economies in the region that have SEZs compared with economies within the same region that do not have SEZs.
(vi) Includes developing and emerging market economies as classified by the International Monetary Fund covering 5 regions (Africa, Asia, Europe, Latin America, Middle East) with information on the existence of SEZ
(vii) Developing Asia refers to the 45 members of ADB, excluding Cook Islands; Hong Kong, China; the Republic of Korea; Nauru; Taipei,China; Singapore, with information on the existence of SEZ.
(viii) Developing Europe includes Bulgaria, Hungary, Lithuania and Romania.
(ix) G7 real GDP growth rate is a proxy for growth in capital exporting countries.
(x) G7 real interest rate is the proxy for international liquidity.
(xi) S&P VIX index is the proxy for the risk environment.
(xii) Average tariff rates on mfg. goods is a proxy for trade liberalization policy. It is the "unweighted average of effectively applied rates for all products subject to tariffs calculated for all traded goods."
(xiii) Corporate tax rates are statutory rates.
Source: ADB calculations using data from Chicago Board Options Exchange; Corporate Tax Rates Table and Corporate Indirect Tax Rate Survey, KPMG; World Tax Database, University of Michigan's Ross School of Business; Deloitte Corporate Tax Rates World Investment Report, UNCTAD; and World Development Indicators, World Bank.

Table 23: GMM Model Estimation Results with SEZ Institutions

[Dependent Variable: Log(FDI)]

Regions	SEZ Law dummy	SEZ Authority dummy
All	0.073 (0.68)	0.002 (0.03)
Developing Asia	0.259 (1.55)	-0.378 (-1.07)
Africa	0.259 (1.55)	-0.378 (-1.07)
Developing Europe	0.183 (0.48)	–
Latin America	0.394** (2.42)	0.195 (1.33)
Middle East	0.326 (1.44)	0.614** (2.21)

– = unavailable, FDI = foreign direct investment, ** = significant at 5%. t-statistics in parentheses.

Notes:
(i) Model includes time dummies for crisis periods.
(ii) Standard errors are heteroskedasticity robust.
(iii) Period coverage is 1990-2013.
(iv) SEZ variable is defined as: 1 for economies with SEZ law (authority), 0 otherwise; See Appendix A for details.
(v) The base of the regional dummies is SEZ economies without law (authority) within the same region. The coefficient is interpreted as the percentage increase (decrease) in FDI levels of economies in the region that have SEZ law (authority) compared with economies within the same region that do not have SEZ law (authority).
(vi) Includes developing and emerging market economies as classified by IMF with information on the existence of SEZ. Developing Asia refers to 45 member economies of ADB excluding Cook Islands; Hong Kong, China; the Republic of Korea; Nauru; Singapore, and Taipei,China; with information on the existence of SEZ law (authority). Developing Europe includes Bulgaria, Hungary, Lithuania, Romania and Poland, with information on the existence of SEZ law (authority)

Source: ADB calculations using data from Chicago Board Options Exchange; *Corporate Tax Rates Table* and *Corporate Indirect Tax Rate Survey*, KPMG; *World Tax Database*, University of Michigan's Ross School of Business; *Deloitte Corporate Tax Rates*; *World Investment Report*, UNCTAD; and *World Development Indicators*, World Bank.

City or municipal level effects of SEZs

There are few studies analyzing how SEZs influence performance at the city or local level. Aggarwal (2005b) and Wang (2013) find that on balance, the effects on the local economy via FDI, productivity, and wages are positive. Using a panel data from 18 Indian states for 1991–2000, Aggarwal (2005b) showed that SEZs significantly influenced the flow of export-oriented FDI.

The PRC was analyzed by Wang (2013) using the difference in difference technique.[102] Wang's panel data on 321 PRC prefecture-level municipalities contained information on GDP, investment, employment, exports, and factor prices, as well as the year SEZs were created in each municipality. Wang's estimates showed that the SEZ affected not only the levels but also the trends in FDI, total factor productivity growth, wages, and the consumer price index. The PRC's SEZ program, on average, increases per capita FDI mainly in the form of foreign-invested and export-oriented industrial enterprises. Wang also found that the FDI inflow does not crowd out domestic investment. More importantly, the majority of the FDI attracted by SEZs was new rather than simply a reallocation from other non-SEZ areas. Finally, there was a significant increase in local worker earnings and a moderate rise in living costs without significant increases in house prices.

Wang's findings are supported by another study using panel data for a 23-year period drawn from 270 prefecture-level PRC cities (Alder et al. 2013). This showed that by establishing a major zone, a city could increase its GDP by 12% on average in post-reform years, with the effect depending on the type of zone. Over the long-term, an SEZ could increase GDP cumulatively by as much as 20%.

Firm-level effects of SEZs

In a study using firm-level data, Lu, Wang, and Zhu (2015) examined the consequences of the place-based economic zones program in the PRC on the performance of firms using detailed information on firm location and zone boundaries. The authors find that firms inside zones on average are larger (in employment, output, and capital), are more capital-intensive, and have larger output-labor ratios. The PRC's zone program also increased the number of firms located in the zones. The zone program has a large and positive effect on newly entered firms and relocated firms, with a modest effect on incumbents. In addition, capital-intensive firms benefit more than labor-intensive firms. Furthermore, firms did better in zones with higher market potential or greater transportation accessibility. Overall, the success of SEZs contributed significantly to the PRC's development in the earlier stages (Aggarwal 2012). The provinces in which SEZs are located transformed themselves from predominantly agrarian areas into metropolitan cities.

---

[102] See D. Zeng. 2015. Global Experience with SEZs: Focus on [the People's Republic of] China and Africa. *World Bank Policy Research Working Papers*. No. 7240. Washington D.C.: World Bank.

EPZ performance in India, Bangladesh, and Sri Lanka was the focus of a study by Aggarwal (2005a) using primary survey data for individual firms and secondary data for national and regional variables. EPZ performance was gauged on the basis of FDI and exports. The primary survey and econometric analysis revealed that economies wishing to take advantage of the opportunities provided by zones need to assemble a coordinated package of incentives, infrastructure and good governance. Results suggested that some aspects of location, facilities and incentives are more important than others. For instance, the presence of social infrastructure within the zones was less important than physical infrastructure; tax benefits are more sought after than subsidies; relaxation in labor laws was more important than relaxation of other laws; locating the zones near bigger cities or ports was more advantageous than locating them near airports or railway stations; and availability of educated disciplined labor was more beneficial to firms than lower wages or skilled labor.

Using the World Bank Enterprise Survey data, we analyze firm-level performance of SEZs for a few economies with available data. The results indicate there are variances across economies in firm-level performance **(Box 7)**.

Cost-benefit analysis

Cost-benefit analyses of SEZs try to account for the investment worthiness of SEZs. Two of the earliest empirical studies on SEZs are the cost-benefit analysis by Warr (1989), which delineated a standard framework for measuring static welfare effects of zones in the Republic of Korea, Malaysia, Indonesia, and the Philippines, and a study by Spinanger (1984), which considered both static and dynamic consequences. The results suggest that SEZs in the Republic of Korea, Malaysia, Sri Lanka, PRC, and Indonesia are economically efficient and generate returns well above estimated opportunity costs. The study by Warr obtained a positive net present value for SEZs located in Indonesia, the Republic of Korea, and Malaysia, and a negative present value for the Philippines. The heavy infrastructure costs involved in setting up zones in the Philippines resulted in a negative net present value. The zones have been an important source of employment in all cases and have promoted local entrepreneurs in some. However, as industrial development proceeds, the gap between market and opportunity costs of labor narrows and the interest in EPZs tends to disappear. Spinanger noted a positive impact in Penang in Malaysia, and in Bataan in the Philippines. Chen (1993) estimated the costs and benefits of the Shenzhen SEZ and found a rate of return of about 10.7%, well above the opportunity cost of capital.

Jayanthakumaran (2003) updated Warr's 1989 study and surveyed the research on performance of EPZs using a cost-benefit analytical framework. The method consists of computing conversion factors, which are the ratio of shadow prices to domestic market price. Benefits are identified as (i) the difference between wages paid to local labor and the shadow wage, (ii) the difference between payments by firms for public utilities and locally purchased inputs and their opportunity cost, (iii) all

Box 7: Measuring the Impact of Special Economic Zones on Firm Performance

We examine whether the performance of manufacturing firms inside a special economic zone (SEZ) is significantly better than those outside SEZs using the World Bank Enterprise Survey (WBES) on Bangladesh, India, and Malaysia.[1] With SEZs as a policy tool, we construct a potential-outcome model for the firm output in measuring the impact of SEZs as follows:[2]

$$y^* = \delta_0 + \delta_1 SEZ + \sum_{i=1}^{n} \gamma_i Z_i + \sum_{i=1}^{n} \beta_i X_i + u$$

The variable Z_i captures the input prices, while X_i captures all other firm characteristics that can affect firm's output such as its size, ownership type, and certain business constraints. SEZ is a dummy variable which indicates if a firm is located within an SEZ or not, with the impact

Estimated Average Treatment Effects

Dependent variable: Log (Sales)	Bangladesh		India		Malaysia	
	ATE[1]	Endogenous ATE[2]	ATE[1]	Endogenous ATE[2]	ATE[1]	Endogenous ATE[2]
SEZ dummy	0.10	-0.24	-0.14**	-0.41**	0.05	0.99**
	(0.10)	(0.20)	(0.03)	(0.06)	(0.10)	(0.48)
Hazard term (test for endogeneity)		0.20*		0.21**		-0.47*
		(0.11)		(0.04)		(0.25)
Log(Wage)	0.18*	0.13**	0.30**	0.28**	0.42**	0.37**
	(0.11)	(0.04)	(0.03)	(0.02)	(0.08)	(0.04)
Log(Raw materials)	0.30**	0.52**	0.51**	0.58**	0.52**	0.35**
	(0.1)	(0.02)	(0.02)	(0.01)	(0.09)	(0.02)
Log(Utilities)	0.15	0.14**	0.16**	0.14**	0.08**	0.07**
	(0.13)	(0.03)	(0.02)	(0.01)	(0.04)	(0.02)
Log(Rental costs)	0.15*	0.09**	0.007	0.0004	0.04	0.04**
	(0.08)	(0.03)	(0.02)	(0.01)	(0.02)	(0.02)
Log(Other costs)	0.29**	0.08**	0.04	0.02**	0.03	0.08**
	(0.09)	(0.02)	(0.02)	(0.01)	(0.03)	(0.02)
Access to electricity dummy	0.69**	-0.17	0.08	-0.003	0.26*	0.09
	(0.30)	(0.17)	(0.06)	(0.03)	(0.14)	(0.06)
Access to telecom dummy	0.36**	0.02	-0.05	0.02	-0.38**	-0.04
	(0.21)	(0.07)	(0.07)	(0.03)	(0.14)	(0.07)
Firm size - medium	-0.02	0.18**	0.06	0.02	-0.04	0.05
	(0.30)	(0.09)	(0.05)	(0.03)	(0.20)	(0.08)
Firm size - large	0.16	0.30**	0.06	0.05	-0.22	0.25**
	(0.37)	(0.13)	(0.10)	(0.06)	(0.26)	(0.11)
Share of foreign ownership	-0.0009	0.003	-0.0002	-0.002	0.001	0.001
	(0.002)	(0.003)	(0.0006)	(0.002)	(0.001)	(0.001)
Sample size	385	385	1318	1318	613	613

ATE = average treatment effects. **= significant at 5%; *= significant at 10%. Standard errors in parentheses.
[1] Results displayed are for firms within SEZ.
[2] Regional dummies were used as instrumental variable (IV) for self-selection (i.e. endogeneity from choosing to locate within SEZ).
Source: ADB calculations using data from World Bank Enterprise Survey.

---

[1] We use the WBES data for Malaysia, Bangladesh, and India for the manufacturing sector held in 2006, 2013, and 2014, respectively. For Bangladesh and India, we tag a firm as SEZ if it is located either within an export processing zone or an industrial park. For Malaysia, we tag a firm as SEZ if it receives any two of the following incentives: (i) benefits from double deduction for promotion of exports; (ii) tax exemption on value of increased exports; (iii) double deduction of export credit insurance premiums; and (iv) industrial building allowance.
[2] See D.B. Rubin. 1974. Estimating Causal Effects of Treatments in Randomized and Non-randomized Studies. *Journal of Educational Psychology*. 66 (5). pp. 688–701.

of SEZ as a policy tool on the firm's output measured by δ_i. In social sciences, we can only observe the outcome of one treatment for each individual and not for both treatments, which prevents us from measuring individual-level outcomes before and after the introduction of policy.[3] Measuring the difference between the treatment and control groups by ordinary least squares (OLS) takes only the average of the observed posttreatment outcome, yielding inconsistent estimates. We should correct for such missing pretreatment outcomes, which can be done using average treatment effects (ATE) regression.[4] To correct for endogeneity of the SEZ, the equation above is augmented similar to Heckman's specification to correct for sample selection. If the parameter associated with the endogeneity of the SEZ is nonzero, then using either OLS or ATE can yield biased estimates. Model estimation results show divergent performance of SEZ firms relative to their non-SEZ counterparts among the three countries included in the analysis.

Measured by firm level output, exports, and productivity, SEZs in some countries have clear, positive impact while in other countries, the impact is not so positive or is even negative **(Box table)**. In Bangladesh, SEZs have no significant impact for both exogenous and endogenous ATE models. For Malaysia, the SEZ dummy is significant and positive for the endogenous ATE model. Results show that those operating within SEZs produce roughly twice as much as their non-SEZ counterparts in Malaysia. For India, we cannot rule out endogeneity since the hazard term for endogenous ATE is significant. Under the endogenous ATE model, SEZ firms' output is lower than that of non-SEZ firms.

SEZ firms in India also show lower labor productivity (proxied by sales-to-employment ratio). SEZs have no impact on productivity for both Bangladesh and Malaysia. We further test if SEZ firms export significantly higher percentage of their outputs relative to non-SEZ firms. Based on the endogenous ATE regression, the results are similar as with the model using labor productivity.

1: Firm Perception Obstacles to Operations
(% of total firm respondents)

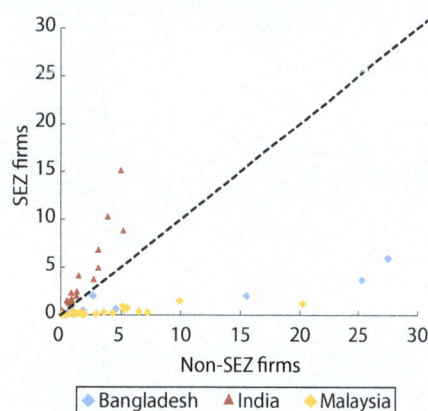

Note: Based on firm respondent rating of factors affecting business operation as major obstacle to operation.
Source: ADB calculations using data from World Bank Enterprise Survey.

The analysis points to the fact that firm level performances in SEZs are diverse across countries. Given diverse historical context of SEZ development and economic and social conditions, this divergence is quite plausible. To shed some light on these issues, we further analyze the information contained in the survey data. In terms of cost of operations, it seems that there is no statistical difference between non-SEZ and SEZ firms for all three economies. However, divergence across countries was found in firms' perception on the different obstacles to their operations **(Box figures 1, 2)**. Based on WBES, 36% of total SEZ firms in Bangladesh point to political instability as the major obstacle in business followed by electricity (22% of SEZ firms), and inadequately educated workforce (12% of SEZ firms). For both India and Malaysia, governance-related and tax issues were identified by SEZ and non-SEZ firms as top obstacles to business operations.

---

[3]   In this case, SEZ is the policy.
[4]   This is typically called the counterfactual outcome. That is, what will be the outcome of the treatment group and the control group if the policy is not yet implemented.

Box 7 continued

2: Top 10 Obstacles in Operation (% of firm respondents per location.)

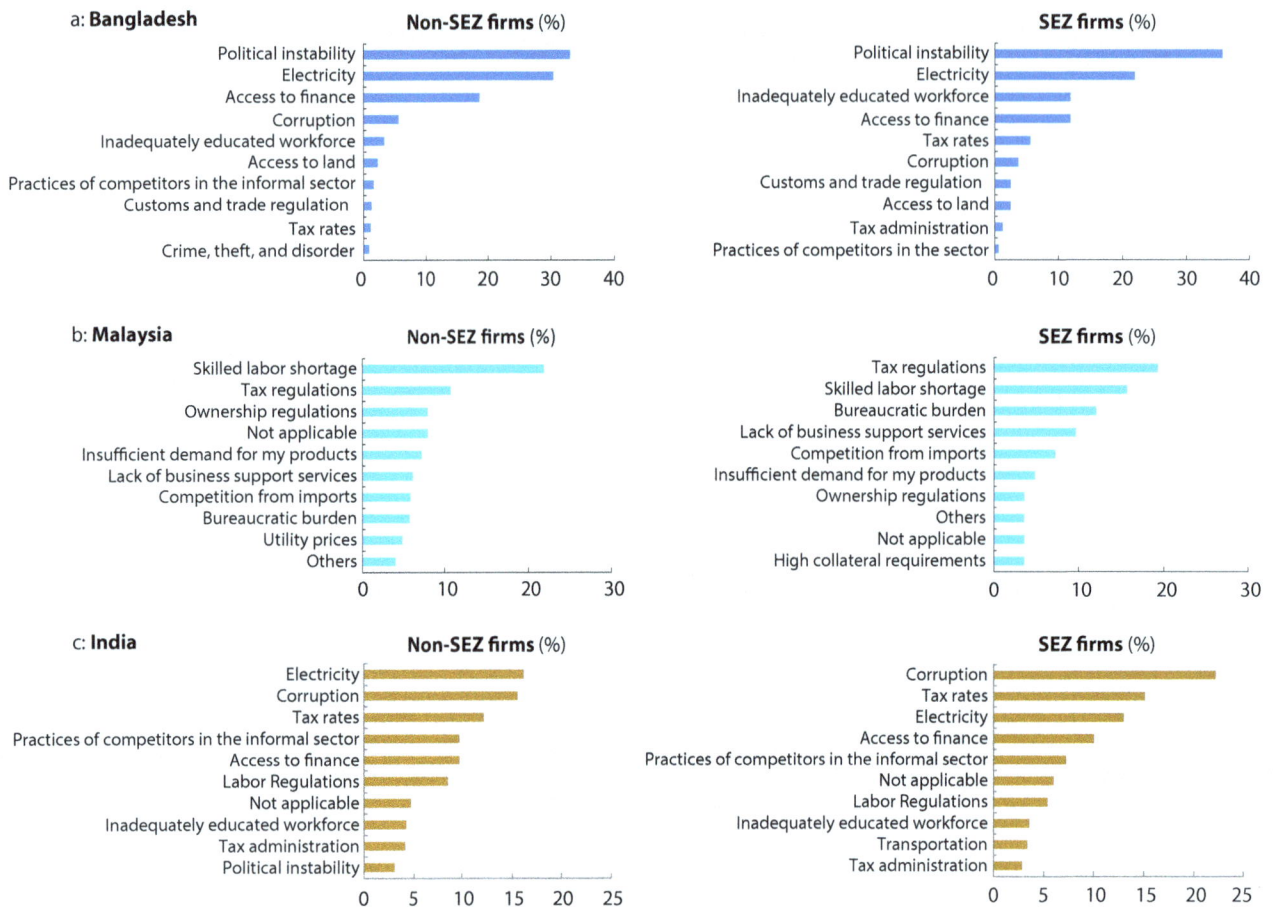

a: Bangladesh

Non-SEZ firms (%)

Political instability	
Electricity	
Access to finance	
Corruption	
Inadequately educated workforce	
Access to land	
Practices of competitors in the informal sector	
Customs and trade regulation	
Tax rates	
Crime, theft, and disorder	

0 10 20 30 40

SEZ firms (%)

Political instability	
Electricity	
Inadequately educated workforce	
Access to finance	
Tax rates	
Corruption	
Customs and trade regulation	
Access to land	
Tax administration	
Practices of competitors in the sector	

0 10 20 30 40

b: Malaysia

Non-SEZ firms (%)

Skilled labor shortage	
Tax regulations	
Ownership regulations	
Not applicable	
Insufficient demand for my products	
Lack of business support services	
Competition from imports	
Bureaucratic burden	
Utility prices	
Others	

0 10 20 30

SEZ firms (%)

Tax regulations	
Skilled labor shortage	
Bureaucratic burden	
Lack of business support services	
Competition from imports	
Insufficient demand for my products	
Ownership regulations	
Others	
Not applicable	
High collateral requirements	

0 10 20 30

c: India

Non-SEZ firms (%)

Electricity	
Corruption	
Tax rates	
Practices of competitors in the informal sector	
Access to finance	
Labor Regulations	
Not applicable	
Inadequately educated workforce	
Tax administration	
Political instability	

0 5 10 15 20 25

SEZ firms (%)

Corruption	
Tax rates	
Electricity	
Access to finance	
Practices of competitors in the informal sector	
Not applicable	
Labor Regulations	
Inadequately educated workforce	
Transportation	
Tax administration	

0 5 10 15 20 25

Note: Based on firm respondent rating of factors affecting business operation as major obstacle to operation.
Source: ADB calculations using data from World Bank Enterprise Survey.

tax payments by firms, and (iv) net profits distributed to local equity shareholders in the EPZ firms. Costs include (i) capital infrastructure cost of the establishment of EPZs and (ii) administrative expenditure for zone operations.

Learning from Experience: Preconditions and Policies

SEZs have a checkered history—a few have matched or exceeded expectations and contributed substantially to economy-wide development. As noted in the previous sections, several SEZs established in the 1970s and the 1980s were well suited for the times and truly catalytic. Others have remained enclaves but nevertheless have been sources of jobs, exports, and GDP growth. Numerous others have failed—and as we close in on the present—successes have become fewer; no SEZ established since the turn of the century has come close to matching the performance of Shenzhen or of the zones set up in Taipei,China and in Malaysia in the 1970s. But hope springs eternal in spite of lengthening odds against the likelihood of a zone returning an adequate return on investment—policy makers continue to pin their hopes on the potentially galvanizing role of zones and, like venture capitalists the world over, believe that one outstanding success will compensate for a dozen failures.

By harvesting a half-century of experience, it is possible to identify a number of preconditions that make it more probable that an SEZ in early stages will in time approach some or all of the desired benchmarks and progress to more advanced stages—irrespective of whether the approach adopted is orthodox, heterodox, or a mixture.

Making SEZs Work: Preconditions

(i)   It is evident that SEZs at every stage should have a clear, coherent, and viable business and economic rationale anchored in local conditions. SEZs must offer investors something significantly better than what is available in the rest of the economy. Marginal improvements will not do. In addition, SEZ development programs should be integrated into the broader economic policy framework and the national investment environment, and be fine-tuned to be consistent with the capacity of the government. SEZ programs should be closely coordinated or linked with wider economic strategies as they evolve, supporting domestic investment in SEZs, and promoting linkages, training, and upgrading along the value chain. At every stage, both the broader development program and the SEZs need clear, consistent, and credible political commitments at the highest levels of government.

(ii) Diagnostic studies should identify a few sectors as growth pillars to be prioritized in SEZ development, promoting specialization and eventually cluster development that jives with an economy's dynamic comparative advantage.

(iii) Individual economies should engage in different approaches depending on policy objectives and development context. The lack of theoretical understanding of policy approaches to SEZs lies at the core of SEZ failure. More often than not, expectations with regard to SEZs are often inflated, objectives are overstated, and strategic planning remains inadequate—resulting in stagnant development, unsustainable growth, or low returns on investment. Using the orthodox approach requires governments to offer attractive fiscal and nonfiscal concessions to firms operating in the zones while shielding them from the wider economy. Economies successfully using this approach at an early stage include Taipei,China and

Malaysia. A heterodox approach to wooing FDI needs to be supported by an attractive platform for MNCs—such as adequate legal and incentive frameworks to promote and protect foreign investments. The Republic of Korea effectively employed this approach and sought to create backward linkages with the domestic economy. The Philippines implemented the same approach with impressive success in attracting FDI and generating trade-related gains.

In contrast, an enclave approach where SEZs are completely separated from the wider economy results in limited success in developing economies in Asia. The commonalities among these economies include (but not limited to) a lack of skilled labor, weak institutional and legal frameworks, limited resources, and inadequate infrastructure, among others. In Central Asia, the SEZ policy in all five economies has not been met with impressive success due to poor investment climates, resource curse, political economy, public sector ownership of SEZs, incoherent zone, and park instruments with policy objectives and inflated vision.

Adopting the agglomeration approach at the initial and evolutionary phase necessitates inherent advantages that attracts more firms and promotes further specialization. Often, successful implementation involves additional strategies such as horizontal expansion and vertical movements and adopting newer innovative SEZ models—as in the PRC. Meanwhile, using the VSI approach requires continuous upgrading of policy and institutional arrangements to promote specialization and technical advancement of domestic firms, including SMEs.

(iv) SEZ progression up the developmental scale needs to be well-timed so as to take advantage of GVC participation, and opportunities such as new FTAs or technological developments affecting outsourcing and transport costs.

(v) Location should be a cost-saving factor—preferably coastal, close to urban centers (which can be a source of agglomeration economies at every stage), and a large consumer market. City-based integrated SEZs help form industrial clusters with social, cultural, educational, technological, business, and related amenities. Inland zones should be well-connected and offer cost-effective transportation. SEZs moving up the development ladder need to assure availability of social services (education, health, and other amenities). Location, objectives, and operation of SEZs should be guided by the quantity and quality of supporting services. In principle, SEZ location should be determined by commercial and economic considerations, which may compromise the regional balance objective. Economies should avoid locating an SEZ in "lagging" or remote regions without due consideration of infrastructure connectivity, availability of labor skills, and supply access during the initial stage. However, balanced economic development should be taken into account for the strategic, logistical positioning over time as the economy matures. Advanced SEZs should be factored into the planning of economic or logistics corridors connecting actual and potential SEZs with markets and regional neighbors—giving impetus to cross-border SEZs and contributing to enhanced regional and subregional cooperation.

If these preconditions are approximately met, an SEZ achieves better footing and with good policies, can become a focus of economic activity.

Making SEZs Work: Policy Regime

(i) A sound policy regime establishes a robust legal and regulatory framework that spells out the rules of the game for all stakeholders and mandates a high degree of transparency and accountability. Ideally, the SEZ authority should enjoy a large measure of autonomy, with a one-stop service for project proposals and outsourcing noncore functions. Involving the private sector financially and managerially, and privileging private zone developers and operators can reinforce this autonomy.

(ii) Land and resource use planning should be prioritized. Rational land use and zoning rules can ensure that longer-term urbanization objectives and those of agricultural production are given due consideration. As many industrial processes are water intensive and a pollution source, aligning zone development with water resource management can minimize water stress and pollution. Good zone design and environmental standards underpin the efficient utilization of scarce resources and contain negative spillovers. Safeguards issues such as household resettlement and environmental protection should be considered during the planning stage.

(iii) SEZs offer a variety of tax and duty exemptions and frequently, competition among zones tend to make these incentives more generous than needed for attracting investment—thereby increasing the fiscal burden. Hence, investment promotion agencies must take care in calibrating the incentive package and should include sunset clauses, so as to enlarge the net gains accruing from SEZ creation. Also, fiscal incentives are usually beneficial at the initial stages of SEZ development. What matters in the long run are the availability and quality of infrastructure and institutional capacity.

(iv) Relatedly, private zones can also be encouraged to reduce the fiscal burden on the government. SEZs have a profit and business objective that encourages private sector development and participation. The entirely privately controlled SEZs are models where the private sector designs, builds, owns, develops, operates, manages and promotes an SEZ with no obligation to transfer it to the government. These models essentially cover Build–Own–Operate (BOO); Build–Develop–Operate (BDO); Design–Construct–Manage–Finance (DCMF); Design–Build–Finance–Operate (DBFO); and Design–Build–Operate–Manage (DBOM) partnerships. SEZs cannot, however, be operated without providing administrative services and customs by the authorities.

(v) In low and lower middle income economies establishing the enclave-type of zones, labor is the key resource; therefore a flexible labor market for unskilled and semi-skilled workers and ease of labor utilization is one of the major attractions—although a too lightly regulated labor market will be prone to abusive practices with workers imperiled by a neglect of safety standards. As economies upgrade to more advanced stages, labor skills can become more important. To draw labor to the zones, providing housing, social services and other amenities can be a major inducement.

(vi) SEZ policy must also address the basic infrastructure requirements of an SEZ—water, power, telecommunications, and transport. Ready and low cost services are a big selling point for the most attractive zones. As many producers in an SEZ export, global connectivity with the help of reliable surface and air transport services can be critical. Increasingly, telecommunications complement transport related ones with good internet access now essential for exporters tied to GVCs.

(vii) SEZ development has proven to be more fruitful when strategically integrated into an economy's overall economic development framework. In other words, an SEZ is more likely to be an effective catalyst when there is an enabling macroeconomic and industrial framework and deepening economic liberalization, economic space planning for optimal land use and cluster development, along with resource use planning utilizing the cost benefit analysis of fiscal and nonfiscal incentives.

Over time, an economy should bring the national investment climate outside SEZ to the same level as the SEZ and, as appropriate, transfer some SEZ privileges to firms outside to enhance profitability. An outward diffusion of technologies from the SEZ needs to be encouraged and domestic firms given access to similar hardware and institutions that will help upgrade skills.

Economies that have not done so should consider shifting from an EPZ to SEZ model, thus eliminating legal restrictions on forward and backward linkages and domestic participation. This should be underpinned by policies supportive of structural change that go beyond the scope of the SEZ program, including: (i) incentivizing skills development, training, technology upgrading, and knowledge sharing; (ii) promoting industry clusters and targeting linkages with economic zone-based firms at the cluster level; (iii) supporting integration with regional value chains; (iv) encouraging public-private coordination and collaboration; and (v) ensuring labor markets are flexible and facilitate the circulation of labor from declining to growing activities.

Furthermore, economies should take advantage of existing industry clusters to develop SEZs rather than the other way around—there are strong historically determined economic, political and social and strategic reasons for the rise of industrial clusters. However, attempts at creating new urban or industrial clusters can be also planned around SEZs—as the PRC has done.

Lastly, using SEZs to further regional cooperation requires several additional initiatives, including: (i) promoting joint ventures at EPZs or SEZs near border crossings as well as cross-border SEZs serving local and regional markets (as in Thailand); (ii) joint ventures that increase the chance of entry into global or regional value chains and boosting value added; (iii) gradual integration of regional economies; and (iv) supporting legal Instruments like signing Investment Promotion and Protection Agreements, Double Taxation Avoidance Agreements and FTAs.

The Future of Zones

The popularity of SEZs remains strong in the second decade of the 21st century in spite of the progress over the past decade in trade liberalization and deregulation, in building institutions and in improving the business environment. EPZs and SEZs were instruments of choice in the latter third of the 20th century for economies with closed and tightly regulated markets and weak institutions. Creating these islands was viewed as a means of exploring the viability of a more open regime and of the institutions needed to make it work. Although many economies are now cognizant of the advantages accruing from deregulation and liberalized trade, they still face opposition from entrenched domestic interests who stand to lose. Hence, policy makers continue to rely on SEZs to bolster development and to test the edge of new initiatives as with the greening of cities and creation of logistics hubs.

Well-designed and managed EPZ-type SEZs are a viable option for low and lower middle-income economies—as in South Asia—which need time to further dismantle trade barriers, other restrictions that cloud the investment climate, and build the institutional scaffolding for industrialization. But many outright SEZ failures and the modest returns of others argue for close attention to the location, design, and management of zones, yoking the establishment of new zones and retaining existing ones to longer term economy-wide policy action. Economies pinning hopes on more advanced zone stages must also consider the global shift toward services. With potential growth forecast to be lower in both advanced and emerging economies, and trade distortions taking a toll, an upturn in merchandise trade appears unlikely in the medium term and an increased focus on services a better bet.[103] Research by Neumark and Kolko (2009) on the US zones suggest those that do better stress marketing and trade facilitation services.

---

[103] World Trade Organization. 2015. Modest trade recovery to continue in 2015 and 2016 following three years of weak expansion. *WTO 2015 Press Releases.* 14 April. https://www.wto.org/english/news_e/pres15_e/pr739_e.htm; S. J. Evenett and J. Fritz. 2015. Crisis-era trade distortions cut LDC export growth 5.5% per year. *Centre for Economic Policy Research's Policy Portal.* 16 June. http://www.voxeu.org/article/crisis-era-trade-distortions-cut-ldc-export-growth-55-year; B. Hoekman, ed. 2015. *The Global Trade Slowdown: A New Normal?* London: CEPR Press.

Until perhaps 2 decades ago, the way forward for a late starting economy was to pursue an export-oriented industrial strategy, starting with the assembly and processing of light manufactures, becoming a part of global production networks with the help of FDI, and gradually diversifying and moving up value chains. For Asia's low and lower middle-income economies, manufacturing might remain the SEZ staple. However, even these economies need to take account of the higher profits to be earned from enlarging the services content of manufactures. This becomes more important as they diversify into more complex and less ubiquitous products and move up the value chain. It is worth noting that FDI in services now accounts for between two-thirds and 70% of investment.[104]

The leading edge of zone development may be in the kinds of entities that are being sponsored by upper middle and advanced economies. They use a mix of public and private initiatives to carve out zones for logistics, financial, knowledge-based, and entertainment services. Zones for services appear to be the wave of the future, mirroring the preponderance of services in GDP and their rising share in trade (Elms and Low 2015). Currently, among Asia's developing economies, only India is a major services exporter (23%)—mainly ICT-based services—and value added by services in exports is also among the highest (51%). The Republic of Korea; the PRC; and Taipei,China all lag behind. Only 14% of the Republic of Korea's exports and 14% of PRC exports are in services; and value added by services in exports is 35% for both economies (Chung 2015). Thus, there is much catching up to do and opportunities to enlarge services exports.

The Republic of Korea's Incheon Free Economic Zone is furnished with multi-modal transport and a suite of amenities, including a golf course. The Songdo ubiquitous city lying within the zone offers an IT-rich environment catering to providers of commercial, medical, educational, and hospitality services. Depending on how well Songdo fares, the Republic of Korea intends to build many more smart and ubiquitous cities. Dalian in the PRC has set up a thriving Software Park and Shanghai is promoting an SEZ that will host an international financial center. Dubai, meanwhile, is a new style SEZ with a port and free zone, an international financial center, an "internet city" and large newly reclaimed areas reserved for housing—mainly for sale to foreigners. The United Kingdom and Japan among others are also on the bandwagon with several zones in the pipeline, and services the primary activity.

The concept of urban development and creation of smart cities will increasingly be an integral part of high-technology and knowledge-based SEZs by combining R&D centers, e-governance, skilled labor and other commercial and recreational centers. Given this changing trend, governments should perceive SEZs not only as a self-contained entity, but also as part of longer-term urban development.

Urban development can also occur through charter cities and special governance zones (SGZs) as proposed by Fuller and Romer (2012) and Wei (1999), respectively. A charter city is a new type of special zone,

---

[104] UNCTAD. 2014. Investing in the SDGs: An Action Plan. *World Investment Report 2014.* Geneva.

one that can serve as an incubator for reform. It extends the concept of an SEZ by increasing its size to city scale and expanding the scope of reforms. During this century of rapid urbanization, charter cities can offer the developing world a choice between several well-run cities, each of which competing to attract residents. This combination of choice and competition is the best strategy for improving the quality of life. A strong argument for charter cities is that urbanization is trending upward in the developing world at a time when the capacity to govern remains in short supply (Fuller and Romer 2014). The potential gains from this strategy are much larger than those from further reducing trade barriers to private goods and services (Clemens 2011, cited by Fuller and Romer 2014).

A related concept is that of the SGZ, as proposed by Wei (1999). An SGZ is a geographically limited area within an economy, in which a comprehensive package of civil service reform, redefined role of government in the economy, enhanced rule of law, and enhanced citizens' voice will take place.[105] At the initial stage, political and fiscal support from the central government and an international organization is crucial. In the long run, the local government in the SGZ will accrue revenues to more than offset the initial cost of the reform.

To a certain extent, an SGZ is similar to an SEZ, but SGZs focus primarily on governance reform, while SEZs are motivated by economic objectives. Another key similarity is that an administrative body using simplified rules and regulations often governs SEZs.

These concepts are perhaps best approximated by the experience of the PRC. At the start of SEZ development in the early 1980s, several top leaders perceived the advantages of reforms despite high uncertainty. Besides fiscal and nonfiscal incentives, the SEZs (especially the comprehensive SEZs and ETDZs) were given greater political and economic autonomy. They had the legislative authority to develop municipal laws and regulations along the basic lines of national laws and regulations, including local tax rates and structures, and to govern and administer zones. At that time, in addition to the PRC's National People's Congress and its Standing Committee, only the provincial-level People's Congress and its Standing Committee had such legislative power. The discretion allowed more freedom in pursuing new policies and development measures deemed necessary to vitalize the economy. At the same time, local governments made great efforts to build a sound business environment. They not only put in place an efficient regulatory and administrative system, but also good infrastructure such as roads, water, electricity, gas, sewers, telecommunications, and ports—in most cases involving heavy government direct investments, especially in the initial stage. These successful SEZs were testing grounds for reforms, pre-selected by virtue of location in coastal regions close to ports with good manpower availability and access to preexisting infrastructure.

Global production networks are becoming increasingly complex with MNCs cutting across industries, dividing their activities more precisely, and searching the globe to find optimum locations for relocating

---

[105]   The actual name could also be "special administrative zone," "clean administration area," and so on, depending on the circumstances of the economy.

production. SEZs that address structural, institutional, and infrastructural bottlenecks—and potentially harness agglomeration economies—not only offer a platform for attracting FDI, but can incentivize firms to take advantage of opportunities and compete on the basis of innovation and learning. When weaved into RCI, SEZs can serve as an effective instrument in further spurring competitiveness and structural transformation by expanding the scope for scale economies and coverage of comparative advantage across regions and borders.

Regional growth initiatives can use SEZs to seed or integrate with domestic industrial clusters, and benefit from local or regional labor markets. This may begin to unlock the potential of zones as catalysts rather than enclaves. By providing strong links to networks that foster horizontal partnerships between SEZs and governments—identifying areas of comparative advantage, economic complementarities and economies of scale—it will be possible to exploit opportunities emerging from international production sharing of MNCs in terms of fragmentation of production value chains and linking to GVCs, cluster development, multimodal transport and logistics, and ICT.

Alongside specifically labeled SEZs, regional economic corridors (REC) have been used as a tool for development. Enhanced trade and transport links centered on SEZ development around economic corridors can facilitate integrated regional trade and development, generating a wider range of economic benefits—including a substantial increase in trade among economies in the region. SEZ development without regional cooperation and the establishment of economic corridors amounts to enclave planning with limited returns that may not always justify the underlying economic and social costs. In the context of GMS, for instance, the development of transport corridors is an integral part of success stories of SEZs (particularly in Viet Nam). However, all potential benefits would accrue to participating economies only through a coordinated strategy that integrates regional trade expansion and growth with SEZ development.

SEZs may also be established to promote industrial clusters as a way to achieve agglomeration. In the PRC, while market forces are usually responsible for initially producing industrial clusters, the government supports or facilitates them in various ways, including setting up an industrial park on the basis of an existing cluster (Zeng 2010). After decades of development, some clusters have begun to grow out of certain SEZs, such as ICT clusters in Zhongguancun (Beijing) and Shenzhen, the electronics and biotech clusters in Pudong (Shanghai), the software cluster in Dalian, and the optoelectronics cluster in Wuhan. The emergence of these clusters actually hinges on SEZ success, which serves as their "greenhouse" and "incubator".

Given how many zones are in play or planned in Asia and across the world, it is vital for economies to ensure they deliver adequate returns. Greater reliance on private developers might be one way of achieving this—because to earn a profit they would try harder to provide a better business climate as well as physical facilities and social milieu (Moberg 2015). In taking the private sector route, governments should support appropriate policy arrangements and basic infrastructure investments.

A second desirable step would be to rigorously evaluate the benefits from zones and determine whether they generate additional activity or merely displace activities that would have occurred in their absence. By designing experiments to effectively conduct this evaluation, instituting a transparent decision-making process, and collecting and making available all relevant data on bids would permit the kind of much-needed assessment but remains lacking even in zones in advanced economies (Overman 2011).[106]

SEZs have enjoyed a long history and by all accounts retain the backing of policy makers the world over. Instead of fading from the scene as economies developed and the initial justification for zones eroded, additional reasons were discovered first for next generation zones that accommodated changing institutional and structural realities. Clearly there are zones for all seasons and economy-wide economic liberalization and institutional strengthening seemingly create new niches. Under these circumstances, a desirable course for governments is to select approaches carefully and spend resources wisely, to evaluate performance with reference to clear criteria, and to be ready to withdraw support from zones that do not make the cut.

[106] H. Overman. 2011. Open evaluation of new enterprise zones stands to increase understanding of the impact of urban policy at little cost. *Spatial Economics Research Centre Blog*. 5 July. http://spatial-economics.blogspot.com/2011/07/open-evaluation-and-future-of-evidence.html

Annex A: Methodology for Coding Data for Regressions

In exploring the economic impact of special economic zones (SEZs) on foreign direct investment (FDI) and exports, we use the method of "dummy coding" which assigns values "1" and "0" to reflect the presence and absence, respectively, of three treatment levels namely—SEZ establishment, SEZ law, and SEZ authority—among specific economies.[107] **Table A1.1** shows the frequency of the values per region across the world.

SEZ establishment[108]

Under this variable, we assign value "1" on the year at which an economy established its first SEZ and successive years until 2014.[109] We assign value "0" for the years preceding SEZ establishment.

Table A1.1: Number of Economies for Each SEZ Variable Used

Region	SEZ Existence		SEZ Law		Independent SEZ Authority		Total
	Without	**With**	**Without**	**With**	**Without**	**With**	
Asia	13	29	3	26	16	13	29
North America	1	1	0	1	0	1	1
Middle East	1	12	4	8	7	5	12
Africa	18	31	4	27	17	14	31
EU	8	18	6	12	15	3	18
Latin America	9	22	3	19	15	7	22
Others	0	6	1	5	4	2	6
Total	**50**	**119**	**21**	**98**	**74**	**45**	**119**

Note:
i) Data on SEZ Dummy is primarily sourced from FIAS 2008 publication on profiles of zone programs. For countries not included in FIAS 2008, data are taken from national sources.
ii) SEZ law and authority data are taken from national sources, country reports from multilateral institutions such as UNCTAD Investment Policy Hub (http://investmentpolicyhub.unctad.org/IPR/Index) and WTO Trade Policy Reviews (https://www.wto.org/english/tratop_e/tpr_e/tp_rep_e.htm#chronologically) and US Department of State Investment Climate Statement 2014 (http://www.state.gov/e/eb/rls/othr/ics/2014/index.htm).

[107] List of economies used to analyze SEZ impact on FDI and exports is based on UN Comtrade trade data partner list.

[108] Data is primarily sourced from FIAS (2008) on profiles of zone programs. For economies not included in FIAS (2008), data are taken from national sources.

[109] As reported on the profiles of zone programs under FIAS (2008), the term "special economic zone" may refer to free trade zones (FTZ), export processing zones (EPZ), hybrid EPZs, free ports, industrial parks (IP), foreign investment zones (FIZ), and foreign access zones (FAZ).

SEZ law[110]

Under this variable, we assign value "1" on the year at which an economy enacted a law on SEZs and successive years until 2014. The law may be in the form of a presidential decree, ministerial decree, government decree, regulation, council directive (EU), ordinance, proclamation, or act. We assign "0" for the years preceding SEZ law enactment.

SEZ authority[111]

Under this variable, we assign value "1" on the year at which an economy established an independent authority and successive years until 2014. The authority is dedicated toward promotion, regulation, monitoring and development of SEZs. Across economies, SEZ authorities have varying scopes of governance—national, regional, provincial, and city-level. We assign "0" for the following criteria:

(i)   For economies without independent SEZ authority;
(ii) For economies with a nonautonomous SEZ authority which delegate a higher and broader body, such as ministries, departments, councils and commissions, to govern special economic zones;
(iii) For economies with SEZ authority, for years preceding SEZ authority establishment.

---

[110] SEZ law data are taken from national sources and country reports from multilateral institutions such as UNCTAD. Investment Policy Hub. http://investmentpolicyhub.unctad.org/; World Trade Organization. Trade Policy Reviews. https://www.wto.org/english/tratop_e/tpr_e/tpr_e.htm; and US Department of State. Investment Climate Statements 2014. http://www.state.gov/e/eb/rls/othr/ics/2014/

[111] Ibid.

Annex B: Country Case Studies

Case Study of SEZs in Bangladesh

The start of economic zones in Bangladesh was triggered by the loss of many jobs in the jute sector. The government wanted to create jobs and was open to establishing a more liberalized environment for trade and investment. The garment sector appeared to offer the main source of hope for large-scale job creation. However, the issues with land accessibility and administrative and logistical obstacles were a major hindrance to attracting investment (Shakir and Farole 2011). The establishment of export processing zones (EPZs) was coined as an innovative and quick way to deal with the issues while nationwide reforms were slowly unfolding. The Bangladesh Export Processing Zone Authority (BEPZA) was established in 1980 and the first EPZ was built in Chittagong in 1983.

Link to development strategy

SEZ policy in Bangladesh is integrated in the 5-year development plan, medium-term expenditure framework and annual budget. SEZ industries are the backbone of policy for the industry or manufacturing sector centered on garments, leather and shoes and electronics. SEZ development is closely aligned with economic corridor policy (transport, port, logistics and trade facilitation). The link with urban development strategy is weak though more important—EPZs are located in the vicinity or inside large cities (Dhaka and Chittagong). SEZ development became an integral part of the economy-wide policy agenda driven by economic liberalization, trade reforms, industrialization based on export diversification, flexible exchange rate management, trade and development-oriented inclusive monetary policy, various types of SEZs, various SEZ modalities, fiscal and nonfiscal incentives for industries (especially export-oriented industries), and forward-looking foreign direct investment (FDI) policy and institutional support.

Types of SEZs

Export processing zones. EPZs in Bangladesh are small industrial enclaves **(Table B.1)** with 429 industries in operation, and 128 under implementation. Land availability is a major operational consideration highlighting the importance of rational land use planning in Bangladesh.

Economic Zones. Private sector orientation, diversity of zone types and adherence to modern labor laws give economic zones (EZs) a distinct edge under the 2010 Bill. Four types of EZs are envisaged: (i) EZ for local and foreign nationals, (ii) private EZ for local or expatriate Bangladesh is and foreigners; (iii) government EZ; and (iv) SEZs for specialized industries under private, PPP, or government initiative.

Table B.1: Overview of EPZs—Bangladesh

Name of EPZ (year of establishment)	Area (in acres)	No. of industrial plots	Standard Factory Buildings (m²)	No. of Industries		Average size of plot (m²)	Tariff for plot/ m² (US$)
				In operation	Under implementation		
Chittagong (1983)	453	501	94,680	170	11	2,000	2.20
Dhaka (1993)	356	451	113,422	102	8	2,000	2.20
Comilla (2000)	267	238	61,122	32	33	2,000	2.20
Mongla (1999)	255	190	18,718	17	13	2,000	1.25
Uttara (2001)	214	180	20,478	12	10	2,000	1.25
Ishwardi (2001)	309	290	20,420	15	12	2,000	1.25
Adamjee (2006)	245	229	56,196	40	23	2,000	2.20
Karnaphuli (2006)	209	255	44,455	41	18	2,000	2.20
Total	**2,308**	**2,334**	**425,070**	**429**	**128**		

EPZ= export processing zone.
Source: Bangladesh Economic Processing Zone Authority. http://www.epzbangladesh.org.bd/

Bangladesh Small and Cottage Industries Corporation (BSCIC). BSCIC was established in 1957 by an Act of Parliament focusing on development of industrial estates or parks for all kinds of industries containing all infrastructure facilities like water, electricity, gas, road and other services. Presently, there are 74 of these industrial estates with 10,399 plots (9,837 allotted for 5,745 industries) developed and managed by BSCIC.

Success outcomes

Employment. Employment has grown rapidly, from less than a thousand in early 1980s to about three million by 2012–2013. The average annual rate of growth of employment in EPZ over 1983-1984 to 2012-2013 was 21.7% but from a low base. Looking at 1995–1996 to 2010, EPZ employment grew 12.0% annually, almost 2.5 times manufacturing (3.6%). The share of women is 64%, 39.3% share in manufacturing as a whole.[112] The high women share in EPZ employment is attributable to the primacy of garment manufacturing in EPZs. (Murayama and Yokota 2009).

Skill Development, Skill Transfer and Labor Mobility. Skill transfer occurs as workers move in and out of a job. The process is dynamic and triggers demand-pull and supply-push in the labor market. Both extend their influence from the factory floor to the village home attracting men and women alike, turning women workers from rural areas into factory labor connected to the global consumer.

Domestic and Foreign Investments. Cumulative investment in EPZs is modest though the trend is upward with some fluctuation **(Figures B.1, B.2)**. Chittagong and Dhaka are considered most attractive in terms of

Figure B.1: Cumulative Investment in EPZs, By Region—Bangladesh
($ million, 2013)

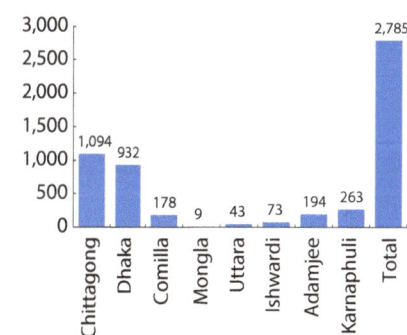

EPZ = export processing zone.
Source: Bangladesh Economic Processing Zone Authority.

Figure B.2: EPZ Investment in Bangladesh ($ million)

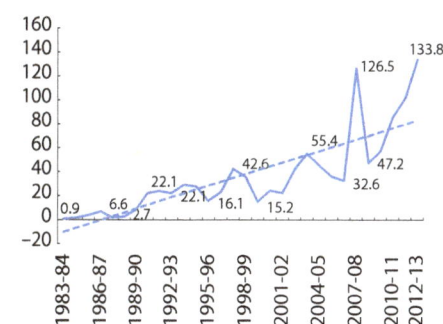

EPZ = export processing zone.
Source: Bangladesh Economic Processing Zone Authority. http://www.epzbangladesh.org.bd/bepza.php?id=about_bepza

---

112   Scribd. 2010. A Case Study on the Export Processing Zones (EPZs) of Bangladesh. http://www.scribd.com/doc/25036973/EPZ-Bangladesh

Figure B.3: EPZ and Garments Exports—Bangladesh (% of total)

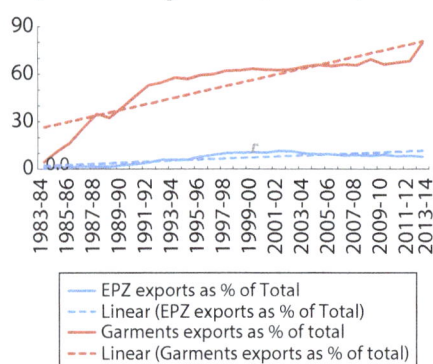

EPZ exports as % of Total
Linear (EPZ exports as % of Total)
Garments exports as % of total
Linear (Garments exports as % of total)

Source: Bangladesh Economic Processing Zone Authority.

Figure B.4: Trend of Labor Productivity in Exports from EPZ—Bangladesh

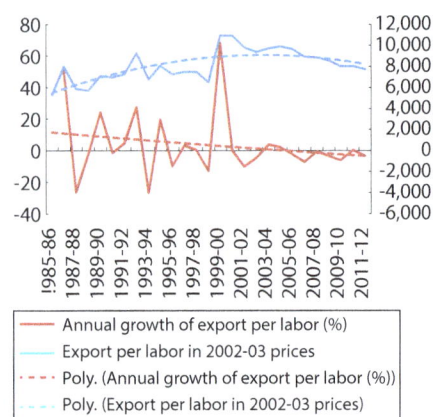

Annual growth of export per labor (%)
Export per labor in 2002-03 prices
Poly. (Annual growth of export per labor (%))
Poly. (Export per labor in 2002-03 prices)

Source: Bangladesh Economic Processing Zone Authority.

location, environment and connectivity as well as support infrastructure. Mongla is an enigma as to why investment is so low despite being located close to the port.

Exports. Ready-made garments (RMG) and leather have boosted Bangladeshi exports in recent years. This has been aided by exports from EPZs **(Figure B.3)**. Over the period 1983-1984 to 2012-2013 EPZ exports grew the fastest (38.67% per annum) as compared with garments (24.95%) and total exports (12.80%).

Labor Productivity. The growth of EPZs and export-oriented industries, boosted both the level and growth of productivity though growth has slowed in recent years **(Figure B.4)**. The higher productivity in EPZs is attributed largely to capital intensity, technology, production processes, management quality and skill level of workers.

Structural Transformation. While the structural transformation of Bangladesh was triggered by EPZs, it was linked to a rural transformation, as the share of agriculture in rural GDP declined and household sources of income became more diversified with remittances and employment in services gaining significance (Ahmed 2014). The transformation process has been manifested in rapid urbanization (from 8% in 1970 to 31% in 2010) increased trade openness from 19% in 1972 to 47% in 2013 (Wahab and Uddin 2014), reduced share of agriculture in GDP (from 30% in 1990 to 16.3% in 2013) and increased share of industry (from 21% in 1990 to 28% in 2013). This growth model now seems to have reached its limit with caps on labor, capital and productivity approaching. There are clear signs that factor productivity growth has decelerated (Chatterjee and Alamgir 2014) and so has total factor productivity (TFP) attributable to technological progress.

Challenges. Bangladesh faces the challenge of diversifying its export base. Almost three-fourths of Bangladesh's EPZ exports and 90% of employment still come from garments, garment accessories and textiles. In addition, most employment, FDI, and exports from the zones are concentrated in Dhaka and Chittagong SEZs. Bangladesh also relies on low-cost labor to attract FDI and by lowering labor standards that threaten EPZ sustainability when wages rise. There is a need to promote greater private sector development and management in the zone program.

Case Study of SEZs in Cambodia

The Cambodian government's purpose in establishing SEZs was to diversify the industrial base beyond electronics, to establish economic linkages between urban and rural areas and to promote industrial investment outside Phnom Penh (World Bank 2012).

The legal framework for SEZs was established by a government sub-decree issued in late 2005. The first SEZ was created in 2006 and by 2014, there were nine zones operating in the economy, with a further 20

Table B.2: SEZs in Cambodia (2014)

Location	Name of SEZ	Year Established	Number of firms operating	Total employment	Employees per firm (average)
Phnom Penh	Phnom Penh SEZ	2008	50	17,000	340
Bavet	Manhattan SEZ	2006	26	28,051	1,079
	Tai Seng Bavet SEZ	2007	17	7,968	469
	Dragon King SEZ	2013	2	280	140
Sihanoukville	Sihanoukville SEZ 1	2009	2	424	212
	Sihanoukville SEZ 2	2008	40	8,967	224
	Sihanoukville Port SEZ	2012	2	416	208
Poi Pet	Poi Pet O'Neang SEZ	2011	2	830	415
Koh Kong	Neang Kok Koh Kong SEZ	2005	4	3,953	988
Total	All Cambodian SEZs	2005	145	67,889	468

SEZ = special economic zone.
Source: Council for the Development of Cambodia (CDC), Government of Cambodia.

authorized to begin operations. Cambodia's SEZs are small and almost entirely privately-owned and managed **(Table B.2)**.[113] This has minimized the large and sometimes wasteful public sector set-up costs associated with SEZ establishment in many other economies. To establish an SEZ, an operator needs at least 50 hectares (124 acres) of land and must establish the roads, electricity and water supply to service prospective firms. SEZs have attracted significant FDI into Cambodia that would not have been present otherwise.

Outside SEZs, garment firms heavily dominate Cambodia's manufacturing sector. This is less true inside SEZs, where the industrial base is more diversified, including a higher proportion of firms producing electronics, electrical products and household furnishings than are found outside the zones. This reduces the vulnerability of Cambodia's industry to a downturn of the global garment industry.

Success outcome

Employment. As a low-income economy, Cambodia is in the initial stage of SEZ development, with employment the primary objective. Total employment in all of Cambodia's SEZs is around 68,000 (see Table B.2). The SEZs represent just under 1% of total employment and 3.7% of total secondary industry employment. By comparison, Cambodia's garments sector mostly outside the SEZs reportedly accounts for about 600,000 employees, about 38% of total secondary industry employment, or 10 times the size of all SEZs combined. At least 95% of production workers employed in the SEZs are women.

---

[113] A partial exception is the small Sihanoukville Port SEZ, which is a public-private joint venture financed by a Japan International Cooperation Agency (JICA) loan.

Figure B.5: Nominal and Real Wages—Cambodia (riel, thousands)

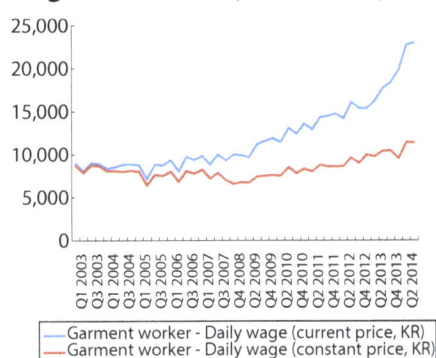

Note: This survey of 120 garment workers is conducted every quarter, except in 2008 q1-q2-q3.
Source: *Vulnerable Worker Survey*, Cambodia Development Resource Institute, Phnom Penh.

Drivers of SEZ performance

Labor Costs. Labor costs are low in Cambodia and this is why firms were initially attracted to the SEZs, together with, in some cases, favorable tariff treatment in the EU and the US for goods produced in Cambodia. Although employment conditions in SEZs seem relatively good, wages paid seldom exceed the legal minimum—currently $100 per month and average total wage is between $160 and $180 per month. Wages in Cambodia's garments sector, a good guide to those paid in the SEZs, are summarized in **Figure B.5**. Real wages have risen in recent years and it is possible, though not at all certain, that the era of cheap labor in Cambodia may be approaching its end, implying rising wages.

Labor Quality and Availability. An ADB survey of SEZ firms found that workers can reach satisfactory levels of productivity but require higher levels of training and longer periods of adjustment to achieve these levels than workers in neighboring Thailand and Viet Nam.[114] The average standard of literacy is not high and 30% of new employees have apparently never attended school and cannot read. A World Bank Enterprise Survey in 2012 also noted there were no significant differences in labor productivity or TFP between SEZ and non-SEZ firms in Cambodia, although value-added per unit of output is slightly higher in SEZs.

Access to Infrastructure. SEZ firms are generally unenthusiastic about the quality of public services available to them and the infrastructure provided **(Table B.3)**. Electricity costs are a frequent source of complaint. Firms choosing to locate in the zones are contractually required to purchase electricity from the zone operator, a source of friction between zone proprietors and firms when cheaper sources of power become available from sources outside the SEZ. In the Phnom Penh SEZ, electricity costs $0.20 per kWh, compared with $0.07 in Thailand and Viet Nam. The availability of water seems to score the highest among firms, although in some locations water quality and waste disposal are problems. All firms surveyed in Phnom Penh and Poipet, and a significant number in the others note high logistics costs (see Table B.3).

Governance. Based on the ADB survey, the general experience seems to be that 'one-stop' administrative service does reduce regulatory compliance costs, but not enough to satisfy firm managers. It also notes that the quality of infrastructure, public services, and variability of government policies range from "good" to "average" **(Table B.4)**.

---

[114] This is based on field work in Cambodia in October 2014, in which SEZs were visited in three locations, including one-on-one interviews with firms operating in various SEZs as well as managers or operators of the SEZs themselves, followed by a questionnaire-based survey of firms operating within Cambodia's SEZs, conducted in October and November of 2014.The ADB team visited 11 SEZ firms—Phnom Penh (3 firms), Bavet (4 firms) and Sihanoukville (4 firms)—in addition to SEZ administrators in each of these locations.

Table B.3: Firm Assessment: Basic Infrastructure, Transport Cost, and Logistics—Cambodia

Location/Industry	Water	Telecommunications	Electricity	Average transport cost per container to port (US$)	Major logistics difficulty		
					High cost	Uncertainty in delivery dates	Lack of multimodal connectivity
Phnom Penh	1.36	2.27	1.82	1500	100	0	0
Bavet	1.90	2.06	2.72	503	78	11	0
Sihanoukville	1.82	2.21	2.29	500	46	11	11
Poipet	2.00	3.00	3.00	250	100	0	0
Footwear	1.70	1.60	2.10	489	57	0	0
Garments	1.90	2.10	2.60	599	64	7	0
Home furnishings	1.60	2.60	2.20	743	71	7	21
Light machinery	1.90	2.30	2.30	738	71	14	0
Luggage and bags	2.00	2.00	2.40	338	80	0	0
Other light mfg.	1.70	2.30	2.40	544	55	18	0
All respondent firms	1.76	2.19	2.35	614	66	9	5

For basic infrastructure: 1 = Good, 2 = Average, 3 = Poor.
For transport cost and logistics problems: Major logistics difficulties may not add to 100 when other problems were mentioned.
Source: *Survey of SEZ Firms,* (October–November 2014), ADB.

Table B.4: Firm Assessment of Overall Business Environment—Cambodia

Location/Industry	Quality of infrastructure	Quality of public services	Variability of government policies
Phnom Penh	2.6	2.7	2.3
Bavet	2.9	3.1	2.1
Sihanoukville	2.3	2.6	1.9
Poipet	3.0	3.0	2.0
Footwear	2.4	2.6	1.7
Garments	2.6	2.9	1.9
Home furnishings	2.3	2.8	2.2
Light machinery	2.9	2.7	1.9
Luggage and bags	2.4	2.2	1.4
Other light mfg.	2.8	3.0	2.5
All respondent firms	2.6	2.8	2.0

Quality of infrastructure and quality of public services: 1 = Very good, 2 = Good, 3 = Average, 4 = Poor, 5 = Very poor.
Variability of government policies: 1 = Very high, 2 = High, 3 = Average, 4 = Low, 5 = Very low.
Source: *Survey of SEZ Firms,* (October–November 2014), ADB.

Case Study of SEZs in the PRC

Over the past half century, one of the most prominent aspects of PRC economic development has been the establishment and development of SEZs, which have successfully helped the PRC reform its economic system toward market development, realize the industrialization process from a weak economic base, and open itself to the world. The development of SEZs originated from the requirement of economic development after the political unrest during 1950s, when there were two major constraints for developing a modern economy:

(i) *Absence of a market system in socialist institutional building.* Because a market system was seen as incompatible with socialism, from 1978 to 1982 there was a long-drawn, convoluted process of recognizing the importance of the markets in a modern economy and institutionalizing SEZs. SEZs were first referred to as special export zones in 1979. After lengthy discussions, SEZs were promoted by Deng Xiaoping in 1980 with the purpose of using "special" to underline their role in exploring the viability of market institutions and using "economic" to emphasize that the objective of the SEZs was to bolster the economy without affecting the political system.

(ii) *Lack of capital to develop a modern economy.* Many developing economies, including the PRC during 1980s–1990s, were constrained by the scarcity of capital. As specially entitled areas, SEZs were expected to offer firms better protection of their property rights and thereby induce much-needed FDI.

Figure B.6: Evolution of SEZs and Theoretical Approaches

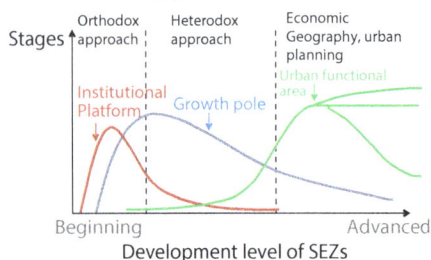

SEZ = special economic zone.
Source: Yang (2015).

Therefore, SEZs became one of the most powerful tools employed by policy makers to implement experimental new policy initiatives, and introduce new industries into the economy. Since the 1980s, SEZs have undergone three key stages: (i) as a new institutional platform, (ii) as a new economic growth pole, and (iii) as a vehicle for rethinking the functions of urban space **(Figure B.6)**. Through this evolution, SEZs have assisted in easing capital and institutional constraints and have enabled the PRC to connect to the global economy, develop new types of economic sectors, and to make a start at urban planning for the purposes of sustainable development.

There are variants of SEZs in the PRC. SEZs became a multilevel concept in the PRC institutional and geographical context. Because of limited resources for investment and constrained scope for policy experiments, the park-oriented concept became a major concern, and often meshed within city and regional concepts. Among others, economic and technological development zones (ETDZs) and first high-technology development zones (HTDZs) are the most important types, as industrial production and technological innovation are crucial for economic development. These two types of SEZs are widely seen in PRC cities with bounded geographical areas, to facilitate certain kinds of management or procedures.

Success Outcomes

Powerhouse of Institutional Reform. SEZs have served as drivers of the PRC policy reform and as areas to demonstrate effects of new policy measures. In particular, they facilitate the institutional decentralization process as the nexus of macro and micro economic policies. Within a limited geographical area and with the benefit of a clear goals, SEZs allow local governments to undertake new policy initiatives and deal with stakeholders in the globalization and marketization processes. They also actively promote the continuing transition from the planning system to a largely market-based economy. The management system in SEZs is relatively more efficient and transparent than the rest of the city, necessary for firms to conduct business.

Driving Economic Development. A huge amount of industrial goods are produced in SEZs, for example, 19% of the total manufacturing GDP produced in national-level ETDZs (NETDZs) in 2012, and 14% in national-level HTDZs (NHTDZs) in 2011 alone **(Figure B.7 and B.8)**. NETDZs and NHTDZs significantly create employment at a compound annual growth rate (CAGR) of 25% and 14%, respectively, during 2006 to 2012, and with production productivity three times that of the PRC as a whole. Moreover, FDI is highly concentrated in SEZs; nearly half of total FDI in the PRC was attracted by NETDZs in 2012, with CAGR at 24%, much higher than the 10% growth for the economy. Further, NHTDZs and NETDZs each shared 14% to 19% of total PRC exports from 2006 to 2012 **(Figure B.9)**.

A Magnet for Urbanization. SEZ-based industrial and urban development has become one of the main modes of urban development. The economic success also greatly sped up urbanization in the PRC. The hot spots for SEZs and fast-urbanized areas are geographically overlapped;

Figure B.8. Industrial Output Value Added, by Ownership in NHTDZs— PRC (RMB billion)

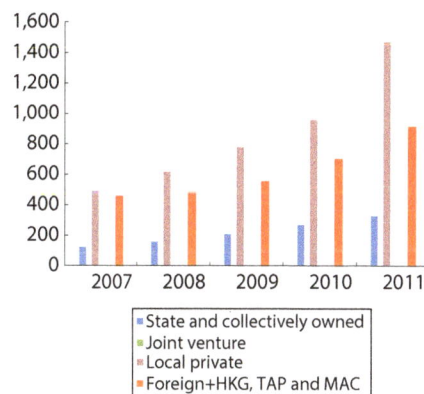

PRC = People's Republic of China; HKG = Hong Kong, China; MAC = Macau, China; NHTDZ = National High-Tech Development Zone; TAP = Taipei,China. Source: [the People's Republic of] China Science and Technology Statistical Yearbook 2008-2012, [the People's Republic of] China Development Zone Statistic Yearbook, 2008-2013.

Figure B.9. Export value form NETDZs and NHTDZs—PRC ($ billion)

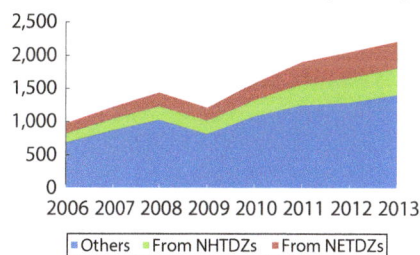

PRC = People's Republic of China, NHTDZ = National High-Tech Development Zone, NETDZ = National Economic and Technology Development Zone. Source: [the People's Republic of] China Science and Technology Statistical Yearbook 2008-2012, [the People's Republic of] China Development Zone Statistic Yearbook, 2008-2013.

Figure B.7: Productivity of NETDZs and NHTDZs—PRC
(RMB per capita)

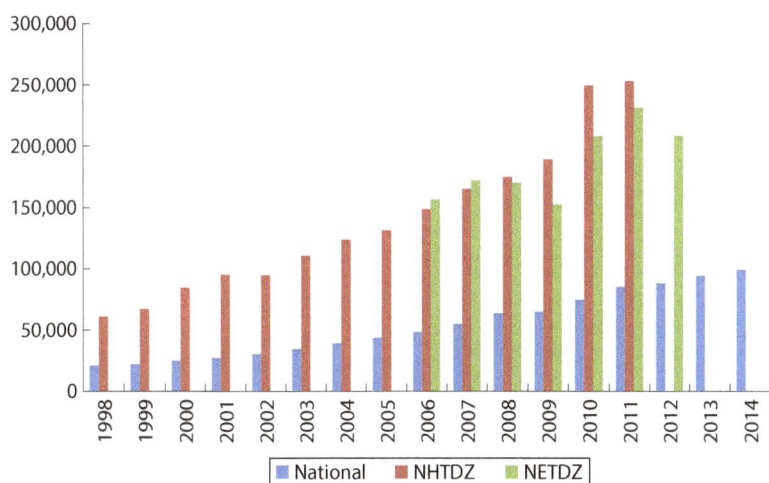

PRC = People's Republic of China, NHTDZ = National High-Tech Development Zone, NETDZ = National Economic and Technology Development Zone. Data for NHTDZ and NETDZ for 2013-2014 not available.
Source: [The People's Republic of] China Science and Technology Statistical Yearbook 2008-2012, [the People's Republic of] China Development Zone Statistic Yearbook, 2008-2013.

most lie in areas in the east coast region. In city spaces, SEZs play a large role in the dynamics of urban space, driving urban expansion and restructuring urban structure, followed by new business opportunities, as well as residential and commercial development.

Drivers of SEZ performance

Institution Building. In general, supportive governance, the right location and investment on infrastructure are the primary factors for SEZs. Various policy incentives also play a key role in developing SEZs, especially in creating the concentration of firms, which reduces marginal costs and improves profitability. The main policy incentives include:

(i) *Reduction or waiver of tax and land rental.* In general, most SEZs give reductions on business tax and land rental charge to attract more firms.
(ii) *Income tax and property tax.* Some SEZs may further reduce the cost of operation for enterprises by reducing property tax, vehicle license tax, education surtax, urban maintenance and construction tax, and local overheads. More importantly, SEZs offer reductions or waivers of tax to people with managerial and technical expertise.
(iii) *Providing a financial platform.* Financial markets have developed relatively slowly in the PRC. In order to remove this constraint, SEZs facilitate the financing of firms. Existing methods include subsidized loans from the development bank especially to SMEs and encouraging ventures, equity, and bond financing of industries that are prioritized by the SEZ.

Subsidies and Facilitation. Infrastructure building subsidies enhance the supply of key services and reduce costs incurred by firms. In addition, SEZs provide investment analysis and facilitation, including collecting market information, helping project management, assigning technical consultants, and holding workshops and training for both employees and employers.

Connection with Host Cities. From the perspective of urbanization, the region and the city are important for the growth of SEZs because cost-savings and benefits of its economic operations are associated with the city or region. This is due to the large size of the potential market, the level of city construction, intermediate goods and services, extensive knowledge spillovers, and a large labor pool. The availability of utilities such as water, electricity, gas, and the urban environment is equally important—their absence can act as constraining factor for SEZs.

The other important aspect is the way SEZs connect with the host city. Experience shows that location is important as it largely determines how the development of SEZs can benefit from the city, including convenient infrastructure, facilities, and even target customers. The mean distance of the NETDZs to the urban center is 19 km, while the maximum distance is 86 km. Ninety percent of NETDZs are located within 60 km of an airport, 20 km of a water port, and 44 km of a railway station (if there are ports or stations in the city). These facts indicate the SEZs in the PRC have access to resources, markets, and the infrastructure of the city that positively affects the firm performance (Lu et al. 2015).

Conditions in the Zone. SEZ conditions affect the costs and the operations of firms. A primary issue is that of serviced land. There is a large variance in the land area of SEZs in the PRC, ranging from 4 to 677 square kilometers with an average of 94 square kilometers. A large area is one key characteristic feature of ETDZs plus availability of services such as water, power, heating and energy. Before 2006, the industrial land was obtained through negotiation between the park authorities and developers. After 2006, the central government created a bidding process for industrial land.

Diminishing Preferential Policies and Privileged Status. While SEZs were granted exclusive policies and other privileges in the early years, later on, those preferential policies had spread to many other parts of the PRC. After the economy's accession to the WTO in 1992, these advantages were further diluted. How SEZs can continue to attract investment, especially FDI in an environment of enhanced competition could be a challenge.

Homogeneity Problem. Many SEZs or industrial parks now competing in the same or similar sectors lack conspicuous sector or product differentiation. While a reasonable level of competition is good for innovation and growth, too much competition might lead to a waste of public resources, because almost all zones or parks are government-sponsored. It would be more desirable to concentrate closely related sectors in a few locations where they have the best comparative advantage.

Lessons from the PRC Experiences

Below are recommendations drawn from firm level surveys of (i) Golmud Industrial Park in Qaidam Basin, Qinghai province, (ii) Liyang Park in Jiangsu province and (iii) industrial parks in Beijing, including Zhongguancun Science Park and Beijing Development Area, along with desk analysis.

Institutional design and approaches

Institutional management should be dedicated to the stage where the SEZ is and designed according to its regional and city contexts:

(i) Land usage—Offering free-of-charge land is inadvisable. The quantity and quality of the land provided, and cost to developers, should be in accordance with the size, production, investment, and associated impact of the firm on the zone and host city.
(ii) Incentives to firms or individuals—Fiscal incentives to firms, such as VAT, are useful to newly established firms, in labor-intensive industries, and/or at the relatively lower stream of the industrial chain. Incentives to individuals with specialized skills are important to the competitiveness of technology-intensive firms.

Industrial design and approaches

Industrial design refers to the economic and business scope of the SEZ and its industries, which is prioritized depending on the vision and position of the SEZ.

(i) Specialization vs. diversification—Both approaches have pros and cons. Possibility of cluster formation and horizontal as well as vertical connectivity across firms should affect relative weight between the two.

(ii) Anchoring firms vs. small firms—The SEZ can be developed based on a few large firms or group of small firms. Both have pros and cons, leading to very different trajectories of SEZs. These two types of models are not mutually exclusive and can be complementary to one another in developing SEZs.

(iii) Industrial chains (backward and forward linkages)—It is desirable that the industrial plan of SEZs be designed to encourage the formation of networks with the domestic economy for achieving greater, long-term effects. However, successful SEZs and firms sometimes may not have strong local backward and forward linkages, simply because of the manner in which GVCs have evolved.

(iv) Marketing and promoting—Management offices should actively engage in marketing and promoting the region, zone, park, industrial chain, sectors, and firms because SEZs also compete in the market.

Spatial design and approaches

Spatial planners should work together with economists, especially for coordinated economic and spatial development, as well as for the sustainability of SEZs. It is also necessary to eventually realize that SEZs are an integral part of urban and regional development.

(i) Facilities—The sufficient, reliable provision of facilities, including electricity, water, gas, heating, and road connectivity is very important to operations. Fast and low-cost provision in terms of both money and time should be the key aspect of SEZs.

(ii) Integration into urban and regional plan—The early integration of SEZs into the urban and regional plan is a win-win situation for SEZs, cities and regions.

(iii) Zoning approach—A good zoning plan can lead to the efficient land use in an SEZ.

(iv) Mixed land use—Although most SEZs are dedicated to manufacturing, mixed land use for industrial, living, and recreational functions is desirable for efficient land use and for providing space and an attractive lifestyle to employees.

Last but not least, there are always exceptions to the development of SEZs, simply because SEZs require coordination among several levels of government and are subject to market forces, all of which give rise to significant uncertainties. Good analysis and adaptation with reference to the social norms, culture, and resources available, are helpful to fit the SEZ plan and development into a local context.

References

Acemoglu, D., S. Johnson, and J. A. Robinson. 2004. Institutions as the Fundamental Cause of Long-Run Growth. *National Bureau of Economic Research (NBER) Working Papers.* No. 10481. Cambridge, MA: NBER.

Acemoglu, D. and J. Robinson. 2008. The Role of Institutions in Growth and Development. *Commission on Growth and Development Working Papers.* No. 10. Washington, D.C.: IBRD/The World Bank.

Aggarwal, A. 2004. Export Processing Zones in India: Analysis of the Export Performance. *Indian Council for Research on International Economic Relations (ICRIER) Working Papers.* No. 148. New Delhi: Indian Council for Research on International Economic Relations.

Aggarwal, A. 2005a. Performance of Export Processing Zones: A Comparative Analysis of India, Sri Lanka, and Bangladesh. *ICRIER Working Papers.* No. 155. New Delhi: Indian Council for Research on International Economic Relations.

Aggarwal, A. 2005b. The Influence of Labor Markets on FDI: Some Empirical Explorations in Export-oriented and Domestic Markets Seeking FDI across Indian States. Paper presented in the seminar on India and Globalization in honor of Professor N.S. Siddharthan. New Delhi. http://www.researchgate.net/publication/266354210_The_Influence_of_Labour_Markets_on_FDI__Some_Empirical_Explorations_in_Export_Oriented_and_Domestic_Market_Seeking_FDI_Across_Indian_States

Aggarwal, A. 2010. Economic Impacts of SEZs: Theoretical Approaches and Analysis of Newly Notified SEZs in India. *Munich Personal RePec Archive Paper.* No. 20902. Munich: Munich University Library.

Aggarwal, A. 2012. *Social and Economic Impact of SEZs in India.* India: Oxford University Press.

Aggarwal, A. 2015. Special Economic Zones: A Conceptual Framework for Success Drivers and Development Outcomes. Background paper for the Asian Development Bank for the Asian Economic Integration Report 2015 Special Chapter. Manila. December.

Ahmed, S. 2014. *The Dynamics of Rural Development and Agricultural Wages in Bangladesh.* Dhaka: Policy Research Institute.

Akhtar, M. H. 2003. An Evaluation of Karachi Export Processing Zone: A Preliminary Investigation. *The Pakistan Development Review.* 42 (4); pp. 927-940. Islamabad: Pakistan Institute of Development Economics.

Akyüz, Y., H. J. Chang and R. Kozul—Wright. 1998. New Perspectives on East Asian Development. *The Journal of Development Studies.* 34 (6). pp. 4-36.

Alamgir, M. 2014. Report on SEZ in Bangladesh (Draft). Asian Development Bank.

Aldaba, R.M. 2013. Twenty Years after Philippine Trade Liberalization and Industrialization: What Has Happened and Where Do We Go from Here. *PIDS Discussion Paper.* 2013-21. Manila: Philippines Institute of Development Studies (PIDS).

Alder, S., et al. 2013. The Effect of Economic Reform and Industrial Policy in a Panel of [People's Republic of China] Chinese Cities. *Working Paper Series.* No. 207. Zurich: Center for Institutions, Policy and Culture in the Development Process, University of Zurich.

Amador, J. and F. di Mauro, eds. 2015. *The Age of Global Value Chains: Maps and Policy Issues.* UK: CEPR Press.

Amsden, A. 1989. *Asia's Next Giant: [The Republic of] Korea and Late Industrialization.* New York: Oxford University Press.

Amsden, A. 2001. *The Rise of the Rest: Challenges to the West from Late-Industrializing Economies.* Oxford: Oxford University Press.

Arbatli, E. 2011. Economic Policies and FDI Inflows to Emerging Market Economies. *International Monetary Fund (IMF) Working Papers.* No. 192. Washington, D.C.: IMF.

Asian Development Bank (ADB). 2014a. Economic Zones: Instruments for Regional Production Networks and Supply Chains. Background paper for the Asian Development Bank RCI Roundtable Conference. Manila. 17–18 November.

ADB. 2014b. *Developing Economic Corridors in South Asia.* Manila.

Baissac, C. 2011. Brief History of SEZs and Overview of Policy Debates. In T. Farole, ed. *Special Economic Zones in Africa: Comparing Performance and Learning from Global Experiences.* Washington, D.C.: The World Bank.

Baldwin, R. 2011. Trade And Industrialization After Globalization's 2nd Unbundling: How Building And Joining A Supply Chain Are Different And Why It Matters. *NBER Working Papers.* No. 17716. Cambridge, MA: NBER.

Bangladesh Export Processing Zones Authority. 2013. Annual Report 2011–2012. http://epzbangladesh.org.bd/files/reports/file_1400670187.pdf

Batith, S. 2009. Assessment of Manhattan Special Economic Zone Development in Cambodia. Chiang Rai: School of Management, Mae Fah Luang University. http://www.ibrarian.net/navon/paper/Assessment_of_Manhattan_Special_Economic_Zone_Dev.pdf?paperid=16005351.

Baumgartner, I.K., E.B. Ruiz and M.L. Franco-Garcia. 2013. Analysis of Sustainability Criteria Applicable to Mexican Industrial Parks. http://doc.utwente.nl/90505/1/TG2013_Kreiner_etal.pdf

Chai, Y.T. and O.C. Im. 2009. The Development of Free Industrial Zones: The Malaysian Experience. Manuscript.

Chatterjee, A. and M. Alamgir. 2014. Economic Zones as Instruments for Regional Production Networks and Supply Chain. Background paper for the Asian Development Bank RCI Roundtable Conference. Manila. 17–18 November.

Cheesman, A. 2012. Special Economic Zones & Development: Geography and Linkages in the Indian EOU Scheme. *Bartlett Development Planning Unit Working Papers.* No. 145. London: Development Planning Unit, University College London.

Chen, J. 1993. Social Cost-Benefit Analysis of [the People's Republic of] China's Shenzhen Special Economic Zone. *Development Policy Review.* 11 (3). pp. 261-71. Oxford: Overseas Development Institute.

Chung, S. 2015. [The Republic of] Korea's Participation in Global Value Chains and Policy Implications. *KDI Focus.* No. 59.

Clemens, M.A. 2011. Economics and Emigration: Trillion Dollar Bills on the Sidewalk? *The Journal of Economic Perspectives.* 25 (3). pp. 83–106.

Cling, J.P., M. Razafindrakoto and F. Roubaud. 2007. Export Processing Zones in Madagascar: The Impact of the Dismantling of Clothing Quotas on Employment and Labour Standards. *Institut de Recherche pour le Développement,* DIAL. Paris. http://www.iza.org/conference_files/worldb2007/cling_J3375.pdf

Constantinescu, C., A. Mattoo and M. Ruta. 2014a. Slow Trade. *IMF Finance and Development.* December.

Constantinescu, C., A. Mattoo and M. Ruta. 2014b. The Global Trade Slowdown: Cyclical or Structural? *IMF Working Papers.* No. WP15/6. Washington, D.C.: IMF.

Cresskoff, S. and P. Wlkenhorst. 2009. Implications of WTO Disciplines for SEZs in Developing Countries. *World Bank Policy Research Working Papers.* No. 4892. Washington, D.C.: The World Bank.

Elms, D. and P. Low, eds. 2015. *Global Value Chains in a Changing World.* Geneva: WTO.

Enright, M.J. 2001. Regional Clusters: What We Know and What We Should Know. In J. BrÖcker, D. Dohse, and R. Soltwedel, eds. 2003. *Innovation Clusters and Interregional Competition.* Berlin: Springer-Verlag Berlin Heidelberg.

Evenett, S. J. and J. Fritz. 2015. Crisis-era trade distortions cut LDC export growth 5.5% per year. Centre for Economic Policy Research's Policy Portal. 16 June. http://www.voxeu.org/article/crisis-era-trade-distortions-cut-ldc-export-growth-55-year

Evans P. 1995. *Embedded Autonomy: States and Industrial Transformation.* Princeton: Princeton University Press.

Farole, T. and G. Akinci, eds. 2011. *Special Economic Zones Progress, Emerging Challenges, and Future Directions.* Washington, D.C.: The World Bank.

Farole, T., ed. 2011. *Special Economic Zones in Africa: Comparing Performance and Learning from Global Experiences.* Washington, D.C.: The World Bank.

Fenwick, A. 1984. Evaluating [the People's Republic of] China's Special Economic Zones. *Berkeley Journal of International Law.* 2 (7).

FIAS: 2008. *Special Economic Zones: Performance, Lessons Learned, and Implications for Zone Development.* Washington, D.C.

Fuller, B. and P. Romer. 2012. *Success and the City: How Charter Cities could Transform the Developing World.* Ottawa: Macdonald-Laurier Institute.

Fuller, B. and P. Romer. 2014. Urbanization as Opportunity. *World Bank Policy Research Working Papers.* No. 6874. Washington, D.C.: The World Bank.

Furby, M. 2005. *Evaluating the Malaysian Export Processing Zones with Special Focus on the Electronic Industry.* Master Thesis for the School of Economics and Management. Lund: Lund University.

Gibbon, P., J. Bair, and S. Ponte. 2008. Governing Global Value Chains: An Introduction. *Economy and Society.* 37 (3). pp. 315-338.

GIZ. 2014a. Expert Hearing on Special Economic Zones in a Regional and Global Context—Economic Significant and Impact. Shanghai. 25-26 August.

Memon, A.A. 2010. *Export Processing Zones/Free Trade Zones: Pakistan Perspective.* www.epza.gov.pk/Brief_EPZ_May_2010.docx

GIZ. 2014b. Special Economic Zones in a Regional and Global Context—Economic Significance and Impact. Expert Hearing on Regional Cooperation and Integration in Asia. Shanghai. 25–26 August.

Henderson, J. and R. Phillips. 2007. Unintended Consequences: Social Policy, State Institutions and the 'stalling'of the Malaysian Industrialization Project. *Economy and Society.* 36 (1). pp. 78-102.

Hoekman, B. ed. 2015. *The Global Trade Slowdown: A New Normal?* London: CEPR Press.

Hummels, D. 2007. Transportation Costs and International Trade in the Second Era of Globalization. *Journal of Economic Perspectives.* 21 (3): pp 131-154.

India Brand Equity Foundation (IBEF). Undated. *SEZ's Role in Indian Manufacturing Growth.* http://www.ibef.org/download/SEZs-Role-in-Indian-Manufacturing-Growth.pdf

IMF. 2001. Global Trade Liberalization and the Developing Countries. *IMF Issue Briefs.* 8 November. https://www.imf.org/external/np/exr/ib/2001/110801.htm

IMF. 2013. *Trade and Interconnectedness: The World with Global Value Chains.* http://www.imf.org/external/np/pp/eng/2013/082613.pdf

Jayanthakumaran, K. 2003. Benefit-Cost Appraisals of Export Processing Zones: A Survey of the Literature. *Development Policy Review.* 21 (1): 51–65. Oxford: Overseas Development Institute.

International Monetary Fund (IMF). 2015. World Economic Outlook. Database—WEO Groups and Aggregates Information. https://www.imf.org/external/pubs/ft/weo/2015/02/weodata/groups.htm

Jeong, H-G. 2011. *Reevaluation of SEZ Development in Viet Nam.* http://cid.kdi.re.kr/upload/20110124_9.pdf

Johansson, H. and L. Nilsson. 1997. Export Processing Zones as Catalysts. *World Development.* 25(12). pp. 2115-2128.

Kaplinsky, R. 1993. Export Processing Zones in the Dominican Republic: Transforming Manufactures into Commodities. *World Development.* 21 (11). pp. 1851–1865.

Karunaratne, C., and A. Abayasekara. 2013. Impact of EPZs on Poverty Reduction and Trade Facilitation in Sri Lanka. *ARTNeT Working Paper Series.* No. 134. Bangkok: United Nations Economic and Social Commission for Asia and the Pacific.

Karzhaubayeva, A. 2013. *Special Economic Zones in Kazakhstan.*

Kundra, A. 2000. *The Performance of India's Export Zones: A Comparison with the Chinese Approach.* New Delhi: Sage Publication.

Leong, C.K. 2013. Special Economic Zones and Growth in [the People's Republic of] China and India: An Empirical Investigation. *International Economics & Economic* Policy. 10 (4). pp. 549-567. Berlin: Springer-Verlag Berlin Heidelberg.

Lester, M. 1982. Export Processing Zones and Technology Transfer in Malaysia. *The Journal of the Flagstaff Institute*. 6. pp 1–37.

Li, K. 1995. *The Evolution of Policy behind [Taipei,China]'s Development Success*. Singapore: World Scientific.

Li, Z. 2004. Problems and Solutions of [the People's Republic of] China Development Zones. *[The People's Republic of] China Accounting*. 2. pp. 46–47.

Liu, X. 2006. Innovation Performance and Channels for International Technology Spillovers: Evidence from the [People's Republic of China] High-Tech Industries. *Research Policy*. 36 (3). pp. 355–366.

Lu, Y., Wang, J., and L. Zhu. 2015. Do Place-Based Policies Work? Microlevel Evidence from [the People's Republic of] China's Economic Zones Program. Manuscript.

Moberg, L. 2015. The Political Economy of Special Economic Zones. *Journal of Institutional Economics*. 11 (1). pp. 167-190.

Murayama, M. and N. Yokota. 2009. Revisiting Labour and Gender Issues in Export Processing Zones: Cases of [the Republic of] Korea, Bangladesh and India. *Economic and Political Weekly*. XLIV (22).

Neumark D. and J. Kolko. 2009. Do Some Enterprise Zones Create Jobs? *NBER Working Papers*. No. w15206. Cambridge, MA: NBER.

Nevmatulina, K.A. 2013. Role of Special Economic Zones in Development of the Republic of Kazakhstan. *Middle-East Journal of Scientific Research*. 15 (11). pp. 1528-1532.

Organisation for Economic Co-operation and Development (OECD). 2009. Towards Best Practice Guidelines for the Development of Economic Zones. A Contribution to the Ministerial Conference by Working Group 1. Marrakech. 23 November.

OECD. 2010. Designing Economic Zones for Effective Investment Promotion. Presentation at Working Group 1: Investment Policies and Promotion. Amman. 15-16 February.

OECD. 2013. *Tax and Development: Principles to Enhance the Transparency and Governance of Tax Incentives for Investment in Developing Countries*. http://www.oecd.org/ctp/tax-global/transparency-and-governance-principles.pdf

Overman, H.G. 2011. Open Evaluation of New Enterprise Zones Stands to Increase Understanding of the Impact of Urban Policy at Little Cost. *Spatial Economics Research Centre Blog*. 5 July. http://spatial-economics.blogspot.com/2011/07/open-evaluation-and-future-of-evidence.html

Penang Skills Development Centre. History. http://psdc.org.my/html/default.aspx?ID=9&PID=155

Rasiah, R. 1995. *Foreign Capital and Industrialization in Malaysia*. Basingstoke: Macmillan.

Rasiah R., V. Crinis and H.A. Lee. 2015. Industrialisation and Labour in Malaysia. *Journal of the Asia Pacific Economy.* 20 (1). pp. 77–99.

Rodrik, D. 2015. Premature Decentralization. *NBER Working Papers.* No.20935. Cambridge, MA: NBER.

Rubin, D. 1974. Estimating Causal Effects of Treatments in Randomized and Non-randomized Studies. *Journal of Educational Psychology.* 66 (5). pp. 688–701.

Sarsembayeva, M. 2012. Economic Impact of Special Economic Zones: Is it Positive or not? http://www.slideshare.net/MeruyertSarsembayeva/economic-impact-of-special-economic-zones

Schrank, A. 2001. Export Processing Zones: Free Market Islands or Bridges to Structural Change? *Development Policy Review.* 19 (2). pp. 223–242. Oxford: Overseas Development Institute.

Schrank, A. 2008. Export Processing Zones in the Dominican Republic: Schools or Stopgaps? *World Development.* 36 (8). pp. 1381–1397.

Scribd. 2010. A Case Study on the Export Processing Zones (EPZs) of Bangladesh. http://www.scribd.com/doc/25036973/EPZ-Bangladesh#scribd

Shakir, M.H. and T. Farole. 2011. The Thin End of the Wedge: Unlocking Comparative Advantage through EPZs in Bangladesh. In T. Farole and G. Akinci, eds. 2011. *Special Economic Zones Progress, Emerging Challenges, and Future Directions.* Washington, D.C.: The World Bank.

Shamsie, Y. 2010. Export Processing Zones: The Purported Glimmer in Haiti's Development Murk. *Review of International Political Economy.* 16 (4). pp. 649—672.

Sivalingam, G. 1994. *The Economic and Social Impact of Export Processing Zones: The Case of Malaysia.* Geneva: International Labour Organization.

Spinanger, D. 1984. Objectives and Impact of Economic Activity Zones: Some Evidence from Asia. *Weltwirftschaftliches Archiv.* 120. pp. 64–89.

The Economist. 2015. Special Economic Zones, Not so Special. 4 April.

The Economist. 2015. Special Economic Zones, Political Priority, Economic Gamble. 4 April.

Tyler, W.G. and A.C.A. Negrete. 2009. Economic Growth and Export Processing Zones: An Empirical Analysis of Policies to Cope with Dutch Disease. *World Development.* 18 (2). pp. 220-241.

UNCTAD. Investment Policy Hub. http://investmentpolicyhub.unctad.org

UNCTAD. 2014. *World Investment Report 2014.* Geneva.

US Department of State. Investment Climate Statements 2014. http://www.state.gov/e/eb/rls/othr/ics/2014/

Uulu A.Z. Undated. *Analysis of Free Economic Zones Legislation of [the] Kyrgyz Republic.*

Vaidlamannati, K.C. and H. Khan. 2012. *Race to the Top or Race to the Bottom? Competing for Investment Proposals in Special Economic Zones (SEZs): Evidence from Indian States, 1998–2010.* http://www.uni-heidelberg.de/md/awi/professuren/intwipol/top_bottom.pdf

Varma, A. 2013. Special Economic Zones: Effect of EXIP Policy on SEZ. http://www.slideshare.net/Akvarma25/special-economic-zone-28640506?related=1

Vernon, R. 1966. International Investment and International Trade in the Product Cycle. *Quarterly Journal of Economics*. 80 (2): pp. 190-207.

Viswadia, S. 2013. Economic Zones in India. http://www.slideshare.net/sejvisa/sez-india

Wade, R. 1990. *Governing the Market. Economic Theory and the Role of Government in [Taipei,China]'s Industrialization*. Princeton: Princeton University Press.

Wahab, Md. A. and Md. M. Uddin. 2014. Country Paper: Bangladesh Management of External Sector Openness: Bangladesh Experiences. Paper for the SAARCFINANCE Seminar. Dhaka. 29-30 April.

Wang, J. 2013. The Economic Impact of Special Economic Zones: Evidence from [the People's Republic of China] Municipalities. *Journal of Development Economics*. 101. pp. 133-147.

Warr, P. 1989. Export Processing Zones: The Economics of Enclave Manufacturing. *The World Bank Research Observer*. 9 (1). pp. 65–88.

Warr, P. and J. Menon. 2014. Cambodia's Special Economic Zones. *ADB Economics Working Paper Series*. No. 459. Manila: Asian Development Bank.

Waters, J. 2013. Achieving WTO Compliance for EPZs while Maintaining Economic Competitiveness for Developing Countries. *Duke Law Journal*. 63 (481). pp. 481-524.

Watson, P. 2001. Export Processing Zones: Has Africa Missed the Boat? Not Yet! *Africa Region Working Paper Series*. No. 17. Washington, D.C.: The World Bank.

Wei, S.J. 1999. *Special Governance Zones: A Practical Entry-point for a Winnable Anticorruption Strategy*. Washington, D.C.: Brookings Institution.

Willmore, L. 1995. Export Processing Zones in the Dominican Republic: A Comment on Kaplinsky. *World Development*. 23(3). pp. 529-535. Won, S.O. 1993. Export Processing Zones in the Republic of Korea: Economic Impact and Social Issues. *Multinational Enterprises Programme Working Papers*. No. 75. Geneva: International Labor Organization.

Wong, K.Y. 1987. [The People's Republic of] China's Special Economic Zone Experiment: An Appraisal. *Geografiska Annaler Serices B, Human Geography*. 69 (1). pp. 27–40.

World Bank. 2012. *Cambodia Enterprise Survey 2012*. Washington, D.C.

World Economic Forum. 2012. *The Shifting Geography of Global Value Chains: Implications for Developing Countries and Trade Policy*. http://www3.weforum.org/docs/WEF_GAC_GlobalTradeSystem_Report_2012.pdf

World Trade Organization (WTO). 2008. *WTO Report: Trade in a Globalizing World*. Geneva.

WTO. 2013. *Trade Policy Review*. Viet Nam. https://www.wto.org/english/tratop_e/tpr_e/tp387_e.htm

WTO. Trade Policy Reviews. https://www.wto.org/english/tratop_e/tpr_e/tp_rep_e.htm#chronologically

WTO. 2015. Modest trade recovery to continue in 2015 and 2016 following three years of weak expansion. *WTO 2015 Press Releases.* 14 April. https://www.wto.org/english/news_e/pres15_e/pr739_e.htm

Yang, Z. 2015. Report on SEZs in the People's Republic of China. Background Paper for the *Asian Economic Integration Report 2015* Special Chapter. Manila. December.

Yang, Z., J. Cai, and C. Fu. 2012. Evolution of Cluster Concept for [the People's Republic of China's] Urban Planning and Development. *Urban Planning.* 36 (12). pp. 60–68.

Zeng, D. Z., ed. 2011. Building Engines for Growth and Competitiveness in [the People's Republic of] China. Experience with Special Economic Zones and Industrial Clusters. Directions in Development: Countries and Regions. Washington, D.C.: The World Bank.

Zeng, D.Z. 2011. [The People's Republic of] China's Special Economic Zones and Industrial Clusters: Success and Challenges. *Let's Talk Development.* 27 April. http://blogs.worldbank.org/developmenttalk/china-s-special-economic-zones-and-industrial-clusters-success-and-challenges

Zeng, D.Z. 2015. Global Experience with SEZs: Focus on [The People's Republic of] China and Africa. *World Bank Policy Research Working Papers.* No. 7240. Washington, D.C.: The World Bank.

STATISTICAL APPENDIX

3

Statistical Appendix

T he statistical appendix is comprised of 11 tables that present selected indicators on economic integration covering the 48 regional members of the Asian Development Bank (ADB). The succeeding notes describe the country groupings and the calculation procedures undertaken.

Regional Groupings

- Asia consists of the 48 regional members of ADB.
- Developing Asia refers to Asia excluding Australia, Japan, and New Zealand.
- European Union (EU) consists of Austria, Belgium, Bulgaria, Cyprus, Czech Republic, Denmark, Estonia, Finland, France, Germany, Greece, Hungary, Ireland, Italy, Latvia, Lithuania, Luxembourg, Malta, the Netherlands, Poland, Portugal, Romania, Slovak Republic, Slovenia, Spain, Sweden, and the United Kingdom.

Table Descriptions

Table A1: Regional Integration Indicators—Asia (% of total)

The table provides a summary of regional integration indicators for three areas: trade and investment, capital (equity and bond holdings), and people movement (migration, remittances and tourism); and for Asian subregions, including ASEAN+3 (including Hong Kong, China). Cross-border flows within and across subregions are shown as well as total flows with Asia and the rest of the world. The definition of each indicators are provided in the description below.

Table A2: Trade Share—Asia (% of total trade)

It is calculated as $(t_{ij}/T_{iw})*100$, where t_{ij} is the total trade of economy "i" with economy "j" and T_{iw} is the total trade of economy "i" with the world. A higher share indicates a higher degree of regional trade integration.

Table A3: FTA Status—Asia

It is the number and status of bilateral and plurilateral free trade agreements (FTA) with at least one of the Asian economies as signatory. FTAs only proposed are excluded. It covers FTAs with the following status: **Framework Agreement signed**—the parties initially negotiate the contents of a framework agreement (FA), which serves as a framework for future negotiations; **Negotiations launched**—the parties, through the relevant ministries, declare the official launch of negotiations or set the date for such, or start the first round of negotiations; **Signed but not yet in effect**—parties sign the agreement after negotiations have been completed, however, the agreement has yet to be implemented; and **Signed and in effect**—provisions of FTA come into force, after legislative or executive ratification.

Table A4: Time to Export and Import—Asia (number of days)

Time to export (import) data measures the number of days required to export (import) by ocean transport, including the processing of documents required to complete the transaction. It covers time used for documentation requirements and procedures at customs and other regulatory agencies as well as the time of inland transport between the largest business city and the main port used by traders. Regional aggregates are weighted averages based on total exports or imports.

Table A5: Logistics Performance Index—Asia (% to EU)

Logistics Performance Index (LPI) scores are based on the following dimensions: (i) efficiency of border control and customs process; (ii) transport and trade-related infrastructure; (iii) competitively priced shipments; (iv) ability to track and trace consignments; and (v) timeliness of shipments. Regional aggregates are computed using total trade as weights. A score above (below) 100 means that it is easier (more difficult) to export or import from that economy compared to EU.

Table A6: Cross-Border Equity Holdings Share—Asia
(% of total cross-border equity holdings)

It is calculated as $(E_{ij}/E_{iw})*100$ where E_{ij} is the holding of economy "i" of the equity securities issued by economy "j" and E_{iw} is the holding of economy "i" of the equity securities issued by all economies except those issued in the domestic market. Calculations are based solely on available data in the Coordinated Portfolio Investment Survey (CPIS) database of the International Monetary Fund (IMF). Rest of the World (ROW) includes equity securities issued by international organizations defined in the CPIS database and "unallocated data". A higher share indicates a higher degree of regional integration.

Table A7: Cross-Border Bond Holdings Share—Asia
(% of total cross-border bond holdings)

It is calculated as $(B_{ij}/B_{iw})*100$ where B_{ij} is the holding of economy "i" of the debt securities issued by partner "j" and B_{iw} is the holding of economy "i" of the debt securities issued by all economies except those issued in the domestic market. Calculations are based solely on available data in the CPIS database of the IMF. ROW includes debt securities issued by international organizations defined in the CPIS database and "unallocated data". A higher share indicates a higher degree of regional integration.

Table A8: FDI Inflow Share—Asia (% of total FDI inflows)

It is calculated as $(F_{ij}/F_{iw})*100$ where F_{ij} is the foreign direct investment (FDI) received by economy "i" from economy "j" and F_{iw} is the FDI received by economy "i" from the world. Figures are based on net FDI inflow data. A higher share indicates a higher degree of regional integration.

Table A9: Remittance Inflows Share—Asia
(% of total remittance inflows)

It is calculated as $(R_{ij}/R_{iw})*100$ where R_{ij} is the remittance received by economy "i" from partner "j" and R_{iw} is the remittance received by economy "i" from the world. Remittances refer to the sum of the following: (i) workers' remittances which are recorded as current transfers under the current account of the IMF's Balance of Payments (BOP); (ii) compensation of employees which includes wages, salaries, and other benefits of border, seasonal, and other non-resident workers and which are recorded under the "income" subcategory of the current account; and (iii) migrants' transfers which are reported under capital transfers in the BOP's capital account. Transfers through informal channels are excluded.

Table A10: Outbound Migration Share—Asia
(% of total outbound migrants)

It is calculated as $(M_{ij}/M_{iw})*100$ where M_{ij} is the number migrants of economy "i" residing in economy "j" and M_{iw} is the number of all migrants of economy "i" residing overseas. This definition excludes those traveling abroad on a temporary basis. A higher share indicates a higher degree of regional integration.

Table A11: Outbound Tourism Share—Asia
(% of total outbound tourists)

It is calculated as $(TR_{ij}/TR_{iw})*100$ where TR_{ij} is the number of nationals of economy "i" travelling as tourists in economy "j" and TR_{iw} is the total number of nationals of economy "i" travelling as tourists overseas. A higher share indicates a higher degree of regional integration.

Table A1: Regional Integration Indicators—Asia

	Movement in Trade and Investment		Movement in Capital		People Movement		
	Trade (%)	FDI (%)	Equity Holdings (%)	Bond Holdings (%)	Migration (%)	Tourism (%)	Remittances (%)
	2014	2014	2014	2014	2013	2013	2014
Within Subregions							
ASEAN+3 (including HKG)[1]	45.5 ▼	85.6 ▼	17.9 ▼	13.0 ▲	40.5 ▲	80.2 ▼	33.3 ▲
Central Asia	7.1 ▲	1.0 ▲	0.9 ▲	-	10.5 ▲	35.8 ▲	6.6 ▲
East Asia	35.5 ▼	58.0 ▲	13.6 ▼	9.0 ▲	33.7 ▼	67.4 ▼	35.8 ▼
South Asia	5.2 ▲	0.6 ▼	0.3 ▲	0.5 ▼	29.8 ▼	10.4 ▼	14.8 ▲
Southeast Asia	24.2 ▼	17.7 ▲	7.6 ▼	11.1 ▲	34.6 ▲	71.0 ▲	12.2 ▲
The Pacific and Oceania	7.1 ▲	0.1 ▼	2.0 ▼	2.8 ▼	55.7 ▲	20.2 ▼	30.9 ▲
Across Subregions							
ASEAN+3 (including HKG)[1]	10.7 ▲	5.1 ▲	4.0 ▼	6.5 ▲	8.7 ▼	5.0 ▲	6.8 ▲
Central Asia	29.6 ▼	13.1 ▲	12.0 ▲	13.9 ▼	0.6 ▲	2.8 ▼	0.7 ▼
East Asia	18.2 ▲	7.0 ▼	3.1 ▼	7.6 ▲	15.2 ▲	15.4 ▲	15.1 ▲
South Asia	30.0 ▲	22.5 ▼	7.5 ▼	28.6 ▲	5.8 ▲	32.3 ▲	5.4 ▼
Southeast Asia	44.2 ▲	31.6 ▼	34.5 ▲	23.6 ▲	14.9 ▼	22.4 ▲	13.7 ▼
The Pacific and Oceania	62.3 ▼	32.9 ▲	10.9 ▲	6.9 ▲	8.2 ▲	42.4 ▼	12.9 ▼
TOTAL (within and across subregions)							
Asia	**55.6** ▼	**52.6** ▲	**20.5** ▼	**18.7** ▲	**38.7** ▼	**77.8** ▼	**29.4** ▲
ASEAN+3 (including HKG)[1]	56.2 ▼	90.7 ▼	21.8 ▼	19.5 ▲	49.2 ▲	85.2 ▼	40.1 ▲
Central Asia	36.6 ▲	14.1 ▲	12.9 ▲	13.9 ▼	11.2 ▲	38.5 ▲	7.2 ▲
East Asia	53.7 ▼	65.0 ▲	16.8 ▼	16.6 ▲	48.8 ▲	82.8 ▼	50.9 ▼
South Asia	35.2 ▲	23.1 ▲	7.7 ▼	29.1 ▲	35.6 ▼	42.7 ▲	20.2 ▲
Southeast Asia	68.4 ▲	49.3 ▲	42.1 ▼	34.8 ▲	49.5 ▲	93.4 ▲	25.9 ▲
The Pacific and Oceania	69.4 ▼	33.0 ▼	12.9 ▼	9.7 ▲	63.9 ▲	62.6 ▼	43.8 ▲
With the rest of the world							
Asia	**44.4** ▲	**47.4** ▼	**79.5** ▲	**81.3** ▼	**61.3** ▲	**22.2** ▲	**70.6** ▼
ASEAN+3 (including HKG)[1]	43.8 ▲	9.3 ▲	78.2 ▲	80.5 ▼	50.8 ▼	14.8 ▲	59.9 ▼
Central Asia	63.4 ▲	85.9 ▲	87.1 ▼	86.1 ▲	88.8 ▼	61.5 ▼	92.8 ▼
East Asia	46.3 ▲	35.0 ▼	83.2 ▲	83.4 ▼	51.2 ▲	17.2 ▲	49.1 ▲
South Asia	64.8 ▼	76.9 ▲	92.3 ▲	70.9 ▼	64.4 ▲	57.3 ▲	79.8 ▼
Southeast Asia	31.6 ▼	50.7 ▼	57.9 ▲	65.2 ▼	50.5 ▼	6.6 ▼	74.1 ▼
The Pacific and Oceania	30.6 ▲	67.0 ▲	87.1 ▲	90.3 ▼	36.1 ▼	37.4 ▲	56.2 ▼

▲ = increase from previous period, ▼ = decrease from previous period, – = data unavailable, HKG = Hong Kong, China.

[1] Includes ASEAN (Brunei Darussalam, Cambodia, Indonesia, the Lao People's Democratic Republic, Malaysia, Myanmar, the Philippines, Singapore, Thailand, and Viet Nam) plus the People's Republic of China; Hong Kong, China; Japan; and the Republic of Korea.

Trade—national data unavailable for Bhutan, Kiribati, Nauru, Palau, Timor-Leste, and Tuvalu; no data available on the Cook Islands, the Marshall Islands, and the Federated States of Micronesia.

Equity and Bond holdings—based on investments from Australia; Bangladesh; Hong Kong, China; India; Indonesia; Japan; Kazakhstan; the Republic of Korea; Malaysia; Mongolia; New Zealand; Pakistan; the Philippines; Singapore; Thailand; and Vanuatu. Data unavailable for Azerbaijan, Bhutan, the Federated States of Micronesia, Palau, Samoa, Tonga, Turkmenistan, and Tuvalu. Data start from 2001.

Migration—share of migrant stock to total migrants in 2013 (compared with 2010).

Source: ADB calculations using data from ASEAN Secretariat; *Asia Regional Integration Center,* Asian Development Bank; CEIC; International Monetary Fund; *Direction of Trade Statistics,* International Monetary Fund; Organisation for Economic Co-operation and Development; *Trends in International Migrant Stock,* United Nations Department of Economic and Social Affairs; United Nations Conference on Trade and Development; United Nations World Tourism Organization; and *World Economic Outlook October 2014 Database,* International Monetary Fund.

Table A2: Trade Share—Asia (% of total trade, 2014)

Reporter	Partner					
	Asia	of which		EU	US	ROW
		PRC	Japan			
Central Asia	**36.6**	**21.8**	**1.1**	**29.7**	**2.7**	**30.9**
Armenia	20.0	9.9	1.9	26.6	3.7	49.6
Azerbaijan	20.8	2.1	0.4	46.5	5.4	27.3
Georgia	30.6	7.2	3.2	26.1	4.3	39.0
Kazakhstan	31.5	22.0	1.4	36.2	2.3	30.0
Kyrgyz Republic	69.0	49.7	1.2	5.4	0.7	24.9
Tajikistan	63.1	42.6	0.3	5.6	0.5	30.8
Turkmenistan	52.6	43.8	0.3	10.9	2.3	34.2
Uzbekistan	55.0	21.5	1.0	11.8	1.2	32.0
East Asia	**53.7**	**14.6**	**6.0**	**11.7**	**11.7**	**22.8**
PRC	45.6	0.0	7.2	14.3	12.8	27.3
Hong Kong, China	77.4	50.2	5.3	8.2	7.1	7.2
Japan	53.9	20.4	0.0	9.9	13.6	22.6
Korea, Rep. of	52.8	21.4	7.8	10.4	10.6	26.2
Mongolia	75.9	65.8	3.5	5.2	1.8	17.1
Taipei,China	69.7	29.2	9.5	7.3	9.9	13.1
South Asia	**35.2**	**10.8**	**2.1**	**13.6**	**7.9**	**43.3**
Afghanistan	61.8	5.2	0.4	8.6	10.6	19.0
Bangladesh	46.2	15.2	2.6	21.9	6.9	25.0
Bhutan	–	–	–	–	–	–
India	31.6	9.2	2.0	12.8	8.2	47.4
Maldives	59.1	6.1	1.5	14.0	2.8	24.1
Nepal	91.1	27.1	0.6	3.1	1.3	4.6
Pakistan	42.3	19.9	2.4	14.0	5.8	37.9
Sri Lanka	53.9	12.3	3.8	16.1	9.7	20.3
Southeast Asia	**68.4**	**15.0**	**9.0**	**9.8**	**8.4**	**13.4**
Brunei Darussalam	91.5	12.7	22.8	3.6	3.8	1.0
Cambodia	69.9	14.4	3.5	14.3	10.5	5.3
Indonesia	71.0	13.6	11.3	8.4	7.0	13.6
Lao PDR	90.8	28.8	2.0	3.7	0.5	4.9
Malaysia	70.6	14.3	9.5	9.9	8.1	11.4
Myanmar	94.9	52.3	4.4	2.2	0.4	2.5
Philippines	68.6	14.1	14.8	11.3	11.2	8.8
Singapore	67.1	12.3	4.7	9.9	8.0	15.0
Thailand	63.6	14.0	12.6	9.3	8.5	18.6
Viet Nam	66.0	20.4	9.6	12.8	12.1	9.0
The Pacific	**73.4**	**11.8**	**10.1**	**5.3**	**2.2**	**19.0**
Cook Islands	–	–	–	–	–	–
Fiji	74.0	9.5	3.2	4.9	6.6	14.5
Kiribati	–	–	–	–	–	–
Marshall Islands	–	–	–	–	–	–
Micronesia, Fed. States of	–	–	–	–	–	–
Nauru	–	–	–	–	–	–
Palau	–	–	–	–	–	–
Papua New Guinea	68.6	9.8	11.8	5.5	1.2	24.7
Samoa	73.8	10.4	2.5	1.5	5.1	19.7
Solomon Islands	82.6	40.0	2.0	6.9	1.3	9.3
Timor-Leste	–	–	–	–	–	–
Tonga	85.1	10.2	5.4	3.3	9.5	2.0
Tuvalu	–	–	–	–	–	–
Vanuatu	86.9	25.9	10.7	2.0	3.8	7.3
Oceania	**69.2**	**25.7**	**11.4**	**11.6**	**7.9**	**11.3**
Australia	70.4	27.0	12.3	11.2	7.5	10.9
New Zealand	61.9	18.5	6.3	13.6	10.5	14.1
Asia	**55.6**	**15.0**	**6.5**	**11.8**	**10.4**	**22.2**
Developing Asia	**55.1**	**13.7**	**7.1**	**12.1**	**10.2**	**22.7**

– = unavailable, PRC = People's Republic of China, EU = European Union (27 members), Lao PDR = Lao People's Democratic Republic, US = United States, ROW = rest of the world.
Source: ADB calculations using data from *Direction of Trade Statistics,* International Monetary Fund.

Table A3: FTA Status—Asia (2015)

Economy	Under Negotiation		Signed but not yet In Effect	Signed and In Effect	TOTAL
	Framework Agreement signed	Negotiations launched			
Central Asia					
Armenia	0	0	0	9	9
Azerbaijan	0	0	5	5	10
Georgia	0	1	0	10	11
Kazakhstan	0	3	3	8	14
Kyrgyz Republic	0	0	1	8	9
Tajikistan	0	0	2	7	9
Turkmenistan	0	0	2	3	5
Uzbekistan	0	0	2	8	10
East Asia					
Hong Kong, China	0	1	0	4	5
PRC	0	6	2	14	22
Japan	0	9	1	14	24
Korea, Rep. of	0	7	4	12	23
Mongolia	0	0	1	0	1
Taipei,China	1	1	0	7	9
South Asia					
Afghanistan	0	0	2	2	4
Bangladesh	0	2	1	3	6
Bhutan	0	1	0	2	3
India	1	14	0	13	28
Maldives	0	1	1	1	3
Nepal	0	1	0	2	3
Pakistan	0	5	2	10	17
Sri Lanka	0	2	0	5	7
Southeast Asia					
Brunei Darussalam	0	3	1	8	12
Cambodia	0	2	0	6	8
Indonesia	0	7	1	9	17
Lao PDR	0	2	0	8	10
Malaysia	1	6	0	14	21
Myanmar	1	3	0	6	10
Philippines	0	3	0	7	10
Singapore	0	10	0	20	30
Thailand	1	7	1	12	21
Viet Nam	0	5	2	8	15
The Pacific					
Cook Islands	0	2	0	2	4
Fiji	0	2	0	3	5
Kiribati	0	2	0	2	4
Marshall Islands	0	2	0	2	4
Micronesia, Fed. States of	0	2	0	2	4
Nauru	0	2	0	2	4
Palau	0	2	0	2	4
Papua New Guinea	0	2	0	4	6
Samoa	0	2	0	2	4
Solomon Islands	0	2	0	3	5
Timor-Leste	0	0	0	0	0
Tonga	0	2	0	2	4
Tuvalu	0	2	0	2	4
Vanuatu	0	2	0	3	5
Oceania					
Australia	0	6	1	11	18
New Zealand	0	6	1	10	17

PRC = People's Republic of China.
FTA = free trade agreement, Lao PDR = Lao People's Democratic Republic.
Notes: Data as of August 2015. Excludes FTAs only proposed.
Source: *Asia Regional Integration Center FTA Database*, Asian Development Bank.

Table A4: Time to Export or Import-Asia (days)

	Time to Export (days)		Time to Import (days)	
	2014	2015	2014	2015
Central Asia	**8.5**	**8.4**	**3.4**	**3.2**
Armenia	2.2	0.2	2.2	0.2
Azerbaijan	2.9	2.9	3.0	3.0
Georgia	2.6	2.6	1.6	1.6
Kazakhstan	11.0	11.0	0.3	0.3
Kyrgyz Republic	2.1	2.1	3.0	3.0
Tajikistan	11.6	5.9	12.5	9.8
Turkmenistan	–	–	–	–
Uzbekistan	11.9	11.9	11.9	11.9
East Asia	**1.7**	**1.7**	**4.0**	**4.0**
Hong Kong, China	0.8	0.8	0.8	0.8
PRC	2.0	2.0	6.6	6.6
Japan	2.1	2.1	2.1	2.1
Korea, Rep. of	0.6	0.6	0.3	0.3
Mongolia	6.3	6.3	5.7	5.7
Taipei,China	2.0	2.0	3.7	3.7
South Asia	**6.5**	**6.5**	**13.8**	**13.8**
Afghanistan	12.1	12.1	18.0	18.0
Bangladesh	10.3	10.3	13.6	13.6
Bhutan	0.2	0.2	0.2	0.2
India	6.3	6.3	14.6	14.6
Maldives	3.8	3.8	6.7	6.7
Nepal	3.5	3.5	3.3	3.3
Pakistan	5.9	5.9	12.3	12.3
Sri Lanka	5.0	5.0	5.4	5.4
Southeast Asia	**2.8**	**2.8**	**4.1**	**4.1**
Brunei Darussalam	10.0	10.0	8.0	8.0
Cambodia	7.4	7.4	5.7	5.7
Indonesia	4.6	4.6	10.1	10.1
Lao PDR	9.1	9.1	9.2	9.2
Malaysia	1.3	1.3	1.4	1.4
Myanmar	12.0	12.0	7.0	7.0
Philippines	4.8	4.8	7.0	7.0
Singapore	0.7	0.7	1.5	1.5
Thailand	2.6	2.6	2.3	2.3
Viet Nam	5.8	5.8	7.1	7.1
The Pacific	**6.7**	**6.7**	**6.5**	**6.3**
Cook Islands	–	–	–	–
Fiji	4.7	4.7	3.2	3.2
Kiribati	4.0	4.0	6.0	6.0
Marshall Islands	5.0	5.0	6.0	6.0
Micronesia, Fed. States of	2.6	2.6	2.6	2.6
Nauru	–	–	–	–
Palau	11.3	11.3	10.5	10.5
Papua New Guinea	7.0	7.0	8.0	8.0
Samoa	1.3	1.3	1.5	1.5
Solomon Islands	7.1	7.1	6.0	6.0
Timor-Leste	5.4	5.4	5.8	5.8
Tonga	9.2	9.2	1.5	1.5
Tuvalu	–	–	–	–
Vanuatu	4.6	4.6	10.3	7.3
Oceania	**0.4**	**1.8**	**1.6**	**1.6**
Australia	0.4	1.8	1.7	1.7
New Zealand	0.4	1.7	1.1	1.1
Asia	**2.2**	**2.3**	**4.8**	**4.8**
Developing Asia	**2.4**	**2.4**	**5.1**	**5.1**

– = unavailable, PRC = People's Republic of China, Lao PDR = Lao People's Democratic Republic.
Source: ADB calculations using data from various issues of *Doing Business Database,* World Bank.

Table A5: Logistics Performance Index (LPI) Scores—Asia (% EU)

	2010	2012	2014
Central Asia	**71.6**	**68.5**	**66.6**
Armenia	65.8	67.4	69.1
Azerbaijan	68.8	65.2	63.3
Georgia	68.1	72.9	64.8
Kazakhstan	73.9	70.8	69.8
Kyrgyz Republic	68.3	61.8	57.1
Tajikistan	61.2	60.0	65.4
Turkmenistan	65.0	–	59.6
Uzbekistan	72.8	64.8	61.9
East Asia	**95.9**	**97.4**	**94.7**
PRC	91.0	92.4	91.3
Hong Kong, China	101.1	108.3	99.0
Japan	103.4	103.3	101.2
Korea, Rep. of	94.9	97.1	94.8
Mongolia	58.7	59.1	60.9
Taipei,China	96.6	97.4	96.1
South Asia	**78.1**	**79.6**	**77.4**
Afghanistan	58.5	60.4	53.5
Bangladesh	71.5	–	66.3
Bhutan	62.1	66.2	59.2
India	81.2	80.8	79.7
Maldives	62.7	66.9	71.1
Nepal	57.5	53.5	66.9
Pakistan	66.0	74.2	73.1
Sri Lanka	59.7	72.3	69.7
Southeast Asia	**89.7**	**90.3**	**89.9**
Brunei Darussalam	–	–	–
Cambodia	61.8	67.3	70.9
Indonesia	72.0	77.4	79.7
Lao PDR	64.2	65.7	61.8
Malaysia	89.7	91.8	92.9
Myanmar	60.7	62.2	58.2
Philippines	81.9	79.5	77.7
Singapore	106.7	108.4	103.6
Thailand	85.9	83.4	88.7
Viet Nam	77.3	78.9	81.6
The Pacific	**56.0**	**58.1**	**59.6**
Cook Islands	–	–	–
Fiji	58.3	63.6	65.8
Kiribati	–	–	–
Marshall Islands	–	–	–
Micronesia, Fed. States of	–	–	–
Nauru	–	–	–
Palau	–	–	–
Papua New Guinea	62.9	62.4	62.8
Samoa	–	–	–
Solomon Islands	60.2	63.4	66.9
Timor-Leste	–	–	–
Tonga	–	–	–
Tuvalu	–	–	–
Vanuatu	–	–	–
Oceania	**99.5**	**96.9**	**97.9**
Australia	100.2	97.9	98.6
New Zealand	95.1	89.9	94.2
Asia	**93.1**	**94.1**	**92.1**
Developing Asia	**92.2**	**93.4**	**91.4**

— = unavailable, PRC = People's Republic of China, EU = European Union (27 members), Lao PDR = Lao People's Democratic Republic.
Source: ADB calculations using data from *Logistics Performance Index,* World Bank.

Table A6: Cross-Border Equity Holdings—Asia (% of total cross-border equity holdings, 2014)

Reporter	Partner					
	Asia	of which:		EU	US	ROW
		PRC	Japan			
Central Asia	**12.9**	**0.1**	**8.8**	**26.1**	**52.2**	**8.8**
Armenia	–	–	–	–	–	–
Azerbaijan	–	–	–	–	–	–
Georgia	–	–	–	–	–	–
Kazakhstan	12.9	0.1	8.8	26.1	52.2	8.8
Kyrgyz Republic	–	–	–	–	–	–
Tajikistan	–	–	–	–	–	–
Turkmenistan	–	–	–	–	–	–
Uzbekistan	–	–	–	–	–	–
East Asia	**16.8**	**11.0**	**0.6**	**19.0**	**22.0**	**42.2**
PRC	–	–	–	–	–	–
Hong Kong, China	31.2	27.7	0.7	13.8	4.3	50.6
Japan	7.1	1.2	–	21.9	30.4	40.6
Korea, Rep. of	21.6	5.7	5.1	22.2	45.0	11.2
Mongolia	66.3	1.3	0.2	5.2	14.6	13.9
Taipei,China	–	–	–	–	–	–
South Asia	**7.7**	**0.0**	**0.3**	**23.3**	**36.1**	**32.9**
Afghanistan	–	–	–	–	–	–
Bangladesh	–	–	–	–	–	–
Bhutan	–	–	–	–	–	–
India	8.7	0.0	0.3	25.8	40.7	24.8
Maldives	–	–	–	–	–	–
Nepal	–	–	–	–	–	–
Pakistan	0.2	0.0	0.0	4.1	0.6	95.1
Sri Lanka	–	–	–	–	–	–
Southeast Asia	**42.1**	**12.3**	**4.0**	**10.4**	**28.6**	**18.9**
Brunei Darussalam	–	–	–	–	–	–
Cambodia	–	–	–	–	–	–
Indonesia	45.1	27.3	0.5	0.0	2.5	52.4
Lao PDR	–	–	–	–	–	–
Malaysia	48.9	1.7	0.6	8.0	38.2	5.0
Myanmar	–	–	–	–	–	–
Philippines	10.2	1.4	0.0	24.2	62.1	3.5
Singapore	42.0	13.5	4.5	10.0	27.6	20.4
Thailand	21.0	2.7	1.5	38.0	34.8	6.2
Viet Nam	–	–	–	–	–	–
The Pacific	**–**	**–**	**–**	**–**	**–**	**–**
Cook Islands	–	–	–	–	–	–
Fiji	–	–	–	–	–	–
Kiribati	–	–	–	–	–	–
Marshall Islands	–	–	–	–	–	–
Micronesia, Fed. States of	–	–	–	–	–	–
Nauru	–	–	–	–	–	–
Palau	–	–	–	–	–	–
Papua New Guinea	–	–	–	–	–	–
Samoa	–	–	–	–	–	–
Solomon Islands	–	–	–	–	–	–
Timor-Leste	–	–	–	–	–	–
Tonga	–	–	–	–	–	–
Tuvalu	–	–	–	–	–	–
Vanuatu	–	–	–	–	–	–
Oceania	**12.9**	**1.0**	**4.0**	**15.9**	**41.8**	**29.5**
Australia	13.4	1.1	4.5	17.5	46.3	22.8
New Zealand	7.9	0.1	0.6	1.9	3.6	86.6
Asia	**20.5**	**9.7**	**1.7**	**17.1**	**26.2**	**36.2**
Developing Asia	**30.3**	**19.6**	**2.4**	**13.5**	**17.7**	**38.5**

– = unavailable, PRC = People's Republic of China, EU = European Union (27 members), Lao PDR = Lao People's Democratic Republic, US = United States, ROW = rest of the world.
Source: ADB calculations using data from *Coordinated Portfolio Investment Survey 2014*, International Monetary Fund.

Table A7: Cross-Border Debt Holdings—Asia (% of total cross-border debt holdings, 2014)

Reporter	Partner					
	Asia	of which:		EU	US	ROW
		PRC	Japan			
Central Asia	**13.9**	**0.1**	**4.8**	**25.6**	**54.3**	**6.2**
Armenia	–	–	–	–	–	–
Azerbaijan	–	–	–	–	–	–
Georgia	–	–	–	–	–	–
Kazakhstan	13.9	0.1	4.8	25.6	54.3	6.2
Kyrgyz Republic	–	–	–	–	–	–
Tajikistan	–	–	–	–	–	–
Turkmenistan	–	–	–	–	–	–
Uzbekistan	–	–	–	–	–	–
East Asia	**16.6**	**6.7**	**0.8**	**32.4**	**35.7**	**15.4**
PRC	–	–	–	–	–	–
Hong Kong, China	59.9	40.5	4.4	13.1	17.0	10.1
Japan	8.2	0.2	–	36.1	39.5	16.2
Korea, Rep. of	17.5	4.2	3.3	31.4	30.7	20.5
Mongolia	94.9	49.2	0.0	1.8	2.8	0.5
Taipei,China	–	–	–	–	–	–
South Asia	**29.1**	**0.0**	**9.9**	**6.8**	**6.3**	**57.8**
Afghanistan	–	–	–	–	–	–
Bangladesh	–	–	–	–	–	–
Bhutan	–	–	–	–	–	–
India	28.8	0.0	1.5	8.6	56.8	5.8
Maldives	–	–	–	–	–	–
Nepal	–	–	–	–	–	–
Pakistan	29.1	0.0	10.9	6.6	0.0	64.2
Sri Lanka	–	–	–	–	–	–
Southeast Asia	**34.8**	**4.0**	**0.0**	**13.4**	**25.7**	**26.1**
Brunei Darussalam	–	–	–	–	–	–
Cambodia	–	–	–	–	–	–
Indonesia	11.5	5.1	0.1	26.3	26.5	35.7
Lao PDR	–	–	–	–	–	–
Malaysia	64.6	2.0	0.5	7.4	9.4	18.6
Myanmar	–	–	–	–	–	–
Philippines	41.8	8.7	0.6	9.0	35.5	13.7
Singapore	33.4	3.7	0.0	14.0	27.6	25.0
Thailand	39.0	9.2	0.3	4.4	3.1	53.6
Viet Nam	–	–	–	–	–	–
The Pacific	**–**	**–**	**–**	**–**	**–**	**–**
Cook Islands	–	–	–	–	–	–
Fiji	–	–	–	–	–	–
Kiribati	–	–	–	–	–	–
Marshall Islands	–	–	–	–	–	–
Micronesia, Fed. States of	–	–	–	–	–	–
Nauru	–	–	–	–	–	–
Palau	–	–	–	–	–	–
Papua New Guinea	–	–	–	–	–	–
Samoa	–	–	–	–	–	–
Solomon Islands	–	–	–	–	–	–
Timor-Leste	–	–	–	–	–	–
Tonga	–	–	–	–	–	–
Tuvalu	–	–	–	–	–	–
Vanuatu	–	–	–	–	–	–
Oceania	**9.7**	**0.5**	**1.4**	**28.0**	**34.4**	**28.0**
Australia	9.0	0.5	1.6	30.7	38.1	22.2
New Zealand	14.5	0.0	0.0	7.9	7.4	70.2
Asia	**18.7**	**5.7**	**0.8**	**29.1**	**34.5**	**17.7**
Developing Asia	**35.9**	**18.2**	**2.2**	**15.1**	**24.3**	**24.8**

– = unavailable, PRC = People's Republic of China, EU = European Union (27 members), Lao PDR = Lao People's Democratic Republic, US = United States, ROW = rest of the world.
Source: ADB calculations using data from *Coordinated Portfolio Investment Survey 2014*, International Monetary Fund.

Table A8: FDI Inflow Share—Asia (2013)

Reporter	Partner					
	Asia	of which		EU	US	ROW
		PRC	Japan			
Central Asia	**10.4**	**7.3**	**1.2**	**40.1**	**5.4**	**44.2**
Armenia	2.3	–	–	51.7	0.7	45.3
Azerbaijan	5.2	–	0.1	7.7	1.7	85.4
Georgia	–	–	–	–	–	–
Kazakhstan	12.1	8.4	1.6	49.5	6.9	31.6
Kyrgyz Republic	28.3	23.2	–	31.4	1.7	38.6
Tajikistan	–	–	–	–	–	–
Turkmenistan	–	–	–	–	–	–
Uzbekistan	–	–	–	–	–	–
East Asia	**64.0**	**15.1**	**6.4**	**6.4**	**-4.6**	**34.1**
PRC	69.6	–	6.6	2.3	2.3	25.8
Hong Kong, China	45.9	42.8	1.4	15.0	-22.2	61.3
Japan	38.8	6.1	–	-175.5	58.9	–
Korea, Rep. of	53.5	2.2	37.1	14.0	19.3	13.1
Mongolia	17.9	7.6	1.1	61.6	2.0	18.6
Taipei,China	13.3	–	7.4	24.8	7.3	54.6
South Asia	**21.8**	**1.1**	**6.6**	**28.3**	**3.5**	**46.4**
Afghanistan	–	–	–	–	–	–
Bangladesh	48.6	1.4	2.3	22.0	3.4	25.9
Bhutan	25.5	–	–	5.9	–	68.6
India	14.0	0.8	7.3	29.0	2.6	54.3
Maldives	–	–	–	–	–	–
Nepal	–	–	–	–	–	–
Pakistan	35.5	8.7	3.4	51.5	25.4	-12.5
Sri Lanka	–	–	–	–	–	–
Southeast Asia	**50.6**	**7.1**	**18.7**	**22.5**	**3.1**	**23.8**
Brunei Darussalam	-5.8	–	2.2	82.9	-0.7	23.6
Cambodia	71.8	22.5	3.0	9.1	2.7	16.5
Indonesia	88.3	3.2	30.1	-3.4	5.8	9.3
Lao PDR	0.5	–	–	–	–	99.5
Malaysia	46.7	1.1	21.4	17.5	1.8	33.9
Myanmar	80.8	30.2	1.4	11.3	–	7.9
Philippines	10.4	0.2	11.3	1.2	-16.9	105.3
Singapore	31.8	8.9	8.1	41.0	2.4	24.8
Thailand	73.8	3.7	53.0	-3.2	12.2	17.1
Viet Nam	85.5	10.7	26.6	3.9	0.6	10.0
The Pacific	**–**	**–**	**–**	**–**	**–**	**–**
Cook Islands	–	–	–	–	–	–
Fiji	–	–	–	–	–	–
Kiribati	–	–	–	–	–	–
Marshall Islands	–	–	–	–	–	–
Micronesia, Fed. States of	–	–	–	–	–	–
Nauru	–	–	–	–	–	–
Palau	–	–	–	–	–	–
Papua New Guinea	–	–	–	–	–	–
Samoa	–	–	–	–	–	–
Solomon Islands	–	–	–	–	–	–
Timor-Leste	–	–	–	–	–	–
Tonga	–	–	–	–	–	–
Tuvalu	–	–	–	–	–	–
Vanuatu	–	–	–	–	–	–
Oceania	**32.2**	**6.5**	**17.9**	**25.6**	**22.6**	**19.6**
Australia	30.3	6.6	18.2	26.2	23.2	20.3
New Zealand	127.7	3.4	-1.3	-5.4	-9.0	-13.3
Asia	**51.8**	**20.8**	**21.6**	**18.7**	**3.1**	**26.4**
Developing Asia	**21.2**	**11.1**	**10.1**	**8.5**	**-1.5**	**71.8**

– = unavailable, FDI = foreign direct investment, PRC = People's Republic of China, EU = European Union (27 members), Lao PDR = Lao People's Democratic Republic, US = United States, ROW = rest of the world.
Source: ADB calculations using data from ASEAN Secretariat, CEIC, OECD, and UNCTAD.

Table A9: Remittance Inflows Share—Asia

(% of total remittance inflows, 2014)

Reporter	Partner				
	Asia	of which Japan	EU	US	ROW
Central Asia	**7.2**	**0.0**	**6.2**	**2.4**	**84.2**
Armenia	4.3	0.0	10.3	13.8	71.6
Azerbaijan	24.1	0.0	3.4	2.0	70.6
Georgia	8.9	0.0	16.7	2.4	71.9
Kazakhstan	4.2	0.0	22.0	0.8	73.1
Kyrgyz Republic	4.5	0.0	12.4	0.6	82.4
Tajikistan	11.9	0.0	4.2	0.9	83.0
Turkmenistan	–	–	–	–	–
Uzbekistan	–	–	–	–	–
East Asia	**50.9**	**15.5**	**8.8**	**27.5**	**12.8**
PRC	52.5	12.5	8.9	25.5	13.1
Hong Kong, China	22.6	0.0	11.6	30.8	35.1
Japan	39.7	0.0	13.1	34.9	12.4
Korea, Rep. of	43.3	61.0	4.5	44.8	7.3
Mongolia	45.1	0.0	19.7	0.3	34.9
Taipei,China	–	–	–	–	–
South Asia	**20.2**	**0.9**	**8.6**	**11.4**	**59.8**
Afghanistan	31.6	0.0	7.6	2.1	58.6
Bangladesh	33.9	0.6	5.4	3.4	57.2
Bhutan	96.9	0.0	1.7	0.2	1.1
India	18.4	0.8	7.9	15.9	57.9
Maldives	58.1	0.0	12.7	0.0	29.2
Nepal	20.7	0.0	2.9	4.8	71.6
Pakistan	16.8	1.0	12.1	6.0	65.2
Sri Lanka	16.7	3.3	18.8	3.1	61.4
Southeast Asia	**25.9**	**10.2**	**10.1**	**32.4**	**31.6**
Brunei Darussalam	–	–	–	–	–
Cambodia	67.7	0.4	7.5	21.6	3.1
Indonesia	39.4	1.8	4.5	2.8	53.3
Lao PDR	73.5	0.0	4.3	20.4	1.8
Malaysia	89.3	0.6	4.3	3.8	2.6
Myanmar	65.7	0.0	0.7	5.4	28.2
Philippines	18.0	19.7	7.0	34.0	41.0
Singapore	–	–	–	–	–
Thailand	36.9	12.3	25.1	27.8	10.2
Viet Nam	19.4	7.2	15.4	56.5	8.8
The Pacific	**58.2**	**0.0**	**2.1**	**25.2**	**14.6**
Cook Islands	–	–	–	–	–
Fiji	59.2	0.0	3.1	23.3	14.3
Kiribati	49.7	0.0	0.8	47.5	2.0
Marshall Islands	2.4	0.0	0.2	94.3	3.0
Micronesia, Fed. States of	1.6	0.0	0.0	71.6	26.8
Nauru	–	–	–	–	–
Palau	–	–	–	–	–
Papua New Guinea	89.3	0.0	1.1	7.8	1.8
Samoa	63.9	0.0	0.2	12.8	23.1
Solomon Islands	88.8	0.0	2.1	4.4	4.7
Timor-Leste	93.8	0.0	5.7	0.0	0.4
Tonga	56.5	0.0	0.3	39.7	3.4
Tuvalu	76.8	0.0	1.3	5.1	16.8
Vanuatu	20.8	0.0	9.8	2.0	67.4
Oceania	**40.5**	**5.8**	**36.0**	**13.0**	**10.5**
Australia	31.5	8.7	41.5	14.9	12.1
New Zealand	84.2	0.7	9.1	3.9	2.8
Asia	**29.4**	**9.7**	**9.1**	**19.8**	**41.8**
Developing Asia	**29.1**	**10.0**	**8.7**	**19.6**	**42.5**

– = unavailable, PRC = People's Republic of China, EU = European Union (27 members), Lao PDR = Lao People's Democratic Republic, US = United States, ROW = rest of the world.

Source: ADB calculations using data from Bilateral Remittance Estimates for 2014 using Migrant Stocks, Host Country Incomes, and Origin Country Incomes,World Bank.

Table A10: Outbound Migration Share—Asia

(% of total outbound migrants, 2013)

Reporter	Partner Asia	of which PRC	of which Japan	EU	US	ROW
Central Asia	**11.2**	**0.0**	**0.0**	**10.9**	**2.3**	**75.7**
Armenia	4.9	0.0	0.0	8.7	11.9	74.5
Azerbaijan	25.0	0.0	0.0	2.6	1.7	70.7
Georgia	10.3	0.0	0.0	14.7	2.0	73.0
Kazakhstan	4.2	0.0	0.0	20.2	0.7	74.9
Kyrgyz Republic	5.8	0.0	0.0	7.9	0.5	85.8
Tajikistan	14.7	0.0	0.0	2.5	0.6	82.2
Turkmenistan	5.9	0.0	0.0	3.1	0.5	90.5
Uzbekistan	20.2	0.0	0.0	2.2	3.3	74.3
East Asia	**48.8**	**3.6**	**20.3**	**8.7**	**29.1**	**13.4**
PRC	53.8	0.0	13.0	9.1	24.0	13.0
Hong Kong, China	24.7	3.4	0.0	11.2	29.8	34.3
Japan	32.5	3.0	0.0	13.8	39.2	14.5
Korea, Rep. of	44.2	19.4	60.9	4.1	44.1	7.6
Mongolia	43.9	0.0	0.0	21.1	0.3	34.6
Taipei,China	0.0	0.0	0.0	0.0	0.0	0.0
South Asia	**35.6**	**0.3**	**0.4**	**8.3**	**8.0**	**48.0**
Afghanistan	46.5	0.0	0.0	4.9	1.4	47.2
Bangladesh	51.1	0.2	0.3	4.9	2.6	41.4
Bhutan	97.9	0.0	0.0	1.3	0.2	0.6
India	24.4	0.4	0.6	7.9	14.5	53.2
Maldives	61.9	0.0	0.0	11.2	0.0	26.9
Nepal	82.1	0.0	0.0	5.9	8.4	3.6
Pakistan	25.1	0.5	0.7	13.4	6.0	55.5
Sri Lanka	27.9	1.8	3.0	26.9	4.3	40.9
Southeast Asia	**49.5**	**2.6**	**3.8**	**7.9**	**23.0**	**19.7**
Brunei Darussalam	75.4	0.0	0.0	11.7	2.1	10.8
Cambodia	75.8	0.0	0.3	6.2	15.5	2.5
Indonesia	57.8	3.4	1.7	6.0	3.6	32.5
Lao PDR	79.7	0.0	0.0	3.5	15.2	1.5
Malaysia	87.2	0.6	0.7	5.1	4.5	3.2
Myanmar	95.3	0.0	0.0	0.6	3.7	0.4
Philippines	14.2	15.5	29.0	7.9	36.4	41.5
Singapore	65.2	0.0	1.4	16.9	12.2	5.6
Thailand	34.0	7.7	15.2	25.1	30.0	10.9
Viet Nam	23.2	5.2	6.3	14.9	53.0	8.8
The Pacific	**63.6**	**0.0**	**0.0**	**1.8**	**20.2**	**14.4**
Cook Islands	99.6	0.0	0.0	0.0	0.3	0.1
Fiji	59.9	0.0	0.0	3.3	22.3	14.6
Kiribati	58.1	0.0	0.0	0.6	39.2	2.1
Marshall Islands	5.2	0.0	0.0	0.2	91.2	3.4
Micronesia, Fed. States of	2.2	0.0	0.0	0.0	67.4	30.4
Nauru	80.8	0.0	0.0	0.8	10.3	8.2
Palau	47.3	0.0	0.0	0.2	30.5	21.9
Papua New Guinea	90.4	0.0	0.0	1.1	6.8	1.7
Samoa	66.1	0.0	0.0	0.2	9.6	24.2
Solomon Islands	92.9	0.0	0.0	1.5	3.0	2.7
Timor-Leste	95.2	0.0	0.0	4.6	0.0	0.2
Tonga	61.6	0.0	0.0	0.3	34.0	4.0
Tuvalu	78.3	0.0	0.0	1.0	3.6	17.2
Vanuatu	25.6	0.0	0.0	9.2	1.7	63.5
Oceania	**64.0**	**1.1**	**2.2**	**21.4**	**8.2**	**6.3**
Australia	33.2	5.2	8.3	40.4	14.6	11.8
New Zealand	83.9	0.0	0.7	9.2	4.1	2.8
Asia	**38.7**	**1.7**	**5.8**	**0.0**	**14.6**	**46.7**
Developing Asia	**38.4**	**1.7**	**2.3**	**8.5**	**14.4**	**38.7**

– = unavailable, PRC = People's Republic of China, EU = European Union (27 members), Lao PDR = Lao People's Democratic Republic, US = United States, ROW = rest of the world.

Source: ADB calculations using data from *Trends in International Migrant Stock: Migrants by Destination and Origin,* United Nations Department of Economic and Social Affairs.

Table A11: Outbound Tourism Share—Asia (% of total outbound tourists, 2013)

Reporter	Partner					
	Asia	of which		EU	US	ROW
		PRC	Japan			
Central Asia	**38.5**	**5.6**	**–**	**0.2**	**0.2**	**61.1**
Armenia	9.5	5.2	–	0.5	0.5	89.6
Azerbaijan	6.2	8.9	–	0.1	0.2	93.5
Georgia	30.5	0.9	–	0.3	0.2	69.1
Kazakhstan	45.9	10.5	–	0.4	0.2	53.5
Kyrgyz Republic	66.4	2.9	–	0.0	0.1	33.4
Tajikistan	30.1	5.1	–	0.0	0.1	69.8
Turkmenistan	31.8	8.1	–	0.1	0.2	67.9
Uzbekistan	46.7	2.0	–	0.1	0.1	53.1
East Asia	**82.8**	**56.4**	**4.2**	**4.7**	**3.8**	**8.6**
PRC	72.0	–	3.3	6.3	3.2	18.5
Hong Kong, China	97.2	95.1	0.9	0.2	0.1	2.4
Japan	57.5	21.9	–	14.5	16.3	11.7
Korea, Rep. of	76.9	30.7	19.0	5.0	8.1	10.1
Mongolia	83.4	90.7	1.3	0.1	–	16.5
Taipei,China	89.7	47.0	20.1	2.1	3.1	5.1
South Asia	**42.7**	**12.5**	**1.6**	**5.7**	**5.3**	**46.3**
Afghanistan	25.5	7.0	–	0.6	0.3	73.6
Bangladesh	71.9	5.9	0.7	1.1	1.7	25.2
Bhutan	94.0	3.6	–	1.0	2.2	2.7
India	41.8	13.8	1.5	7.8	7.3	43.1
Maldives	96.4	2.9	–	0.1	0.2	3.4
Nepal	70.8	14.8	4.5	0.1	2.3	26.8
Pakistan	17.0	22.2	1.9	3.7	1.9	77.4
Sri Lanka	75.6	7.5	1.9	2.4	1.6	20.4
Southeast Asia	**93.4**	**10.3**	**2.0**	**1.0**	**1.1**	**4.4**
Brunei Darussalam	99.7	0.6	0.1	0.0	0.1	0.2
Cambodia	99.4	3.4	0.5	0.0	0.4	0.2
Indonesia	90.9	7.6	1.7	0.7	1.0	7.4
Lao PDR	99.8	1.2	0.2	0.0	0.1	0.1
Malaysia	93.4	12.7	1.9	1.5	0.8	4.4
Myanmar	97.7	21.5	1.5	0.0	0.5	1.8
Philippines	78.3	22.9	2.5	1.0	3.6	17.1
Singapore	96.6	5.0	1.0	1.1	0.8	1.6
Thailand	93.7	8.3	5.8	1.5	1.1	3.8
Viet Nam	96.3	27.8	1.7	0.1	1.3	2.4
The Pacific	**87.4**	**4.8**	**–**	**0.4**	**4.0**	**8.3**
Cook Islands	97.5	–	–	0.0	0.4	2.1
Fiji	87.6	5.1	–	0.3	8.5	3.7
Kiribati	86.7	36.0	–	0.6	3.9	8.7
Marshall Islands	42.2	46.2	–	0.7	–	57.2
Micronesia, Fed. States of	–	–	–	–	–	–
Nauru	91.9	10.9	–	3.5	2.9	1.7
Palau	11.1	8.8	–	1.2	–	87.7
Papua New Guinea	97.7	1.7	–	0.1	1.1	1.1
Samoa	93.9	4.3	–	0.4	4.7	1.0
Solomon Islands	94.1	8.8	–	1.7	3.3	0.9
Timor-Leste	96.4	8.0	–	0.4	0.3	3.0
Tonga	93.4	6.1	–	0.1	5.7	0.8
Tuvalu	88.5	32.3	–	2.3	2.2	7.1
Vanuatu	77.5	2.6	–	0.4	1.0	21.1
Oceania	**61.5**	**8.4**	**2.8**	**18.9**	**8.6**	**11.0**
Australia	59.2	9.1	3.1	19.4	9.0	12.4
New Zealand	71.8	6.0	1.7	9.6	7.0	11.6
Asia	**77.8**	**39.9**	**3.4**	**4.4**	**3.3**	**14.5**
Developing Asia	**80.4**	**34.1**	**3.6**	**2.4**	**1.9**	**15.3**

– = unavailable, PRC = People's Republic of China, EU = European Union (27 members), Lao PDR = Lao People's Democratic Republic, US = United States, ROW = rest of the world.
Source: ADB calculations using *Data on Outbound Tourism*, United Nations World Tourism Organization.

www.ingramcontent.com/pod-product-compliance
Lightning Source LLC
Chambersburg PA
CBHW061220270326
41926CB00032B/4790